image comics p...

CHU

VOL. II

(SHE) DRUNK HISTORY

written & lettered by
John Layman

drawn & coloured by
Dan Boultwood

IMAGE COMICS, INC. • TODD MCFARLANE: President • JIM VALENTINO: Vice President • MARC SILVESTRI: Chief Executive Officer • ERIK LARSEN: Chief Financial Officer • ROBERT KIRKMAN: Chief Operating Officer • ERIC STEPHENSON: Publisher / Chief Creative Officer • NICOLE LAPALME: Controller • LEANNA CAUNTER: Accounting Analyst • SUE KORPELA: Accounting & HR Manager • MARLA EIZIK: Talent Liaison • JEFF BOISON: Director of Sales & Publishing Planning • DIRK WOOD: Director of International Sales & Licensing • ALEX COX: Director of Direct Market Sales • CHLOE RAMOS: Book Market & Library Sales Manager • EMILIO BAUTISTA: Digital Sales Coordinator • JON SCHLAFFMAN: Specialty Sales Coordinator • KAT SALAZAR: Director of PR & Marketing • DREW FITZGERALD: Marketing Content Associate • HEATHER DOORNINK: Production Director • DREW GILL: Art Director • HILARY DILORETO: Print Manager • TRICIA RAMOS: Traffic Manager • MELISSA GIFFORD: Content Manager • ERIKA SCHNATZ: Senior Production Artist • RYAN BREWER: Production Artist • DEANNA PHELPS: Production Artist • **IMAGECOMICS.COM**

Dedications:

JOHN: To the Divided Vine crew of Clayton, Jeff, Lennon, Ty
and of course Chef Rico. Magic alcohol indeed!

DAN: To Eleanor.

Thanks:

Deanna Phelps, for the production.
Melissa Gifford, for the proffreaderin.
Tom B. Long, for the logo.
Comicbookfonts.com, for the fonts.
David Baron, for being freakin' awesome!!!!!

And More Thanks:

Kim Peterson, Carter Layman, Drew Gill, Rob Guillory,
Thierry Mornet, Kathryn & Israel Skelton, Jeff Boison,
Eric Stephenson, and all the wonderful people at Image.

characters created by
John Layman & Dan Boultwood

characters created by
John Layman & Rob Guillory

Book Design: John Layman with Rob Guillory

Chapter 1

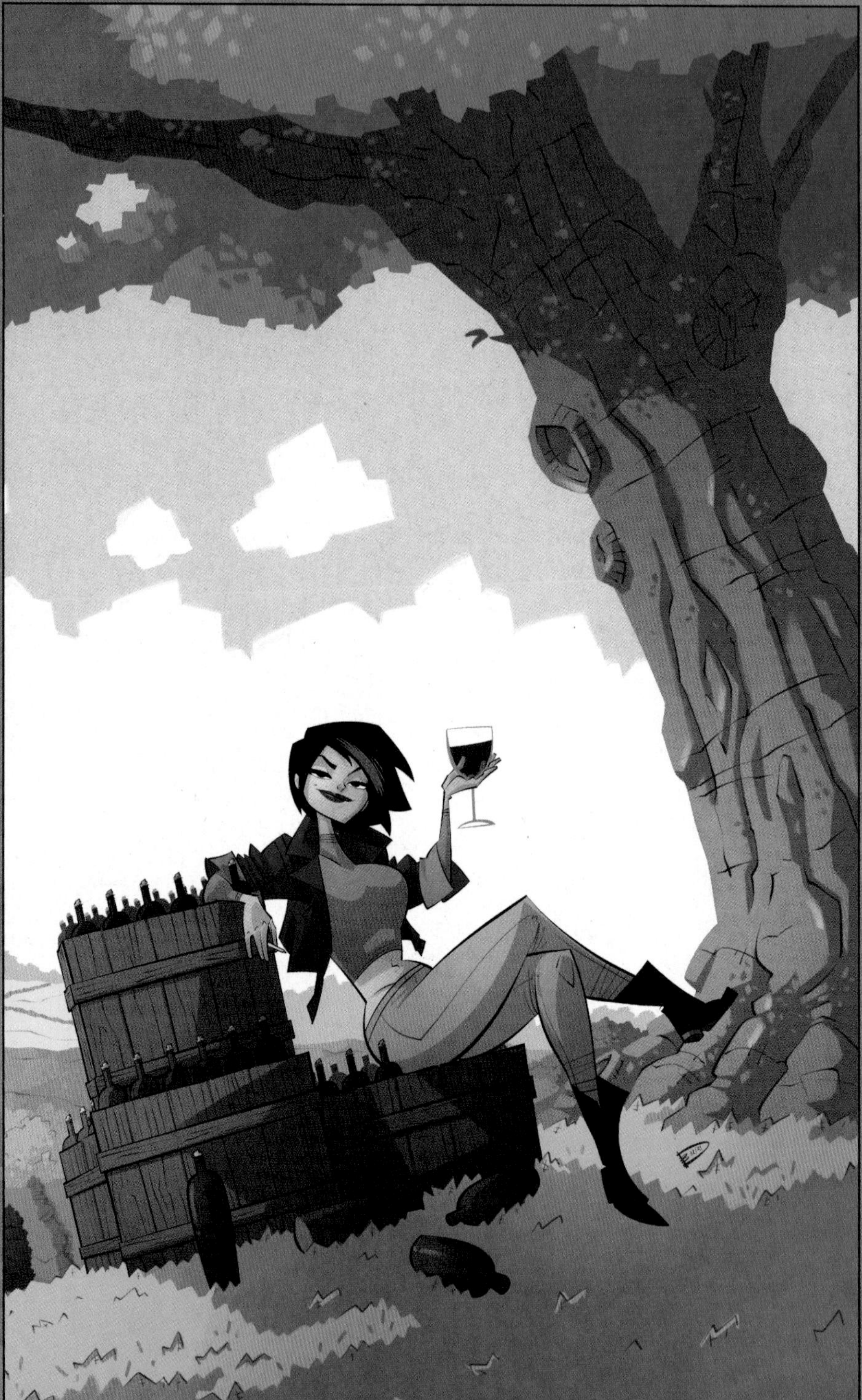

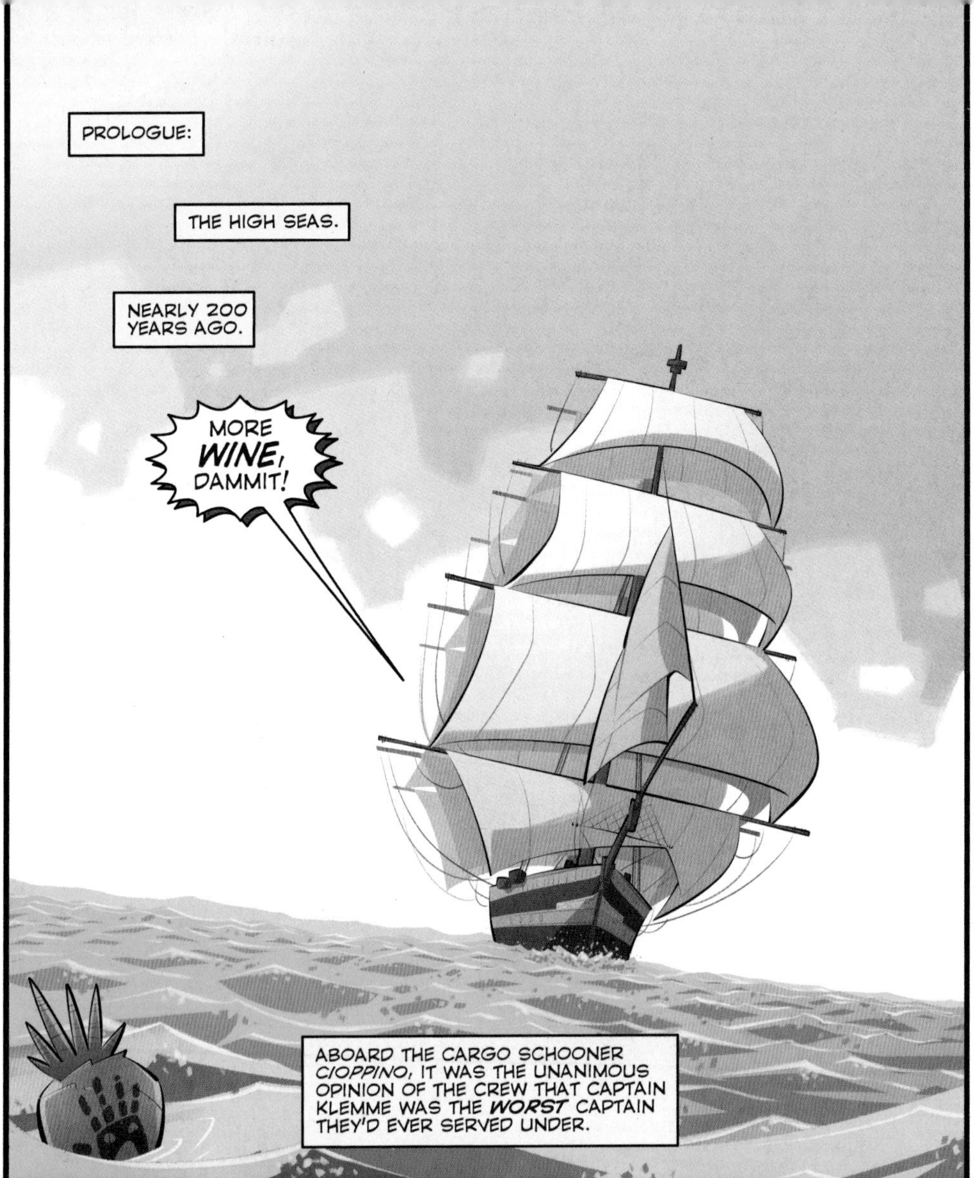
PROLOGUE:
THE HIGH SEAS.
NEARLY 200 YEARS AGO.
MORE *WINE*, DAMMIT!
ABOARD THE CARGO SCHOONER *CIOPPINO*, IT WAS THE UNANIMOUS OPINION OF THE CREW THAT CAPTAIN KLEMME WAS THE *WORST* CAPTAIN THEY'D EVER SERVED UNDER.

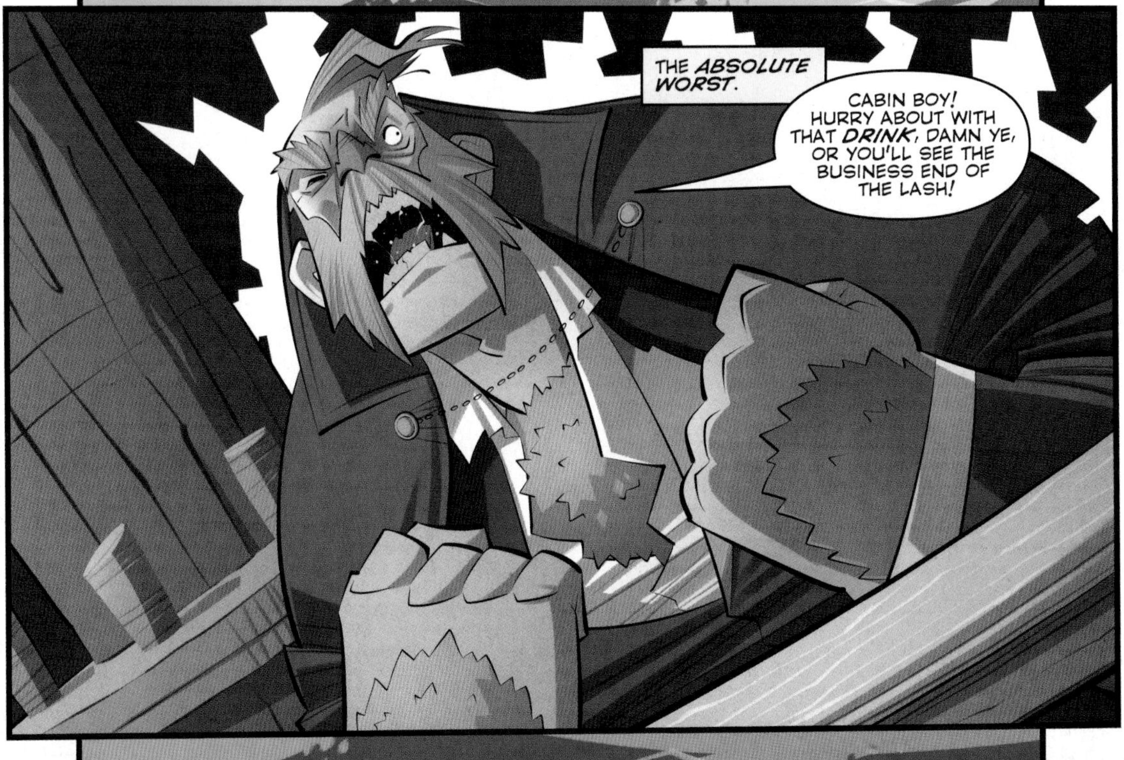
THE *ABSOLUTE WORST*.
CABIN BOY! HURRY ABOUT WITH THAT *DRINK*, DAMN YE, OR YOU'LL SEE THE BUSINESS END OF THE LASH!

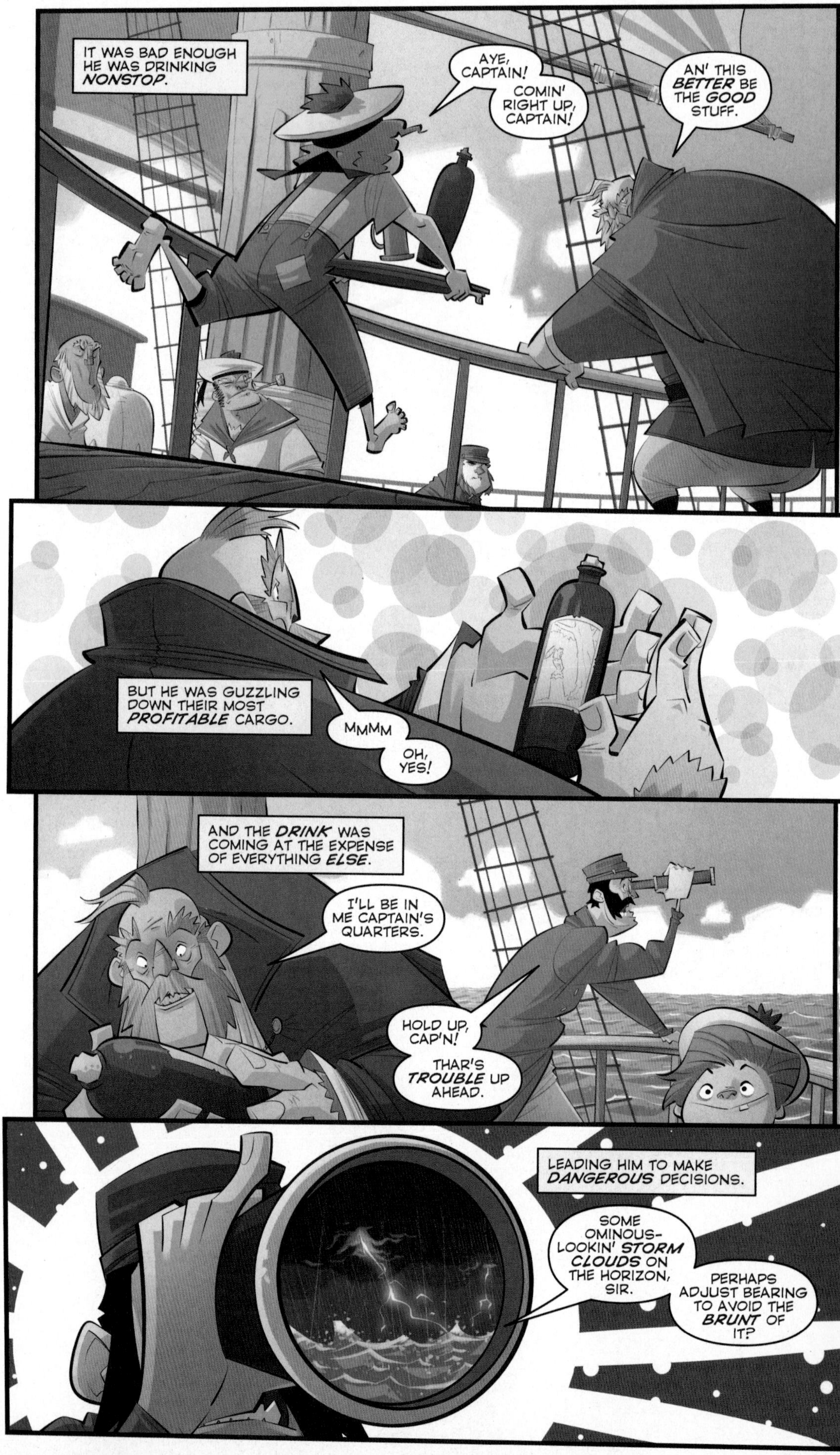

IT WAS BAD ENOUGH HE WAS DRINKING NONSTOP.
AYE, CAPTAIN!
COMIN' RIGHT UP, CAPTAIN!
AN' THIS BETTER BE THE GOOD STUFF.
BUT HE WAS GUZZLING DOWN THEIR MOST PROFITABLE CARGO.
MMMM
OH, YES!
AND THE DRINK WAS COMING AT THE EXPENSE OF EVERYTHING ELSE.
I'LL BE IN ME CAPTAIN'S QUARTERS.
HOLD UP, CAP'N!
THAR'S TROUBLE UP AHEAD.
LEADING HIM TO MAKE DANGEROUS DECISIONS.
SOME OMINOUS-LOOKIN' STORM CLOUDS ON THE HORIZON, SIR.
PERHAPS ADJUST BEARING TO AVOID THE BRUNT OF IT?

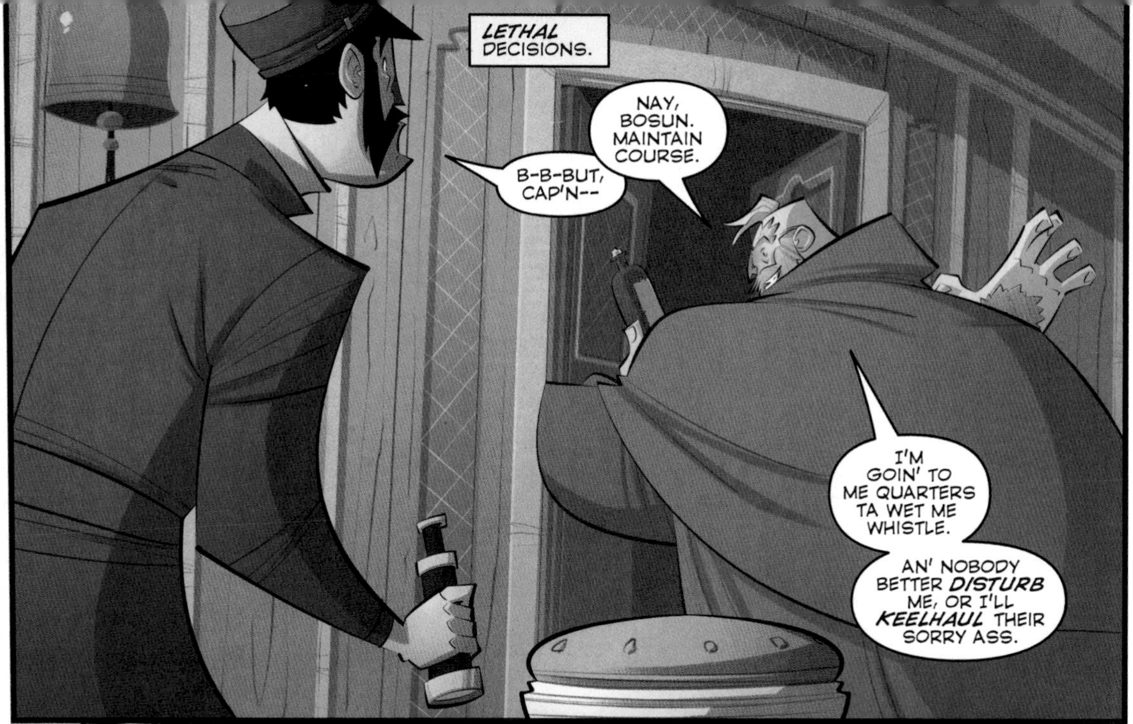
LETHAL DECISIONS.
B-B-BUT, CAP'N--
NAY, BOSUN. MAINTAIN COURSE.
I'M GOIN' TO ME QUARTERS TA WET ME WHISTLE.
AN' NOBODY BETTER DISTURB ME, OR I'LL KEELHAUL THEIR SORRY ASS.

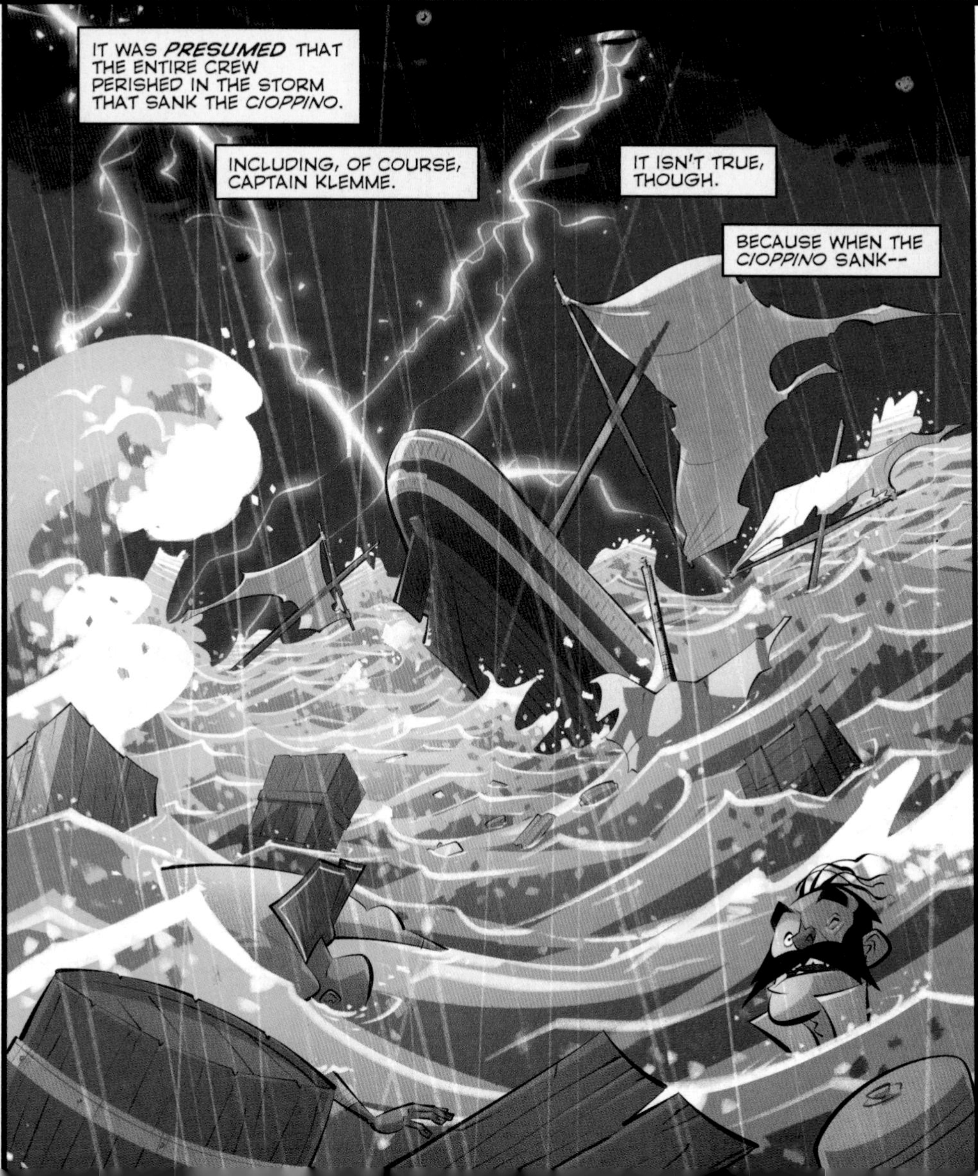
IT WAS PRESUMED THAT THE ENTIRE CREW PERISHED IN THE STORM THAT SANK THE CIOPPINO.
INCLUDING, OF COURSE, CAPTAIN KLEMME.
IT ISN'T TRUE, THOUGH.
BECAUSE WHEN THE CIOPPINO SANK--

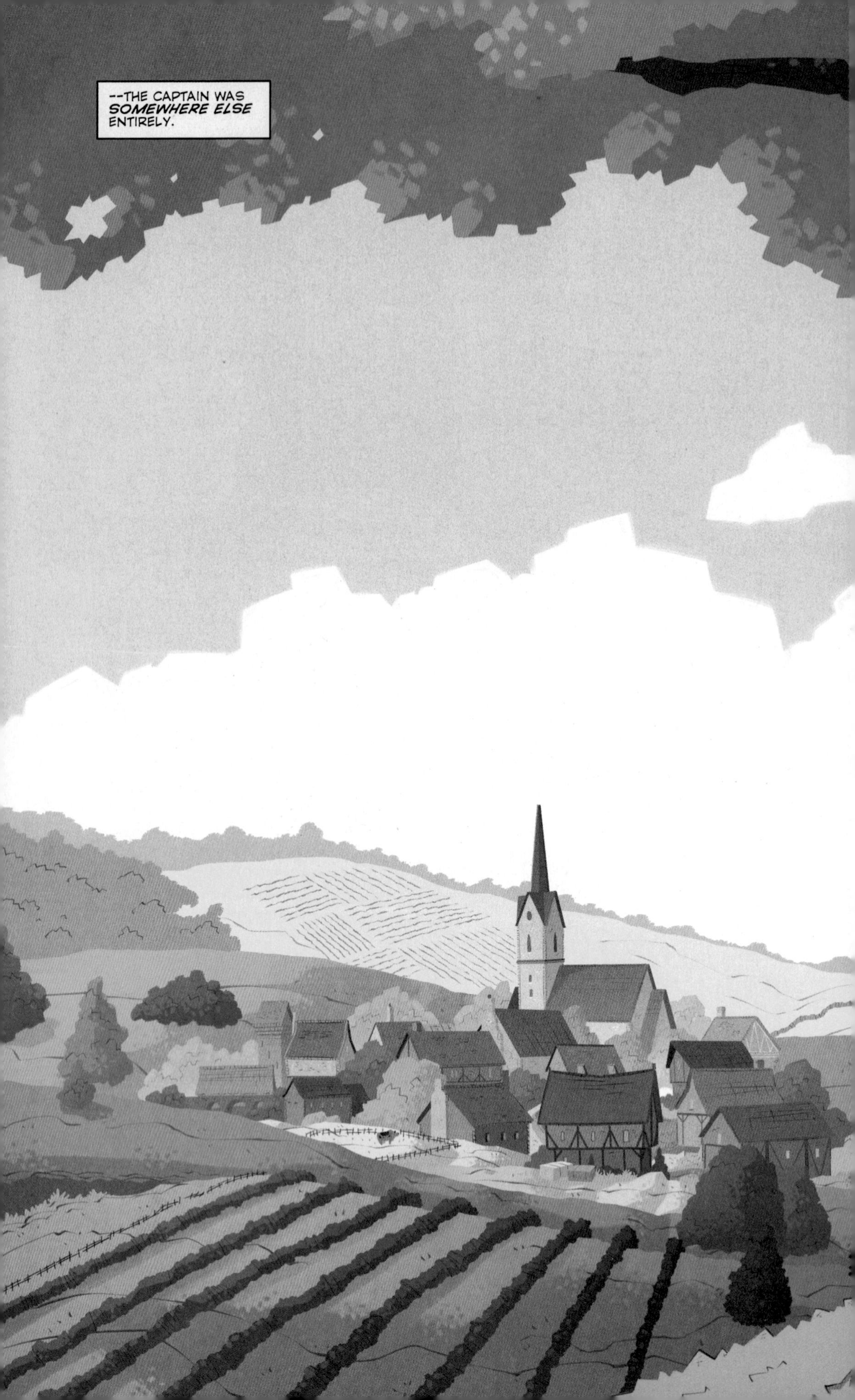
--THE CAPTAIN WAS SOMEWHERE ELSE ENTIRELY.

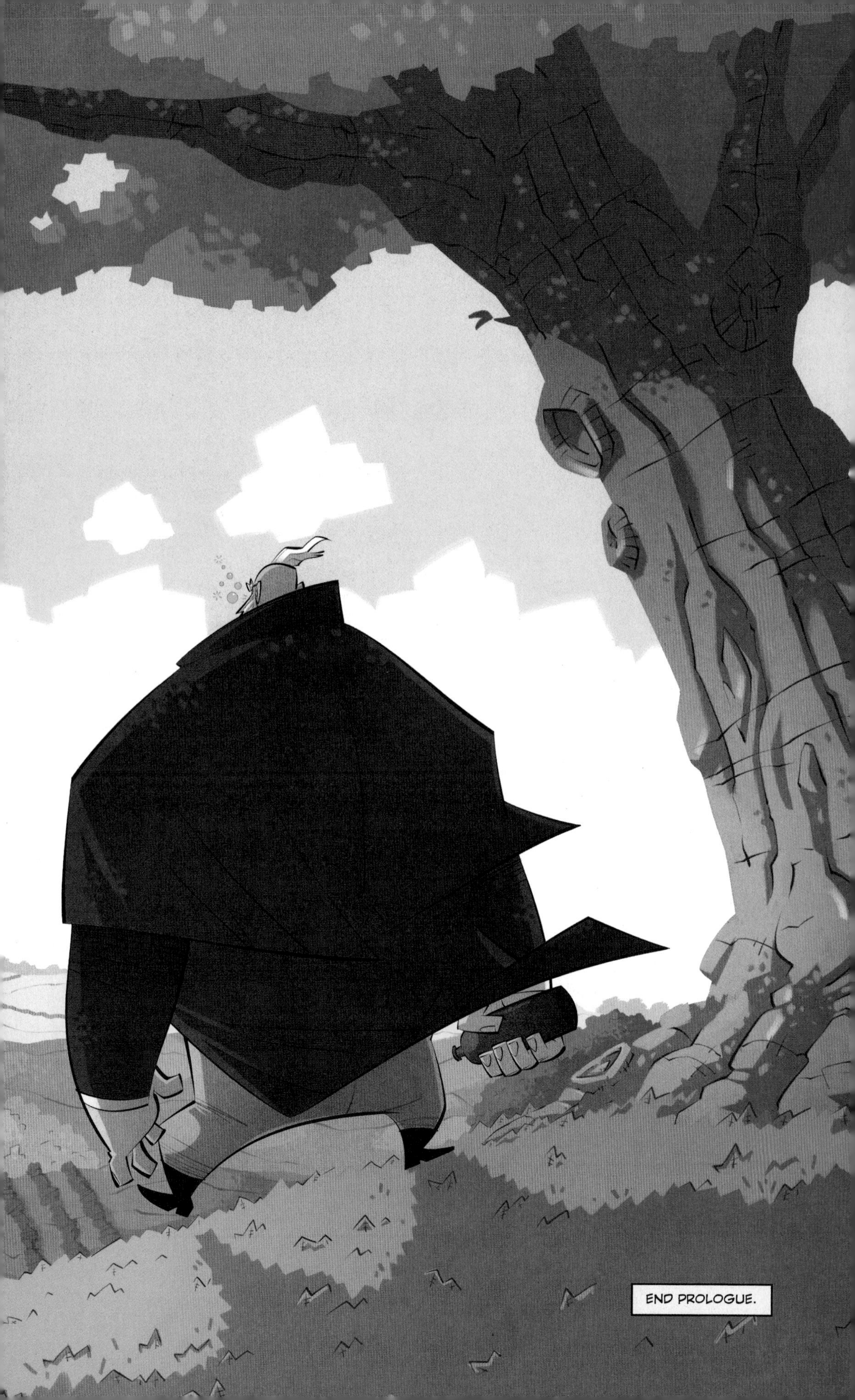
END PROLOGUE.

THE HIGH SEAS.
TWO YEARS AGO.
THE SALVAGE BOAT *ASAM PEDA*.
CAPTAIN, I'VE *FOUND* IT!
THE *WRECKAGE* WE'RE LOOKING FOR.
John Layman
Dan Boultwood
And image

THE WRECK OF THE CARGO SCHOONER CIOPPINO, TO BE PRECISE.
WHAT'S ITS CONDITION?
ANYTHING LOOK SALVAGEABLE?
"SALVAGEABLE"?
YEAH, YOU MIGHT SAY THAT.
ARE PROUD TO Present
CHU
(SHE) DRUNK HISTORY
Part 1 of 5

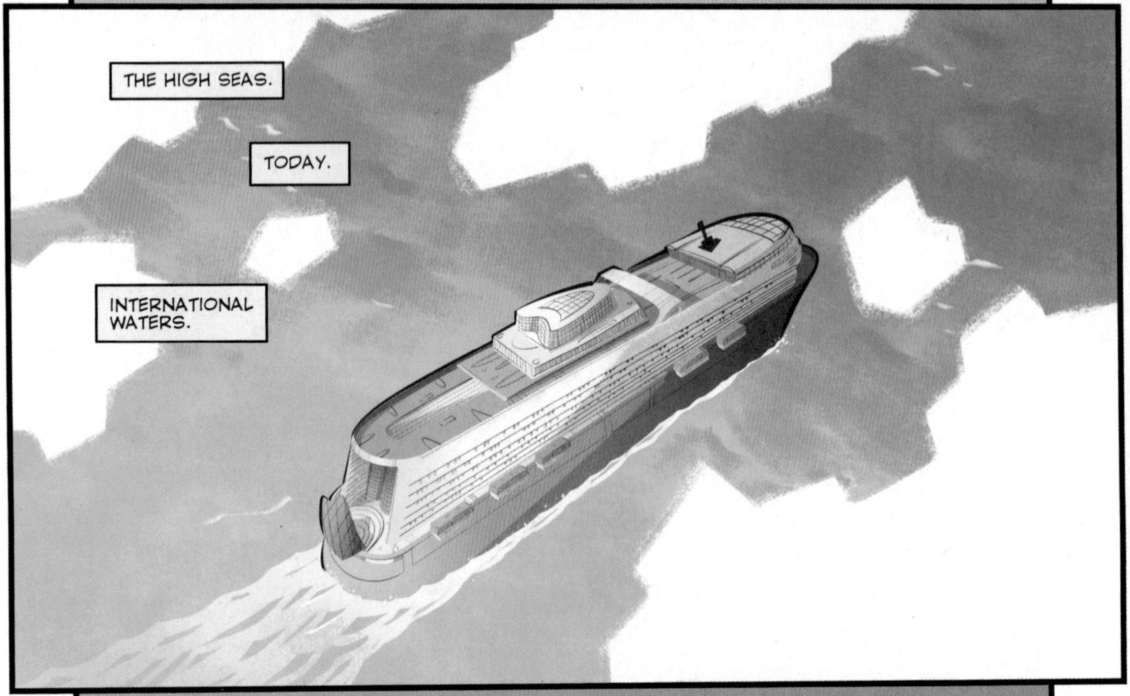
THE HIGH SEAS.
TODAY.
INTERNATIONAL WATERS.

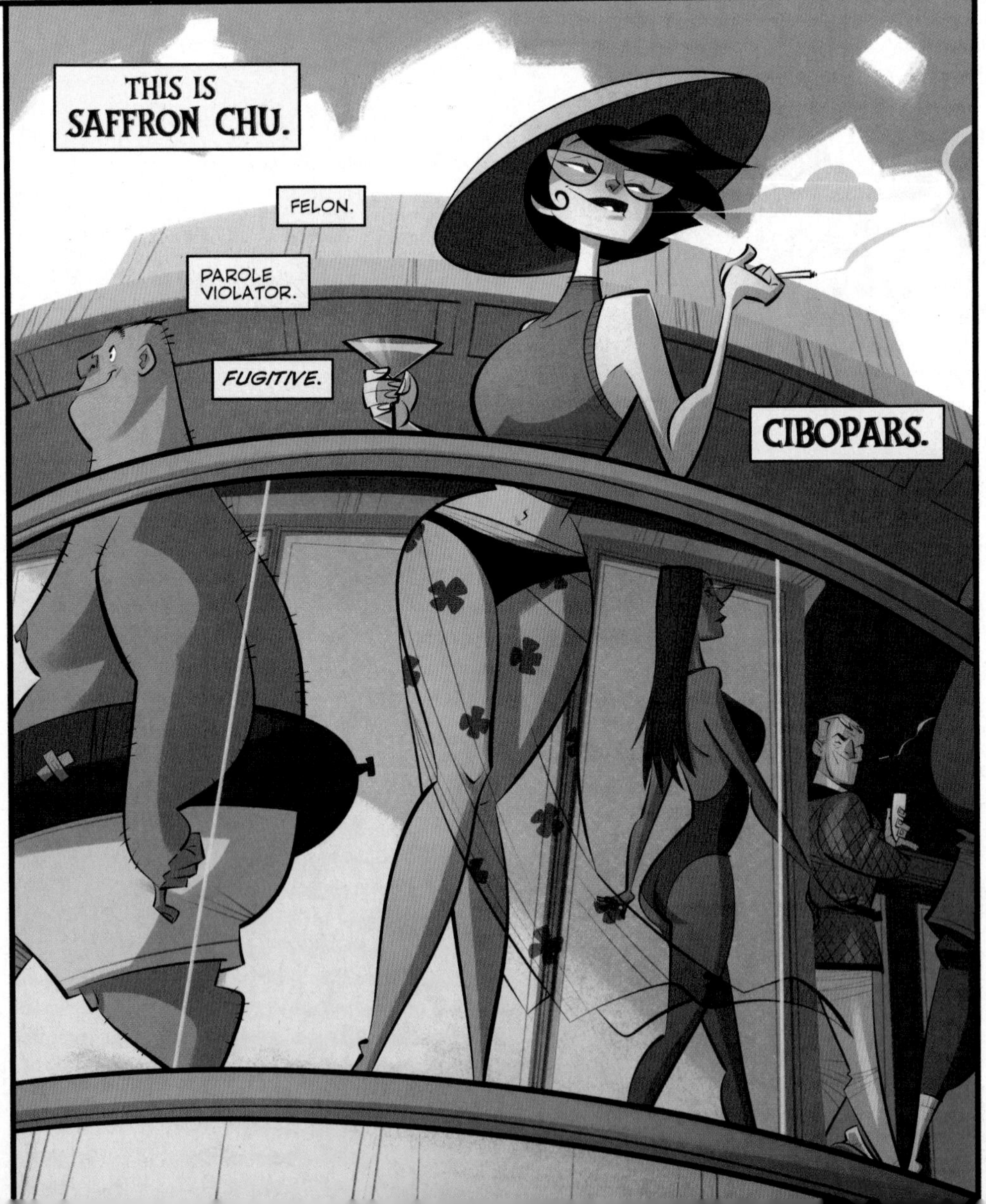
THIS IS SAFFRON CHU.
FELON.
PAROLE VIOLATOR.
FUGITIVE.
CIBOPARS.

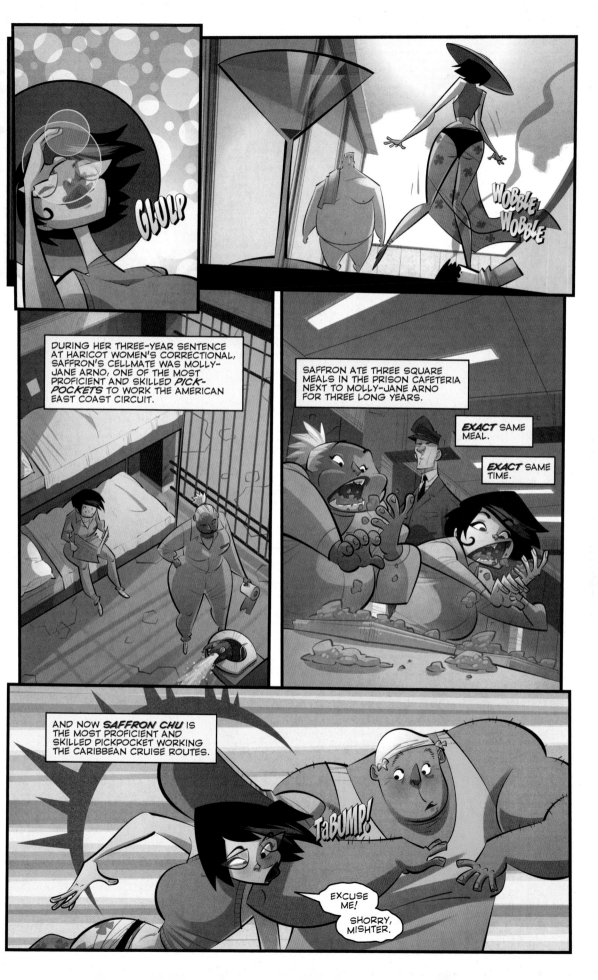

GLULP

WOBBLE WOBBLE

DURING HER THREE-YEAR SENTENCE AT HARICOT WOMEN'S CORRECTIONAL, SAFFRON'S CELLMATE WAS MOLLY-JANE ARNO, ONE OF THE MOST PROFICIENT AND SKILLED *PICK-POCKETS* TO WORK THE AMERICAN EAST COAST CIRCUIT.

SAFFRON ATE THREE SQUARE MEALS IN THE PRISON CAFETERIA NEXT TO MOLLY-JANE ARNO FOR THREE LONG YEARS.

EXACT SAME MEAL.

EXACT SAME TIME.

AND NOW *SAFFRON CHU* IS THE MOST PROFICIENT AND SKILLED PICKPOCKET WORKING THE CARIBBEAN CRUISE ROUTES.

TABUMP!

EXCUSE ME!

SHORRY, MISHTER.

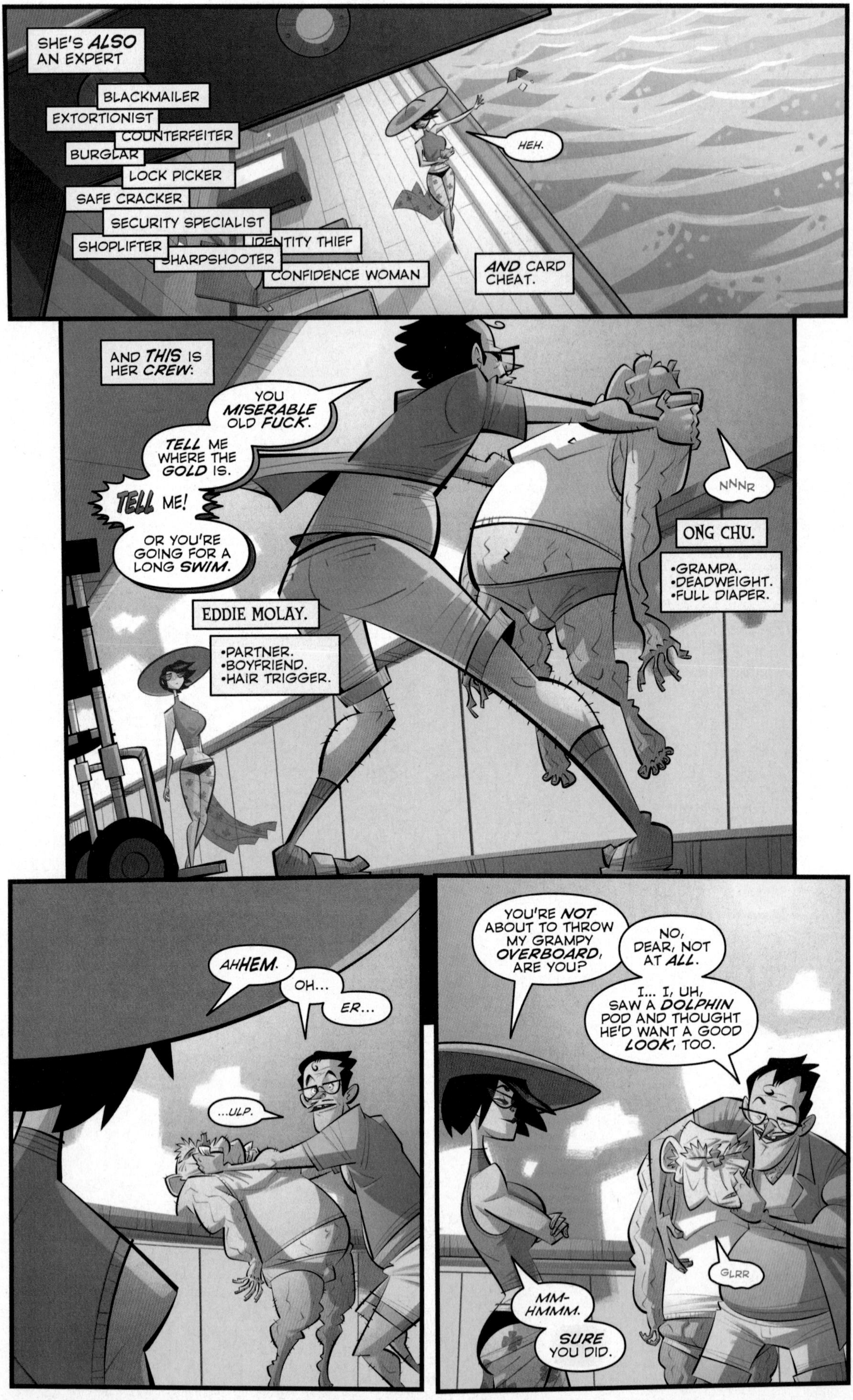

SHE'S ALSO AN EXPERT
BLACKMAILER
EXTORTIONIST
COUNTERFEITER
BURGLAR
LOCK PICKER
SAFE CRACKER
SECURITY SPECIALIST
SHOPLIFTER
IDENTITY THIEF
SHARPSHOOTER
CONFIDENCE WOMAN
HEH.
AND CARD CHEAT.
AND THIS IS HER CREW:
YOU MISERABLE OLD FUCK.
TELL ME WHERE THE GOLD IS.
TELL ME!
OR YOU'RE GOING FOR A LONG SWIM.
NNNR
ONG CHU.
•GRAMPA.
•DEADWEIGHT.
•FULL DIAPER.
EDDIE MOLAY.
•PARTNER.
•BOYFRIEND.
•HAIR TRIGGER.
AHHEM.
OH...
ER...
...ULP.
YOU'RE NOT ABOUT TO THROW MY GRAMPY OVERBOARD, ARE YOU?
NO, DEAR, NOT AT ALL.
I... I, UH, SAW A DOLPHIN POD AND THOUGHT HE'D WANT A GOOD LOOK, TOO.
GLRR
MM-HMMM.
SURE YOU DID.

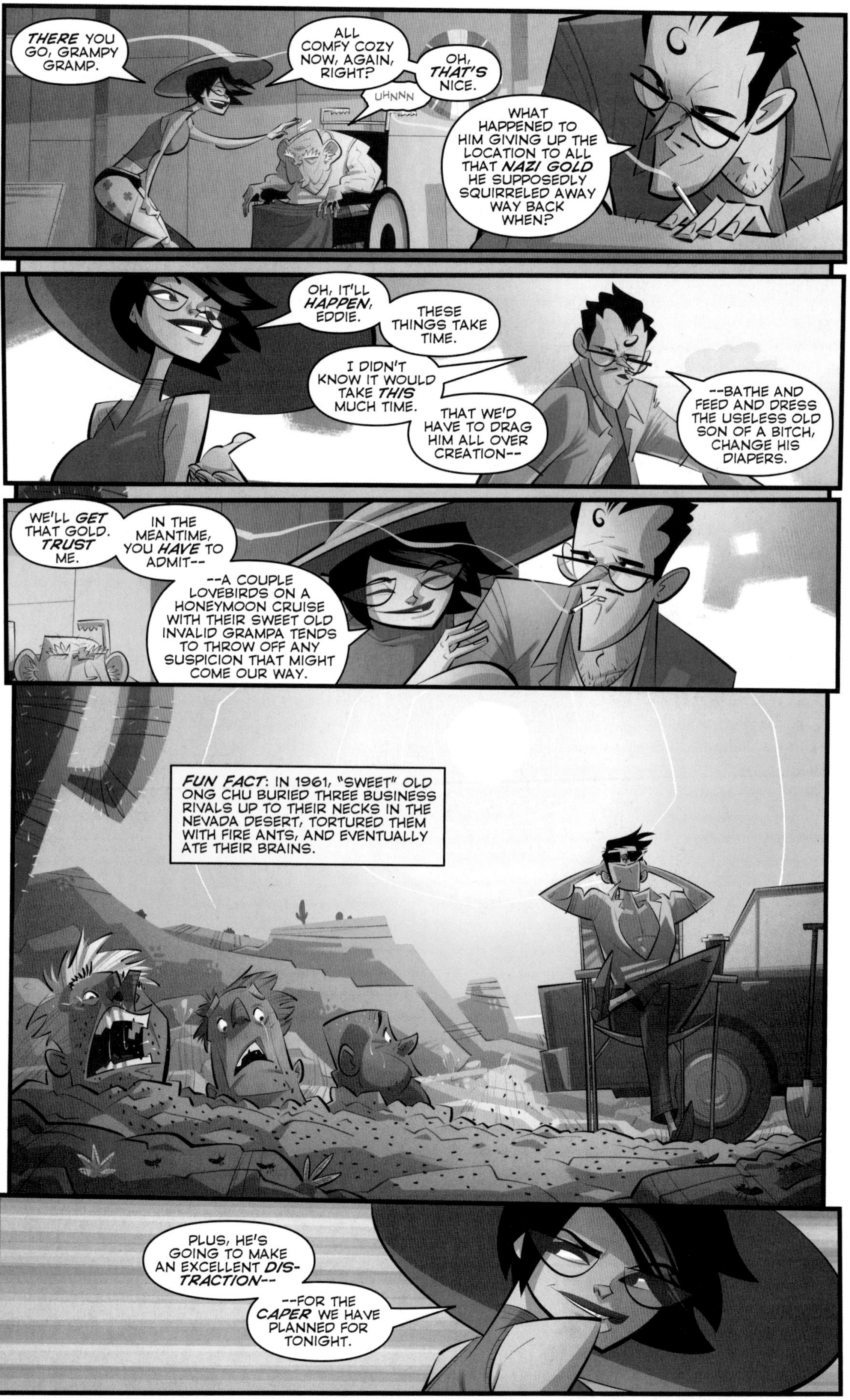
THERE YOU GO, GRAMPY GRAMP.
ALL COMFY COZY NOW, AGAIN, RIGHT?
UHNNN
OH, THAT'S NICE.
WHAT HAPPENED TO HIM GIVING UP THE LOCATION TO ALL THAT NAZI GOLD HE SUPPOSEDLY SQUIRRELED AWAY WAY BACK WHEN?
OH, IT'LL HAPPEN, EDDIE.
THESE THINGS TAKE TIME.
I DIDN'T KNOW IT WOULD TAKE THIS MUCH TIME.
THAT WE'D HAVE TO DRAG HIM ALL OVER CREATION--
--BATHE AND FEED AND DRESS THE USELESS OLD SON OF A BITCH, CHANGE HIS DIAPERS.
WE'LL GET THAT GOLD. TRUST ME.
IN THE MEANTIME, YOU HAVE TO ADMIT--
--A COUPLE LOVEBIRDS ON A HONEYMOON CRUISE WITH THEIR SWEET OLD INVALID GRAMPA TENDS TO THROW OFF ANY SUSPICION THAT MIGHT COME OUR WAY.
FUN FACT: IN 1961, "SWEET" OLD ONG CHU BURIED THREE BUSINESS RIVALS UP TO THEIR NECKS IN THE NEVADA DESERT, TORTURED THEM WITH FIRE ANTS, AND EVENTUALLY ATE THEIR BRAINS.
PLUS, HE'S GOING TO MAKE AN EXCELLENT DIS-TRACTION--
--FOR THE CAPER WE HAVE PLANNED FOR TONIGHT.

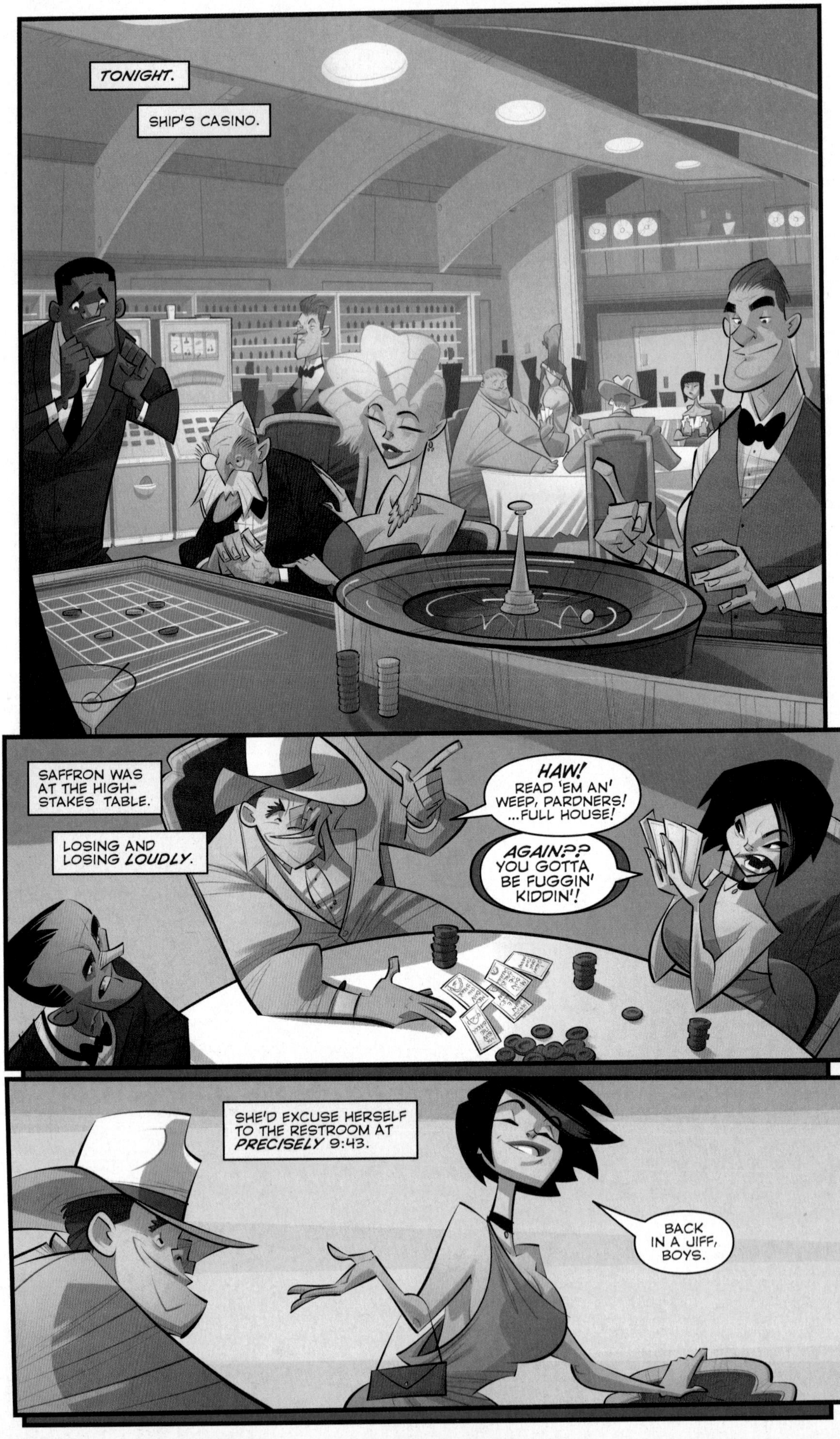
TONIGHT.
SHIP'S CASINO.
SAFFRON WAS AT THE HIGH-STAKES TABLE.
LOSING AND LOSING LOUDLY.
HAW! READ 'EM AN' WEEP, PARDNERS! ...FULL HOUSE!
AGAIN?? YOU GOTTA BE FUGGIN' KIDDIN'!
SHE'D EXCUSE HERSELF TO THE RESTROOM AT PRECISELY 9:43.
BACK IN A JIFF, BOYS.

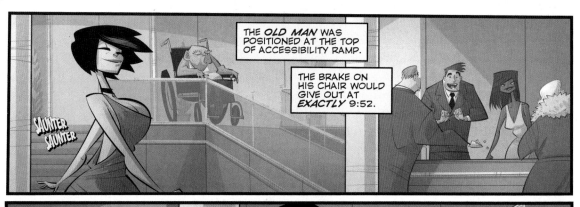

THE *OLD MAN* WAS POSITIONED AT THE TOP OF ACCESSIBILITY RAMP.

THE BRAKE ON HIS CHAIR WOULD GIVE OUT AT *EXACTLY* 9:52.

SAUNTER SAUNTER

EDDIE MOLAY WAS SEATED AT A SLOT MACHINE ADJACENT TO THE CASHIER'S STATION.

STRUT STRUT

MR. CARD, THEIR INSIDE MAN, WAS WORKING THE BLACKJACK TABLE DIRECTLY ACROSS FROM THE COUNTING ROOM.

SWISH SWISH

PIT BOSS KASSOLAY WAS THE ONLY PERSON WHO *MIGHT* HAVE BEEN ABLE TO SUSS OUT WHAT WAS HAPPENING.

BUT HE CALLED IN *SICK* THAT SHIFT--

--HAVING EATEN SOMETHING EARLIER IN THE DAY THAT LEFT HIM *VIOLENTLY* ILL.

BLEGHORFF!

EARLIER THAT DAY:

OR *SOMETHING* LIKE THAT.

DISTRACT DISTRACT

PLINK PLINK

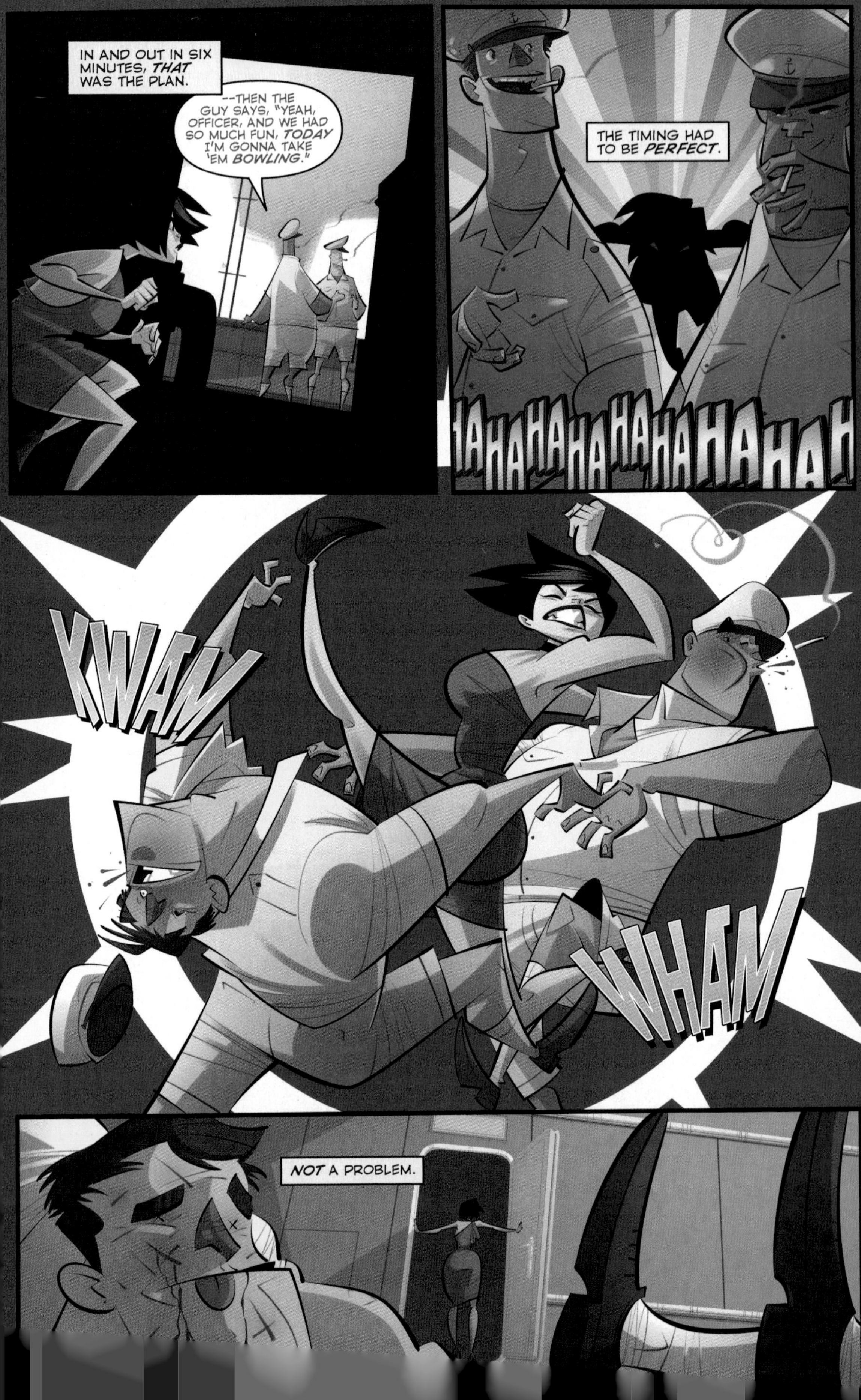
IN AND OUT IN SIX MINUTES, *THAT* WAS THE PLAN.
--THEN THE GUY SAYS, "YEAH, OFFICER, AND WE HAD SO MUCH FUN, *TODAY* I'M GONNA TAKE 'EM *BOWLING*."
THE TIMING HAD TO BE *PERFECT*.
HAHAHAHAHAHAHAHAHAH
KWAM
WHAM
NOT A PROBLEM.

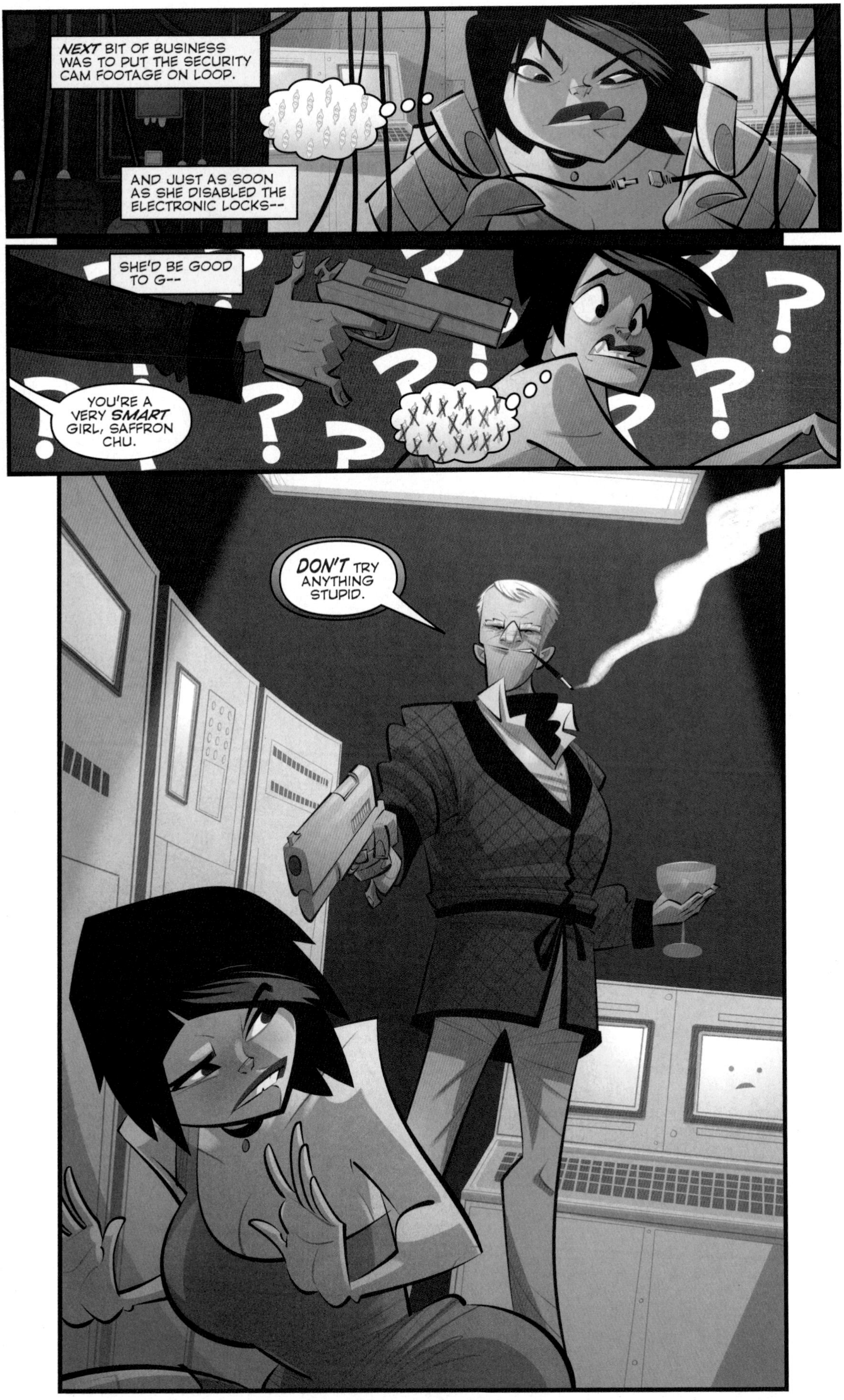
NEXT BIT OF BUSINESS WAS TO PUT THE SECURITY CAM FOOTAGE ON LOOP.
AND JUST AS SOON AS SHE DISABLED THE ELECTRONIC LOCKS--
SHE'D BE GOOD TO G--
YOU'RE A VERY SMART GIRL, SAFFRON CHU.
DON'T TRY ANYTHING STUPID.

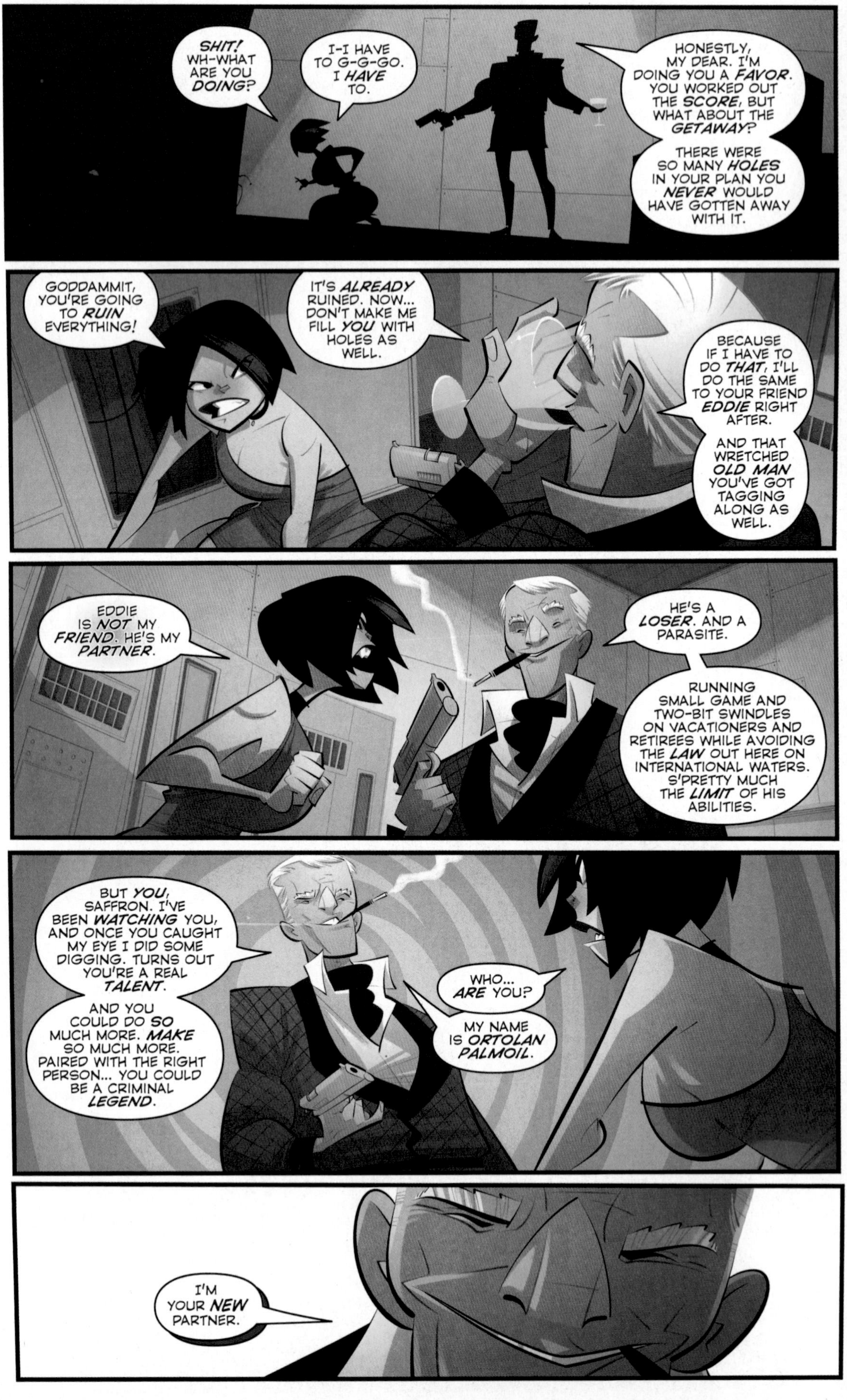
SHIT! WH-WHAT ARE YOU DOING?
I-I HAVE TO G-G-GO. I HAVE TO.
HONESTLY, MY DEAR. I'M DOING YOU A FAVOR. YOU WORKED OUT THE SCORE, BUT WHAT ABOUT THE GETAWAY?
THERE WERE SO MANY HOLES IN YOUR PLAN YOU NEVER WOULD HAVE GOTTEN AWAY WITH IT.
GODDAMMIT, YOU'RE GOING TO RUIN EVERYTHING!
IT'S ALREADY RUINED. NOW... DON'T MAKE ME FILL YOU WITH HOLES AS WELL.
BECAUSE IF I HAVE TO DO THAT, I'LL DO THE SAME TO YOUR FRIEND EDDIE RIGHT AFTER.
AND THAT WRETCHED OLD MAN YOU'VE GOT TAGGING ALONG AS WELL.
EDDIE IS NOT MY FRIEND. HE'S MY PARTNER.
HE'S A LOSER. AND A PARASITE.
RUNNING SMALL GAME AND TWO-BIT SWINDLES ON VACATIONERS AND RETIREES WHILE AVOIDING THE LAW OUT HERE ON INTERNATIONAL WATERS. S'PRETTY MUCH THE LIMIT OF HIS ABILITIES.
BUT YOU, SAFFRON. I'VE BEEN WATCHING YOU, AND ONCE YOU CAUGHT MY EYE I DID SOME DIGGING. TURNS OUT YOU'RE A REAL TALENT.
AND YOU COULD DO SO MUCH MORE. MAKE SO MUCH MORE. PAIRED WITH THE RIGHT PERSON... YOU COULD BE A CRIMINAL LEGEND.
WHO... ARE YOU?
MY NAME IS ORTOLAN PALMOIL.
I'M YOUR NEW PARTNER.

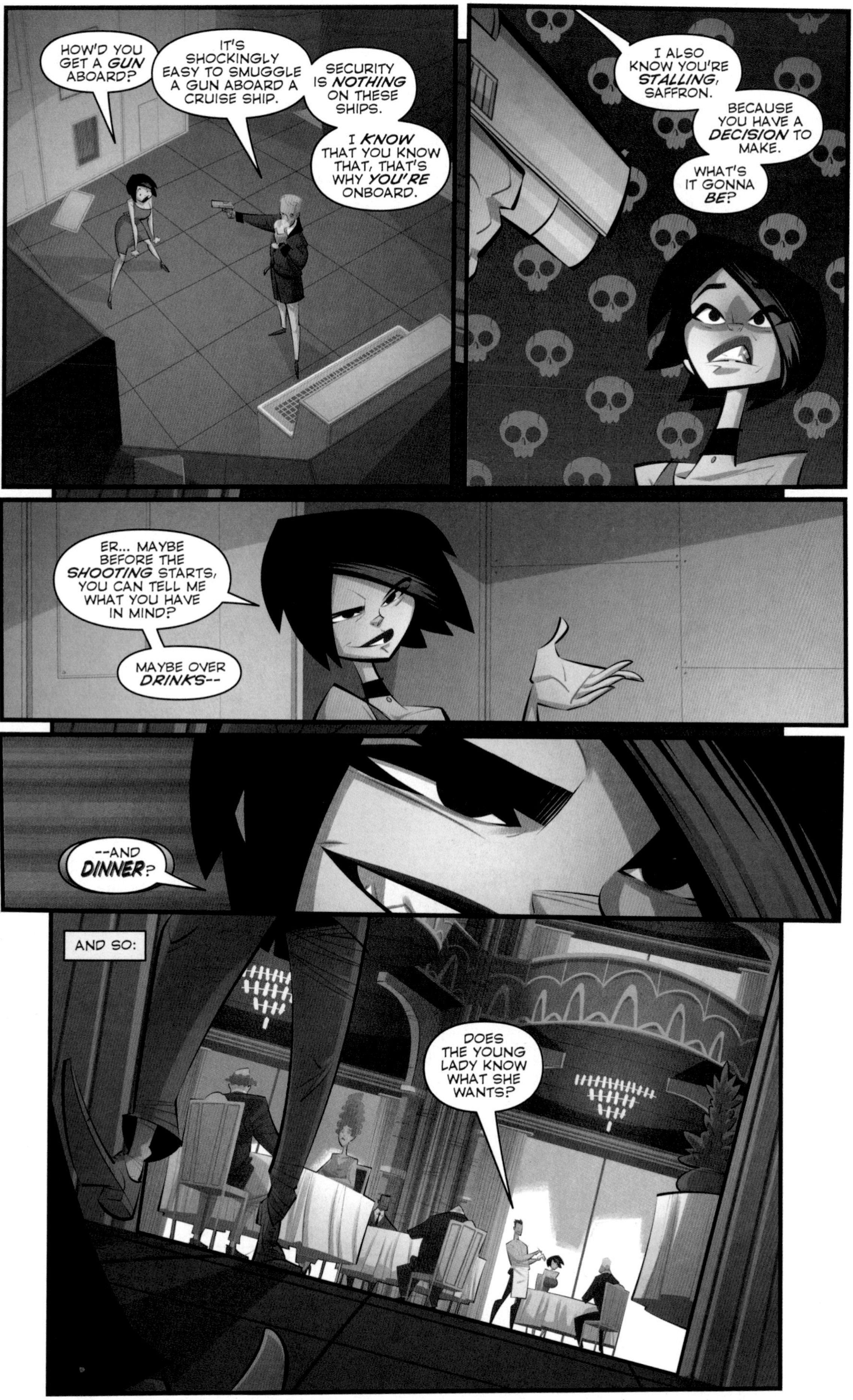
HOW'D YOU GET A GUN ABOARD?
IT'S SHOCKINGLY EASY TO SMUGGLE A GUN ABOARD A CRUISE SHIP.
SECURITY IS NOTHING ON THESE SHIPS.
I KNOW THAT YOU KNOW THAT, THAT'S WHY YOU'RE ONBOARD.
I ALSO KNOW YOU'RE STALLING, SAFFRON.
BECAUSE YOU HAVE A DECISION TO MAKE.
WHAT'S IT GONNA BE?
ER... MAYBE BEFORE THE SHOOTING STARTS, YOU CAN TELL ME WHAT YOU HAVE IN MIND?
MAYBE OVER DRINKS--
--AND DINNER?
AND SO:
DOES THE YOUNG LADY KNOW WHAT SHE WANTS?

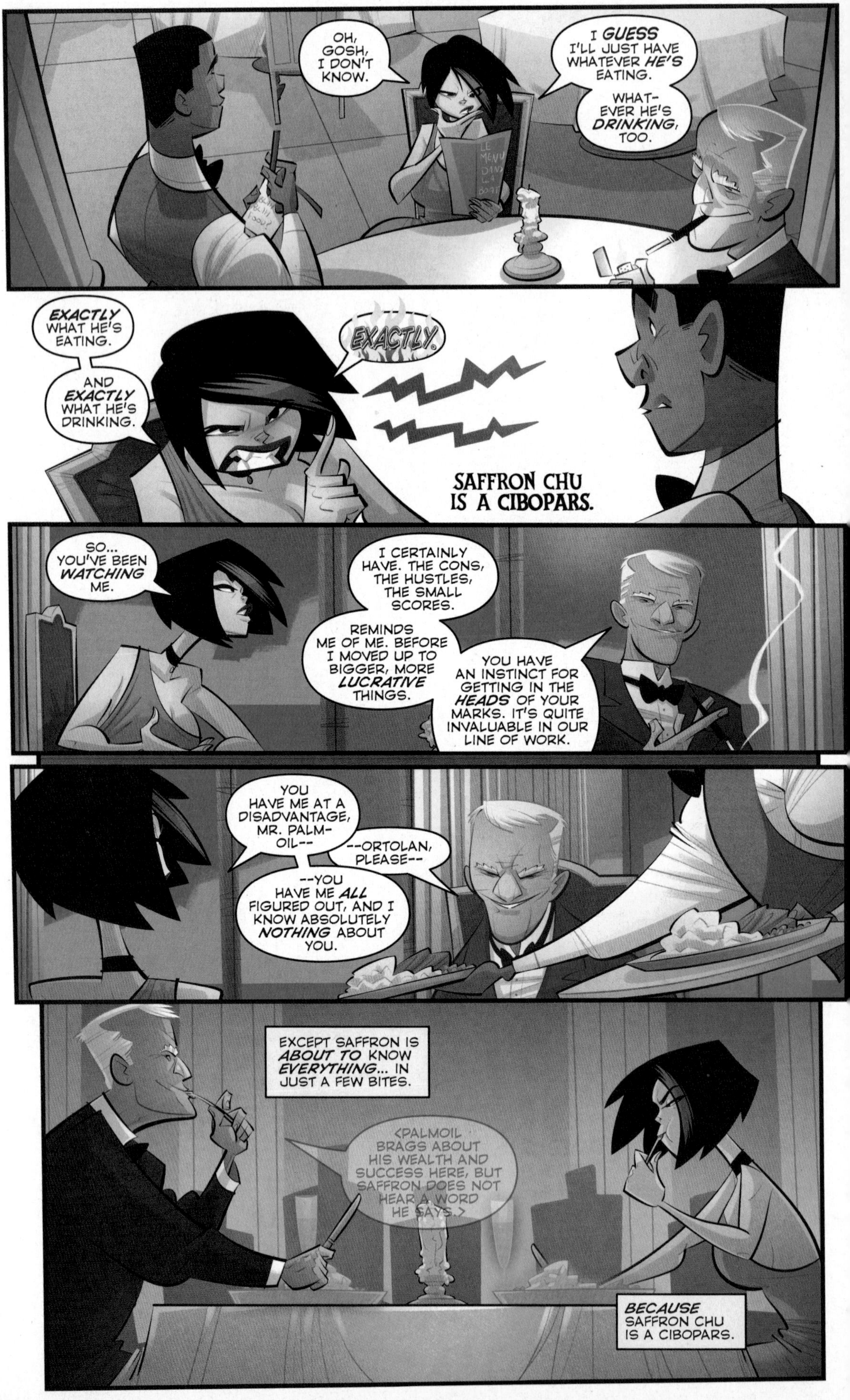
OH, GOSH, I DON'T KNOW.
I GUESS I'LL JUST HAVE WHATEVER HE'S EATING.
WHAT-EVER HE'S DRINKING, TOO.
LE MENU
EXACTLY WHAT HE'S EATING.
AND EXACTLY WHAT HE'S DRINKING.
EXACTLY.
SAFFRON CHU IS A CIBOPARS.
SO... YOU'VE BEEN WATCHING ME.
I CERTAINLY HAVE. THE CONS, THE HUSTLES, THE SMALL SCORES.
REMINDS ME OF ME. BEFORE I MOVED UP TO BIGGER, MORE LUCRATIVE THINGS.
YOU HAVE AN INSTINCT FOR GETTING IN THE HEADS OF YOUR MARKS. IT'S QUITE INVALUABLE IN OUR LINE OF WORK.
YOU HAVE ME AT A DISADVANTAGE, MR. PALM-OIL--
--ORTOLAN, PLEASE--
--YOU HAVE ME ALL FIGURED OUT, AND I KNOW ABSOLUTELY NOTHING ABOUT YOU.
EXCEPT SAFFRON IS ABOUT TO KNOW EVERYTHING... IN JUST A FEW BITES.
<PALMOIL BRAGS ABOUT HIS WEALTH AND SUCCESS HERE, BUT SAFFRON DOES NOT HEAR A WORD HE SAYS.>
BECAUSE SAFFRON CHU IS A CIBOPARS.

...BUT ON A MUCH LARGER SCALE, AND ONCE YOU'VE HAD A *TASTE* FOR IT, IT'S HARD TO GIVE UP.

AND SO I *COLLECT*. THE FINEST WINES, THE FASTEST CARS, THE MOST EXPENSIVE ART, SCULPTURE, INTERNATIONAL PROPERTIES.*

AND I CAN *AFFORD* TO, TOO.

THIS COULD BE *YOUR* LIFE AS WELL, SAFFRON.

*BUT DEFINITELY *NOT* COMIC BOOKS!

THIS IS WHAT I'M OFFERING YOU.

INTERESTED?

OH, I'M *VERY* INTERESTED.

BUT WHAT I'M EVEN *MORE* INTERESTED IN--

--IS THAT GOLDEN *INVITATION* IN YOUR INSIDE LEFT POCKET.

ASTONISHING. WHEN I SAID YOU HAD A TALENT FOR GETTING INTO PEOPLE'S HEADS, I WAS SPEAKING FIGURATIVELY.

BUT YOU... YOU'RE SOMETHING *TRULY* UNIQUE, AREN'T YOU?

(CIBOPARS.)

THE INVITATION, PALMOIL.

SPILL.

THIS... IS A TICKET. A TICKET TO UNTOLD *MILLIONS.*

DO YOU KNOW WHAT A *VINÉTEMPORUS* IS, SAFFRON?

L'Invitation

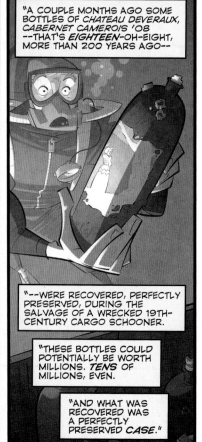

"A COUPLE MONTHS AGO SOME BOTTLES OF *CHATEAU DEVERAUX, CABERNET CAMEROIS '08* --THAT'S *EIGHTEEN*-OH-EIGHT, MORE THAN 200 YEARS AGO--

"--WERE RECOVERED, PERFECTLY PRESERVED, DURING THE SALVAGE OF A WRECKED 19TH-CENTURY CARGO SCHOONER.

"THESE BOTTLES COULD POTENTIALLY BE WORTH MILLIONS. *TENS* OF MILLIONS, EVEN.

"AND WHAT WAS RECOVERED WAS A PERFECTLY PRESERVED *CASE.*"

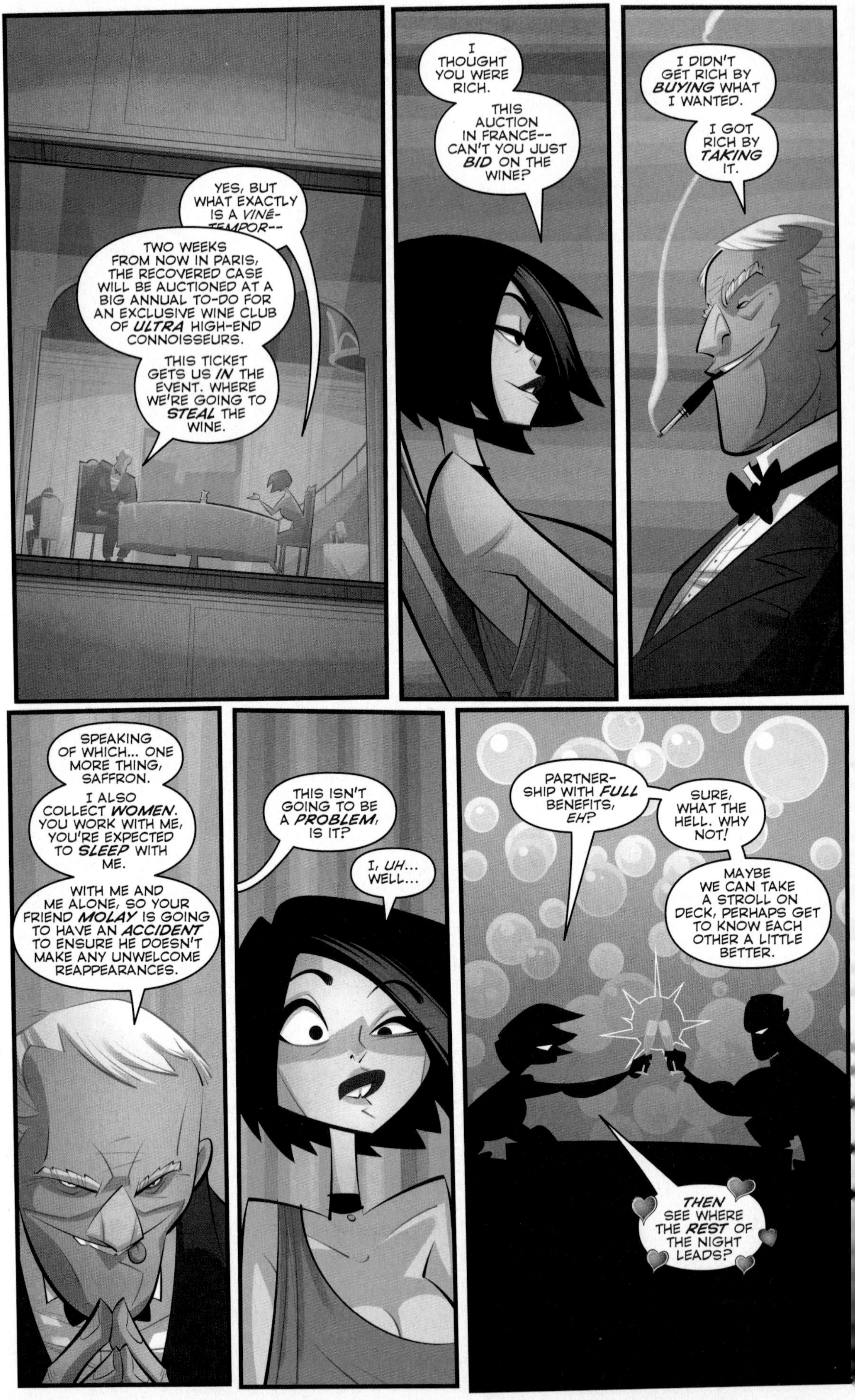

YES, BUT WHAT EXACTLY IS A VINÉ-TEMPOR--
TWO WEEKS FROM NOW IN PARIS, THE RECOVERED CASE WILL BE AUCTIONED AT A BIG ANNUAL TO-DO FOR AN EXCLUSIVE WINE CLUB OF ULTRA HIGH-END CONNOISSEURS.
THIS TICKET GETS US IN THE EVENT. WHERE WE'RE GOING TO STEAL THE WINE.
I THOUGHT YOU WERE RICH.
THIS AUCTION IN FRANCE-- CAN'T YOU JUST BID ON THE WINE?
I DIDN'T GET RICH BY BUYING WHAT I WANTED.
I GOT RICH BY TAKING IT.
SPEAKING OF WHICH... ONE MORE THING, SAFFRON.
I ALSO COLLECT WOMEN. YOU WORK WITH ME, YOU'RE EXPECTED TO SLEEP WITH ME.
WITH ME AND ME ALONE, SO YOUR FRIEND MOLAY IS GOING TO HAVE AN ACCIDENT TO ENSURE HE DOESN'T MAKE ANY UNWELCOME REAPPEARANCES.
THIS ISN'T GOING TO BE A PROBLEM, IS IT?
I, UH... WELL...
PARTNERSHIP WITH FULL BENEFITS, EH?
SURE, WHAT THE HELL. WHY NOT!
MAYBE WE CAN TAKE A STROLL ON DECK, PERHAPS GET TO KNOW EACH OTHER A LITTLE BETTER.
THEN SEE WHERE THE REST OF THE NIGHT LEADS?

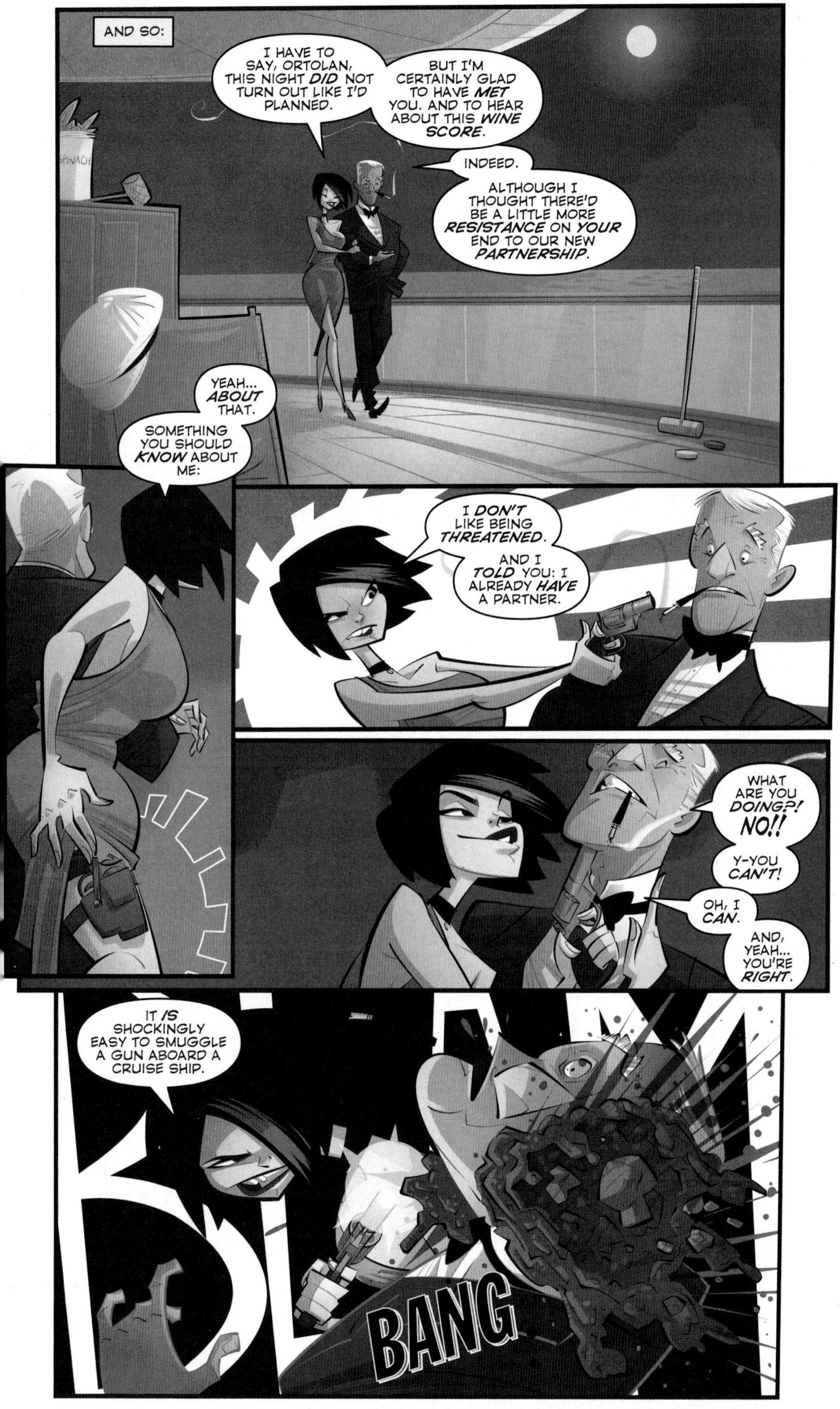
AND SO:
I HAVE TO SAY, ORTOLAN, THIS NIGHT *DID* NOT TURN OUT LIKE I'D PLANNED.
BUT I'M CERTAINLY GLAD TO HAVE *MET* YOU. AND TO HEAR ABOUT THIS *WINE SCORE*.
INDEED.
ALTHOUGH I THOUGHT THERE'D BE A LITTLE MORE *RESISTANCE* ON *YOUR* END TO OUR NEW *PARTNERSHIP*.
SPINACH
YEAH... *ABOUT* THAT.
SOMETHING YOU SHOULD *KNOW* ABOUT ME:
I *DON'T* LIKE BEING *THREATENED*.
AND I *TOLD* YOU: I ALREADY *HAVE* A PARTNER.
WHAT ARE YOU *DOING?!* NO!!
Y-YOU *CAN'T*!
OH, I *CAN*.
AND, YEAH... YOU'RE *RIGHT*.
IT *IS* SHOCKINGLY EASY TO SMUGGLE A GUN ABOARD A CRUISE SHIP.
BANG

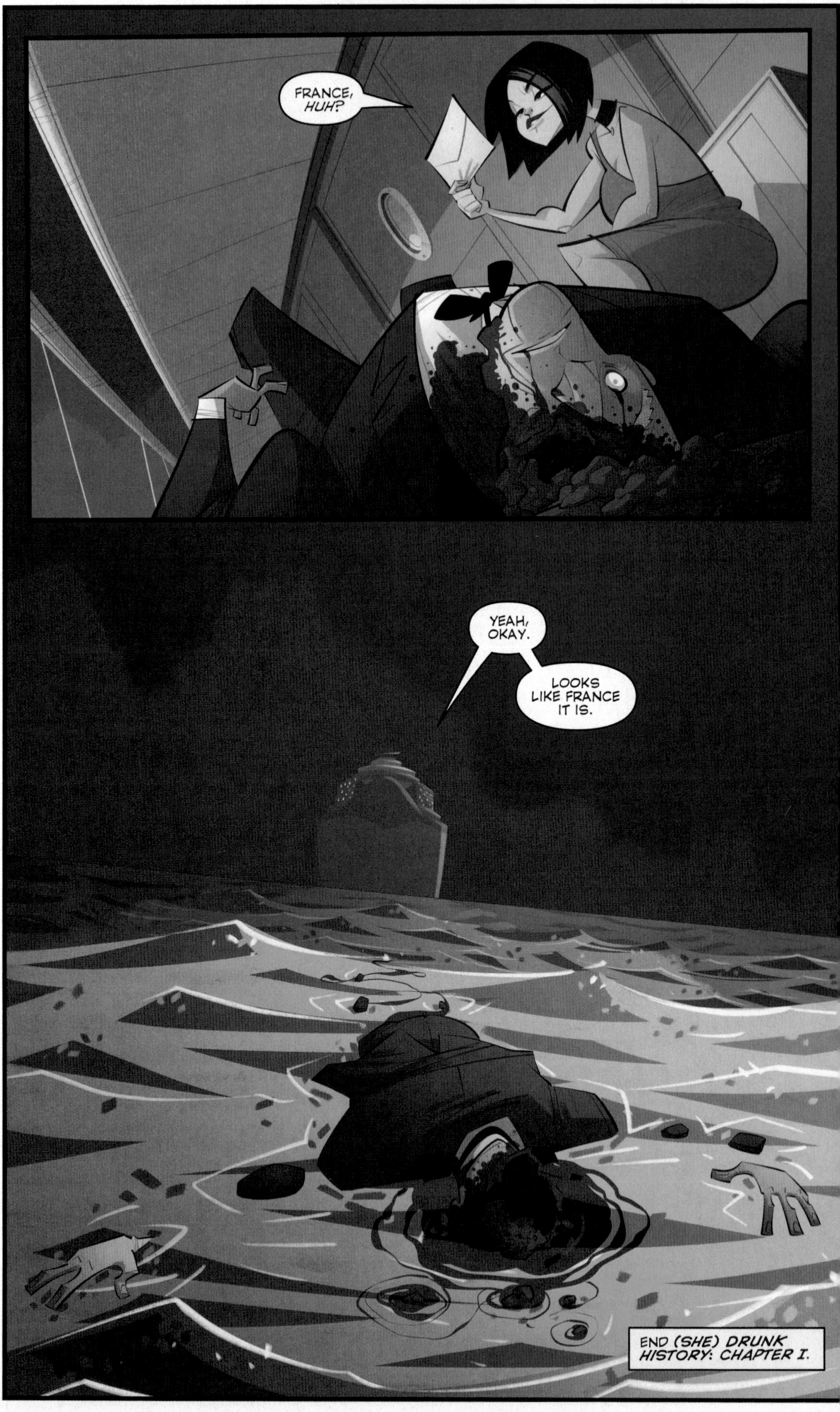
FRANCE, *HUH?*
YEAH, OKAY.
LOOKS LIKE FRANCE IT IS.
END (SHE) *DRUNK HISTORY: CHAPTER I.*

Chapter 2

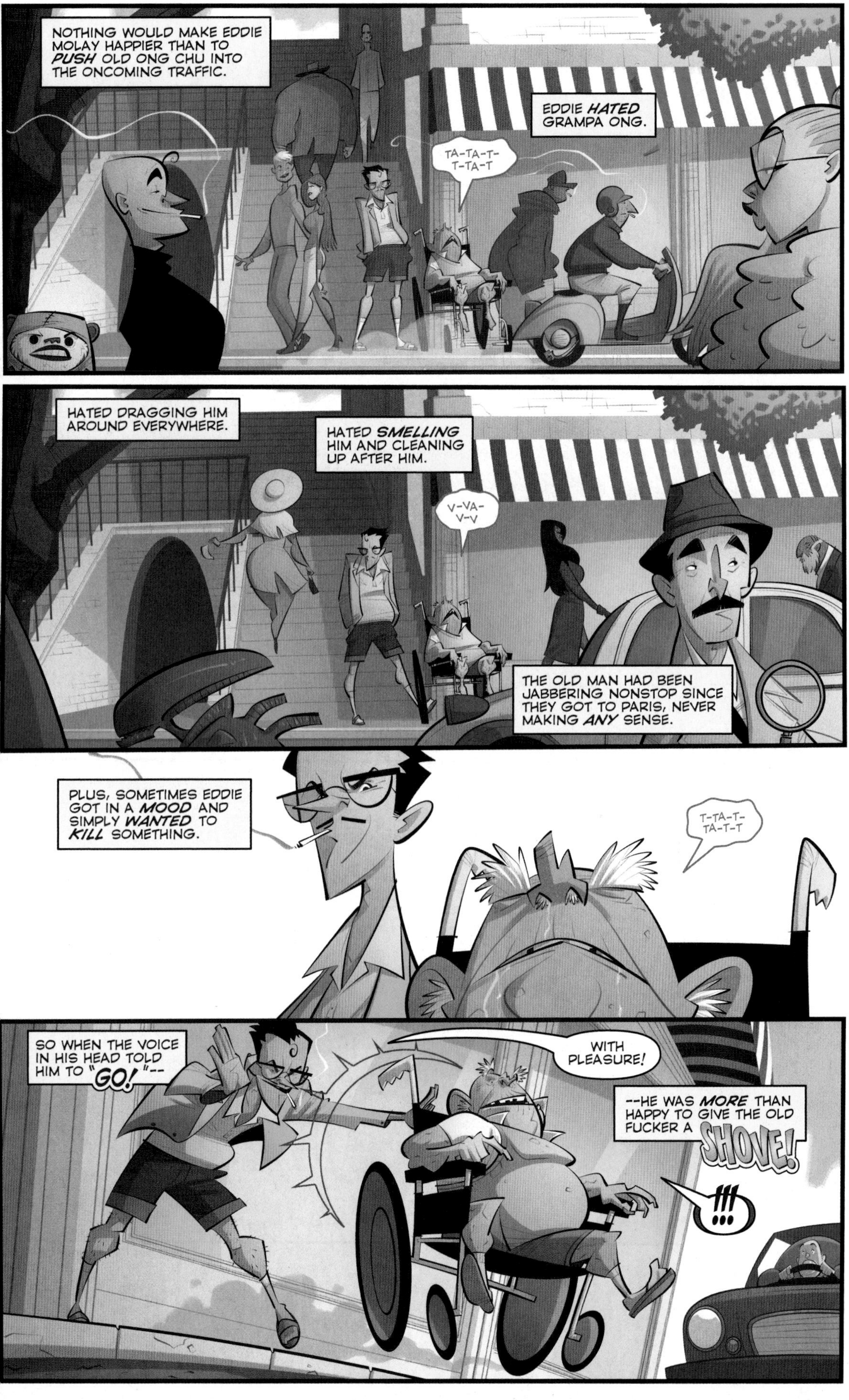
NOTHING WOULD MAKE EDDIE MOLAY HAPPIER THAN TO PUSH OLD ONG CHU INTO THE ONCOMING TRAFFIC.
EDDIE HATED GRAMPA ONG.
TA-TA-T-T-TA-T
HATED DRAGGING HIM AROUND EVERYWHERE.
HATED SMELLING HIM AND CLEANING UP AFTER HIM.
V-VA-V-V
THE OLD MAN HAD BEEN JABBERING NONSTOP SINCE THEY GOT TO PARIS, NEVER MAKING ANY SENSE.
PLUS, SOMETIMES EDDIE GOT IN A MOOD AND SIMPLY WANTED TO KILL SOMETHING.
T-TA-T-TA-T-T
SO WHEN THE VOICE IN HIS HEAD TOLD HIM TO "GO!"--
WITH PLEASURE!
--HE WAS MORE THAN HAPPY TO GIVE THE OLD FUCKER A SHOVE!
!!!

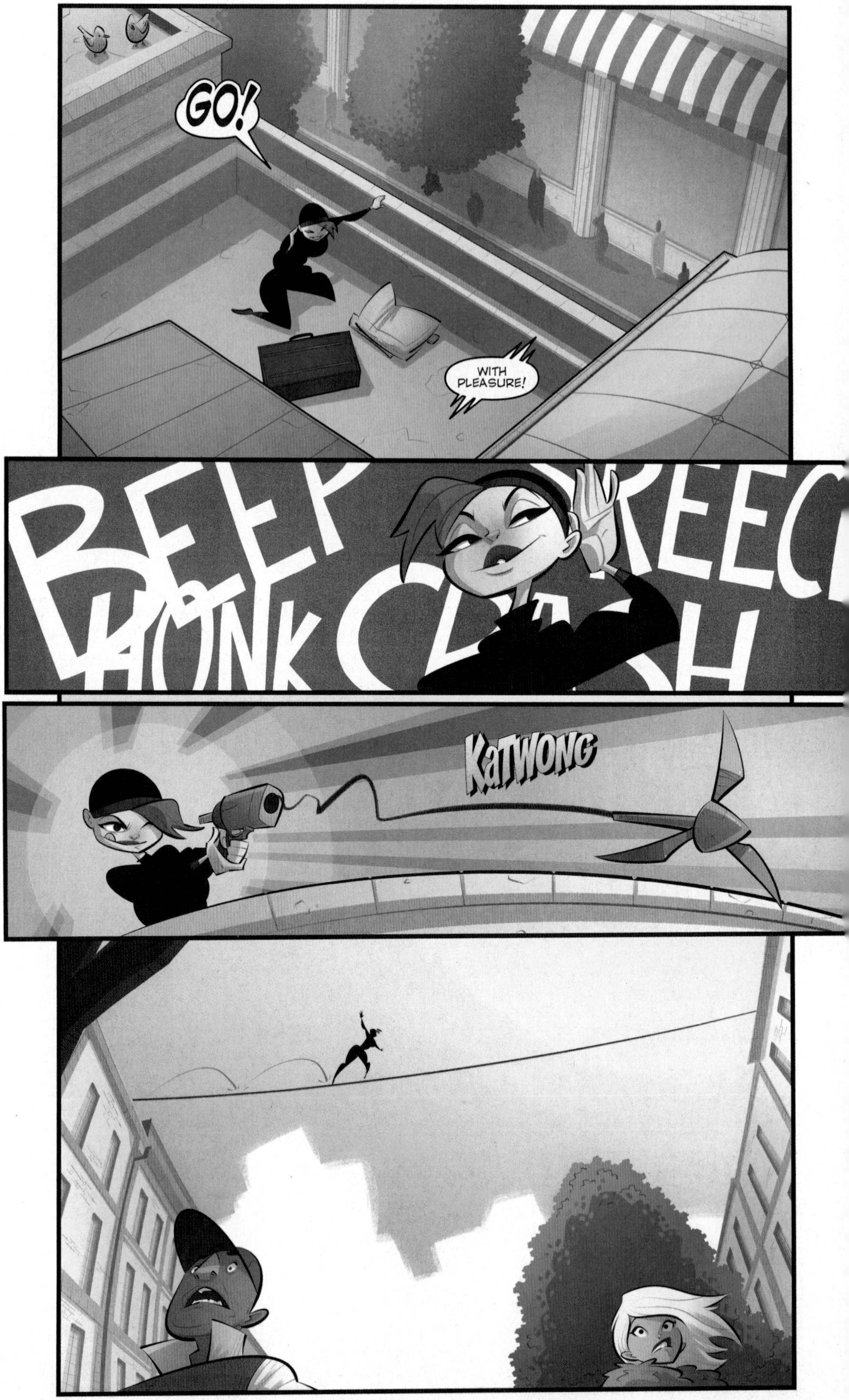
GO!
WITH PLEASURE!
BEEP
HONK
KaTWONG

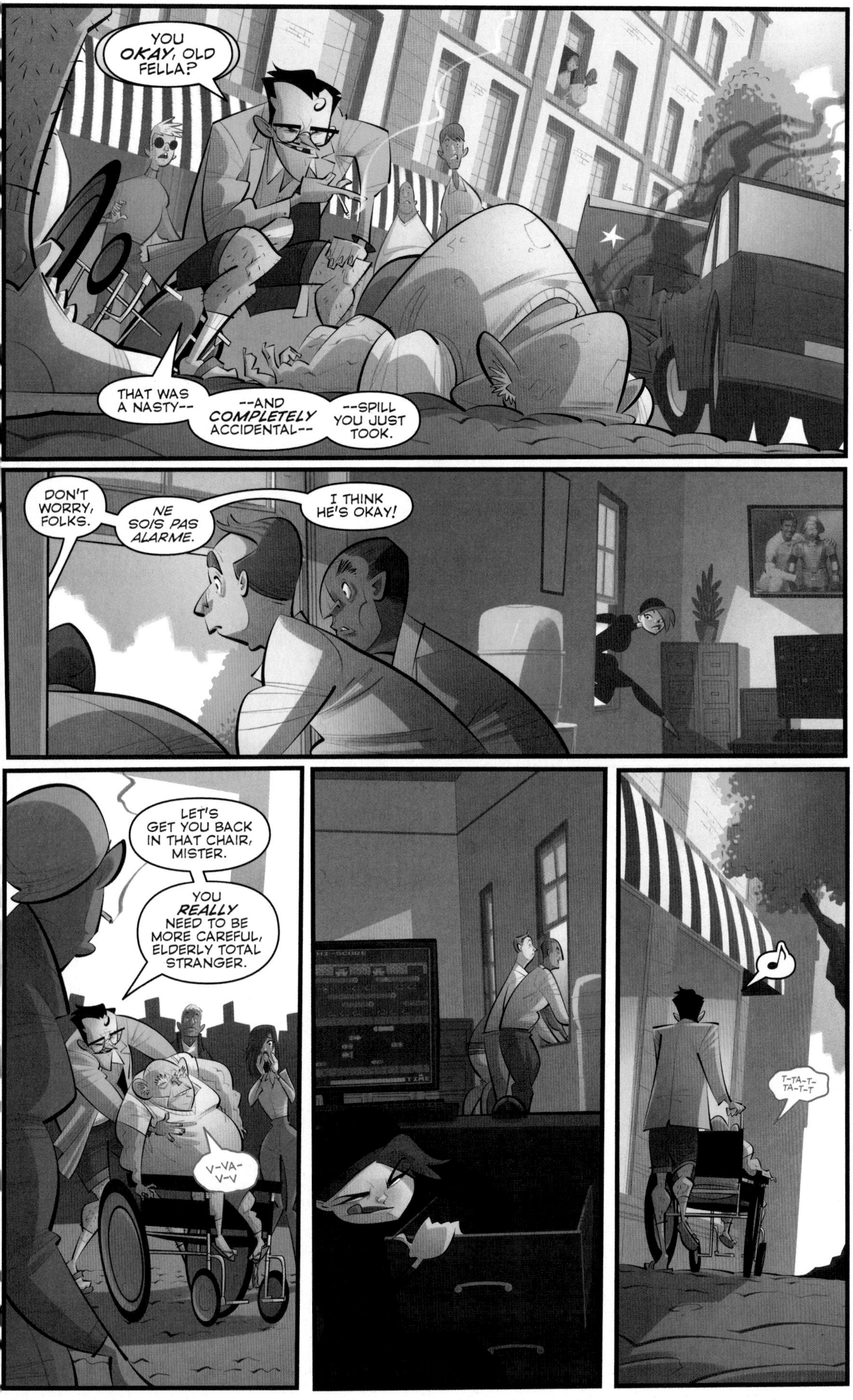
YOU OKAY, OLD FELLA?
THAT WAS A NASTY--
--AND COMPLETELY ACCIDENTAL--
--SPILL YOU JUST TOOK.
DON'T WORRY, FOLKS.
NE SOIS PAS ALARME.
I THINK HE'S OKAY!
LET'S GET YOU BACK IN THAT CHAIR, MISTER.
YOU REALLY NEED TO BE MORE CAREFUL, ELDERLY TOTAL STRANGER.
V-VA-V-V
HI-SCORE
TIME
T-TA-T-TA-T-T

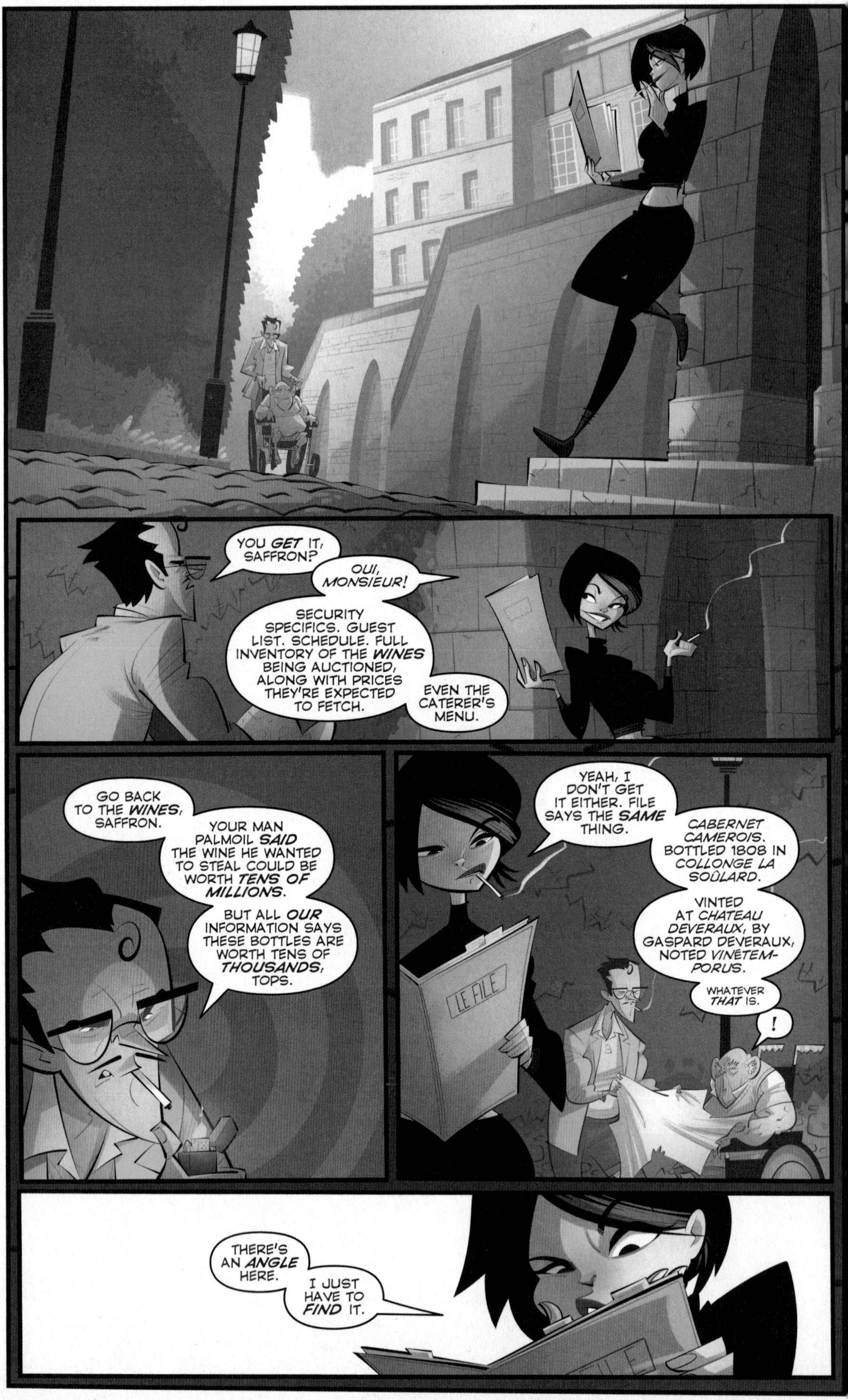
YOU GET IT, SAFFRON?
OUI, MONSIEUR!
SECURITY SPECIFICS. GUEST LIST. SCHEDULE. FULL INVENTORY OF THE WINES BEING AUCTIONED, ALONG WITH PRICES THEY'RE EXPECTED TO FETCH.
EVEN THE CATERER'S MENU.
GO BACK TO THE WINES, SAFFRON.
YOUR MAN PALMOIL SAID THE WINE HE WANTED TO STEAL COULD BE WORTH TENS OF MILLIONS.
BUT ALL OUR INFORMATION SAYS THESE BOTTLES ARE WORTH TENS OF THOUSANDS, TOPS.
YEAH, I DON'T GET IT EITHER. FILE SAYS THE SAME THING.
CABERNET CAMEROIS. BOTTLED 1808 IN COLLONGE LA SOÛLARD.
VINTED AT CHATEAU DEVERAUX, BY GASPARD DEVERAUX, NOTED VINÉTEMPORUS.
WHATEVER THAT IS.
!
LE FILE
THERE'S AN ANGLE HERE.
I JUST HAVE TO FIND IT.

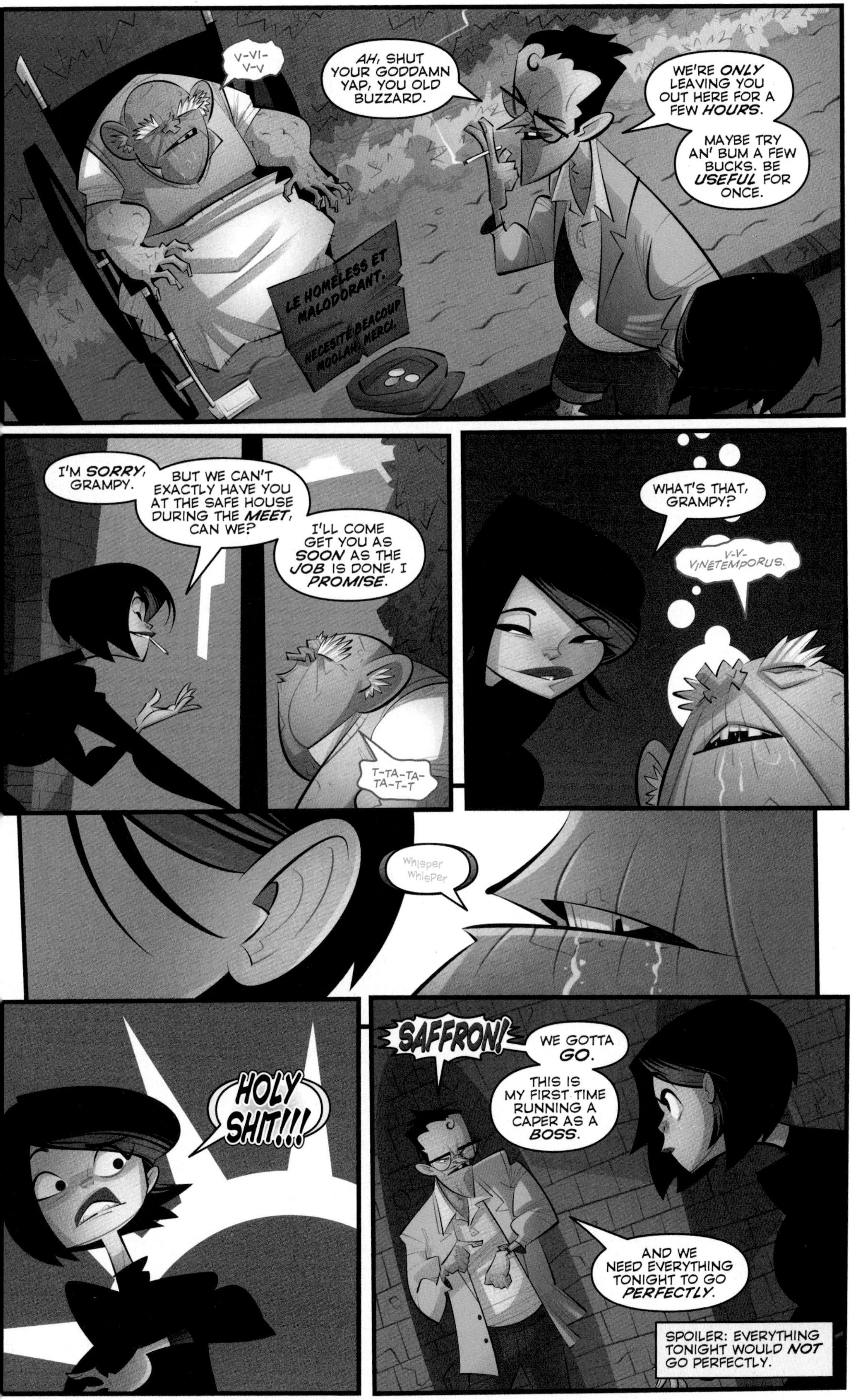

V-VI-
V-V
AH, SHUT YOUR GODDAMN YAP, YOU OLD BUZZARD.
WE'RE ONLY LEAVING YOU OUT HERE FOR A FEW HOURS.
MAYBE TRY AN' BUM A FEW BUCKS. BE USEFUL FOR ONCE.
LE HOMELESS ET MALODORANT.
NECESITÉ BEACOUP MOOLAH, MERCI.
I'M SORRY, GRAMPY.
BUT WE CAN'T EXACTLY HAVE YOU AT THE SAFE HOUSE DURING THE MEET, CAN WE?
I'LL COME GET YOU AS SOON AS THE JOB IS DONE, I PROMISE.
T-TA-TA-TA-T-T
WHAT'S THAT, GRAMPY?
V-V-VINETEMPORUS.
Whisper whisper
HOLY SHIT!!!
SAFFRON!
WE GOTTA GO.
THIS IS MY FIRST TIME RUNNING A CAPER AS A BOSS.
AND WE NEED EVERYTHING TONIGHT TO GO PERFECTLY.
SPOILER: EVERYTHING TONIGHT WOULD NOT GO PERFECTLY.

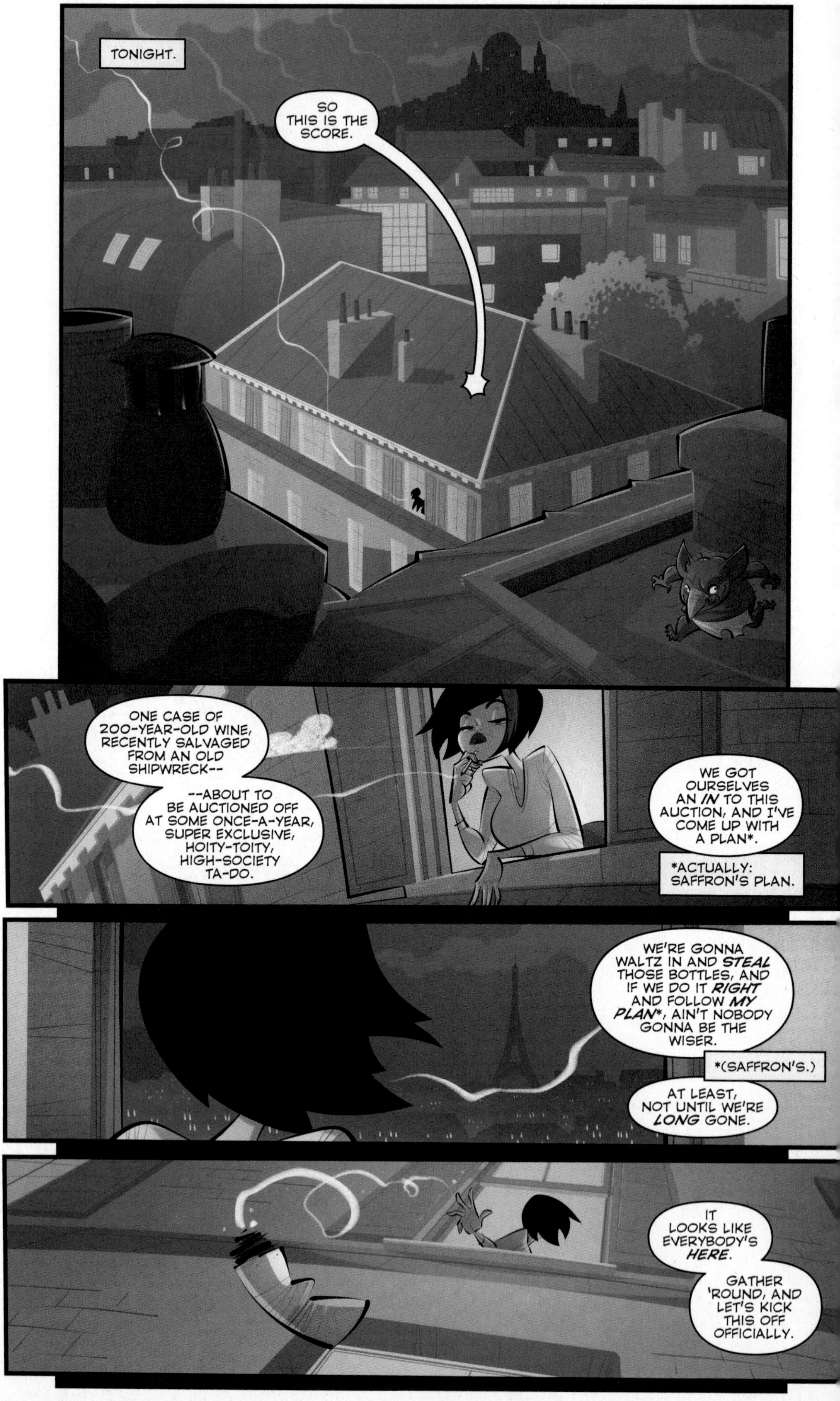
TONIGHT.
SO THIS IS THE SCORE.
ONE CASE OF 200-YEAR-OLD WINE, RECENTLY SALVAGED FROM AN OLD SHIPWRECK--
--ABOUT TO BE AUCTIONED OFF AT SOME ONCE-A-YEAR, SUPER EXCLUSIVE, HOITY-TOITY, HIGH-SOCIETY TA-DO.
WE GOT OURSELVES AN *IN* TO THIS AUCTION, AND I'VE COME UP WITH A PLAN*.
*ACTUALLY: SAFFRON'S PLAN.
WE'RE GONNA WALTZ IN AND ***STEAL*** THOSE BOTTLES, AND IF WE DO IT ***RIGHT*** AND FOLLOW ***MY PLAN****, AIN'T NOBODY GONNA BE THE WISER.
*(SAFFRON'S.)
AT LEAST, NOT UNTIL WE'RE ***LONG*** GONE.
IT LOOKS LIKE EVERYBODY'S ***HERE***.
GATHER 'ROUND, AND LET'S KICK THIS OFF OFFICIALLY.

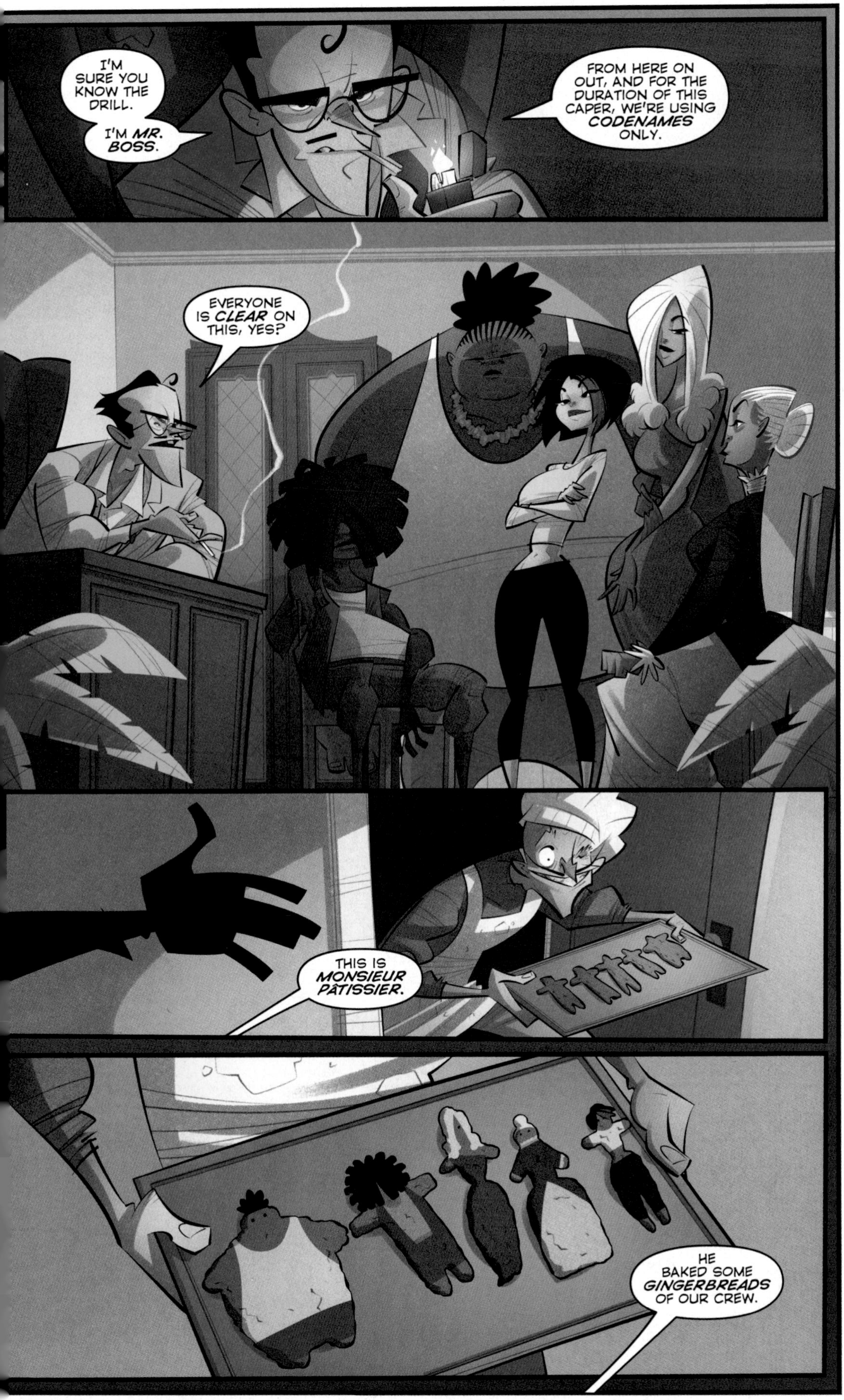
I'M SURE YOU KNOW THE DRILL.
I'M MR. BOSS.
FROM HERE ON OUT, AND FOR THE DURATION OF THIS CAPER, WE'RE USING CODENAMES ONLY.
EVERYONE IS CLEAR ON THIS, YES?
THIS IS MONSIEUR PÂTISSIER.
HE BAKED SOME GINGERBREADS OF OUR CREW.

EAT, *MES AMIS!* EAT AND ENJOY!

THESE COOKIES... THEY, UH, *DO* ANYTHING?

THEY ARE *VERY* SPECIAL. VERY DELICIOUS.

MUNCH MUNCH

MUNCH MUNCH

DISCLAIMER: THE GINGERBREADS, WHILE TASTY, ARE PERFECTLY ORDINARY.

FOR *YOU,* MADEMOISELLE?

MUNCH MUNCH

MUNCH MUNCH

MERCI, NON. NEVER BEFORE A JOB, DAHLING.

HELLO THERE, DEAR. I'M *LILY.* LILY VAN D—

UH... CODENAMES *ONLY,* REMEMBER?

I'M JUST HERE FOR THE *PAYCHECK,* SWEETIE.

I DON'T GIVE A FIG TOSS ABOUT YOUR DREARY MR. BOSS-MAN'S PRECIOUS "RULES."

WE NEED TO *TALK,* EDDIE.

WE GOT A *BIG PROBLEM* WITH *ONE* OF OUR CREW.

LATER, SAFFRON.

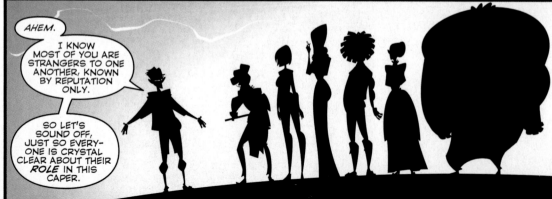

AHEM. I KNOW MOST OF YOU ARE STRANGERS TO ONE ANOTHER, KNOWN BY REPUTATION ONLY.

SO LET'S SOUND OFF, JUST SO EVERY- ONE IS CRYSTAL CLEAR ABOUT THEIR *ROLE* IN THIS CAPER.

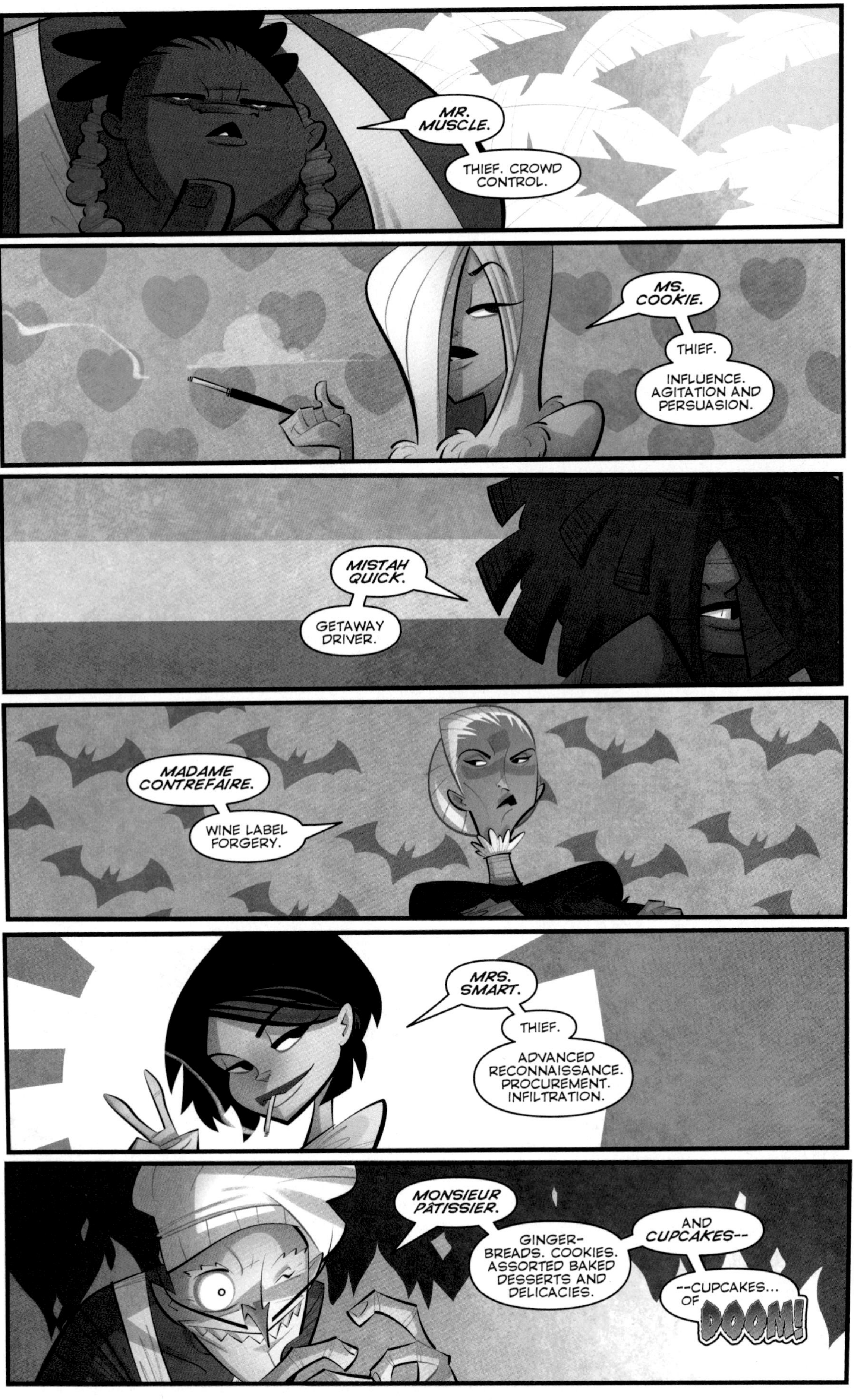
MR. MUSCLE.
THIEF. CROWD CONTROL.
MS. COOKIE.
THIEF.
INFLUENCE. AGITATION AND PERSUASION.
MISTAH QUICK.
GETAWAY DRIVER.
MADAME CONTREFAIRE.
WINE LABEL FORGERY.
MRS. SMART.
THIEF.
ADVANCED RECONNAISSANCE. PROCUREMENT. INFILTRATION.
MONSIEUR PÂTISSIER.
GINGER-BREADS. COOKIES. ASSORTED BAKED DESSERTS AND DELICACIES.
AND CUPCAKES--
--CUPCAKES... OF DOOM!

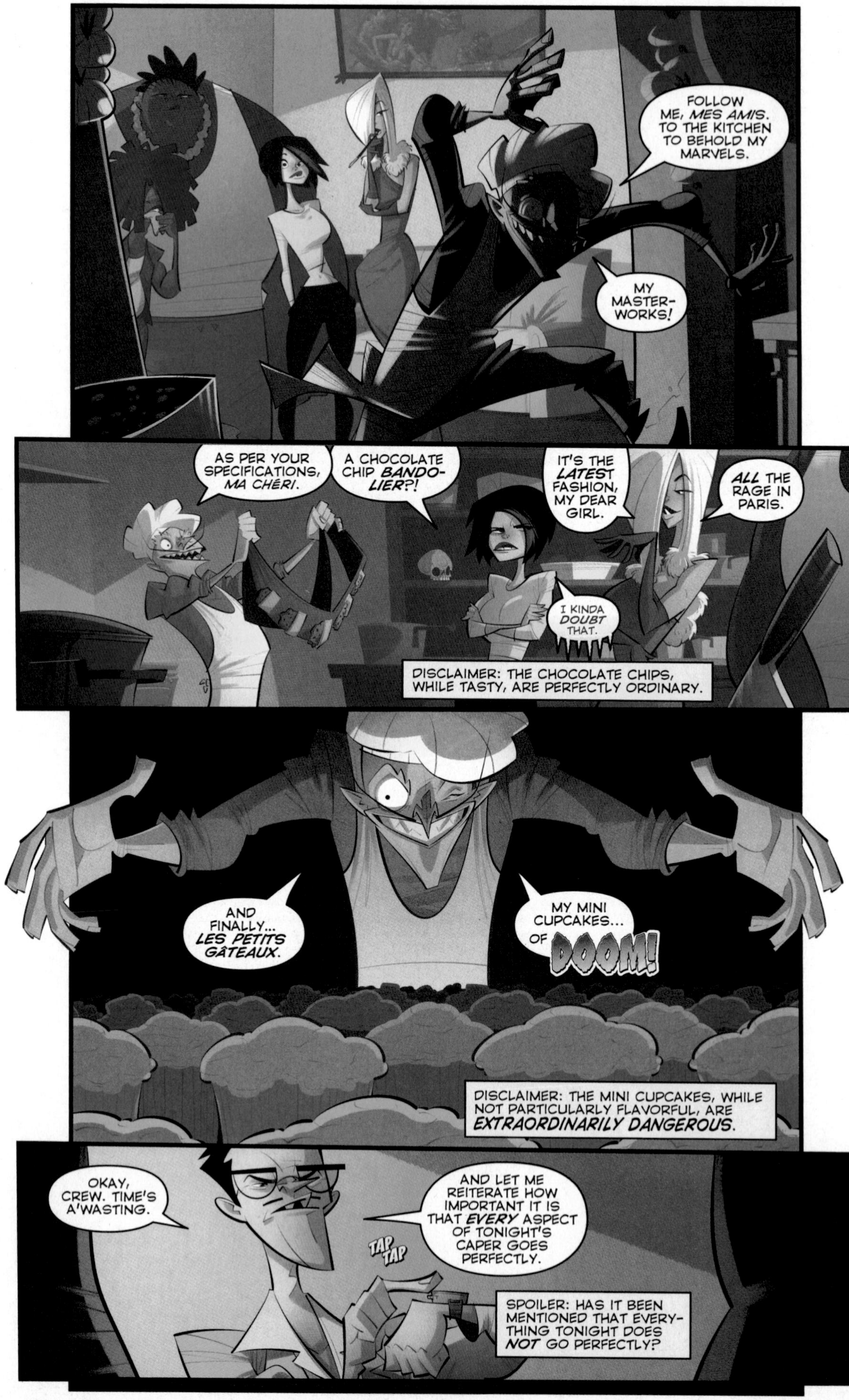
FOLLOW ME, MES AMIS. TO THE KITCHEN TO BEHOLD MY MARVELS.
MY MASTER-WORKS!
AS PER YOUR SPECIFICATIONS, MA CHÉRI.
A CHOCOLATE CHIP BANDOLIER?!
IT'S THE LATEST FASHION, MY DEAR GIRL.
ALL THE RAGE IN PARIS.
I KINDA DOUBT THAT.
DISCLAIMER: THE CHOCOLATE CHIPS, WHILE TASTY, ARE PERFECTLY ORDINARY.
AND FINALLY... LES PETITS GÂTEAUX.
MY MINI CUPCAKES... OF DOOM!
DISCLAIMER: THE MINI CUPCAKES, WHILE NOT PARTICULARLY FLAVORFUL, ARE EXTRAORDINARILY DANGEROUS.
OKAY, CREW. TIME'S A'WASTING.
AND LET ME REITERATE HOW IMPORTANT IT IS THAT EVERY ASPECT OF TONIGHT'S CAPER GOES PERFECTLY.
TAP TAP
SPOILER: HAS IT BEEN MENTIONED THAT EVERY-THING TONIGHT DOES NOT GO PERFECTLY?

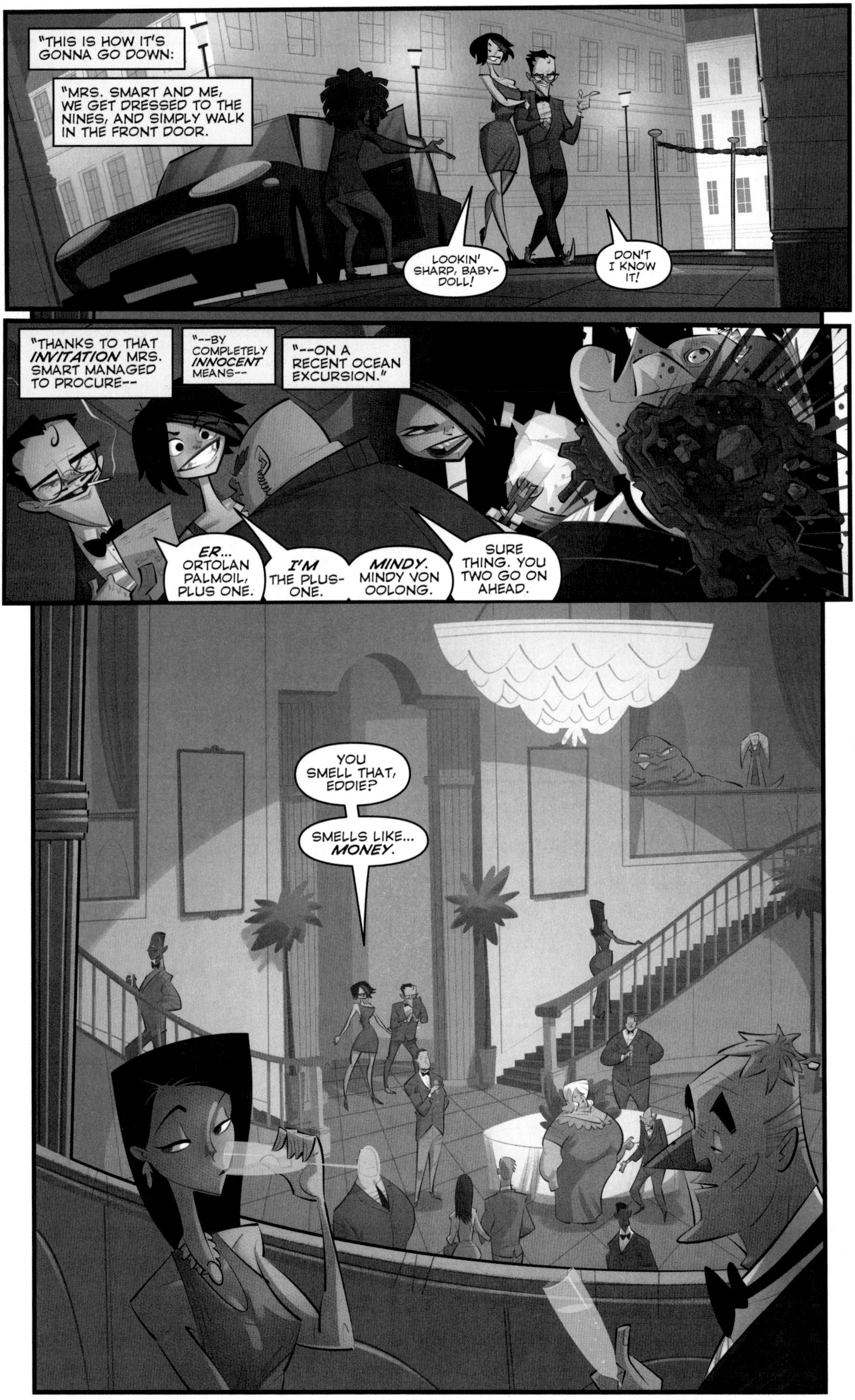
"THIS IS HOW IT'S GONNA GO DOWN:
"MRS. SMART AND ME, WE GET DRESSED TO THE NINES, AND SIMPLY WALK IN THE FRONT DOOR.
LOOKIN' SHARP, BABY-DOLL!
DON'T I KNOW IT!
"THANKS TO THAT *INVITATION* MRS. SMART MANAGED TO PROCURE--
"--BY COMPLETELY *INNOCENT* MEANS--
"--ON A RECENT OCEAN EXCURSION."
ER... ORTOLAN PALMOIL, PLUS ONE.
I'M THE PLUS-ONE.
MINDY. MINDY VON OOLONG.
SURE THING. YOU TWO GO ON AHEAD.
YOU SMELL THAT, EDDIE?
SMELLS LIKE... *MONEY*.

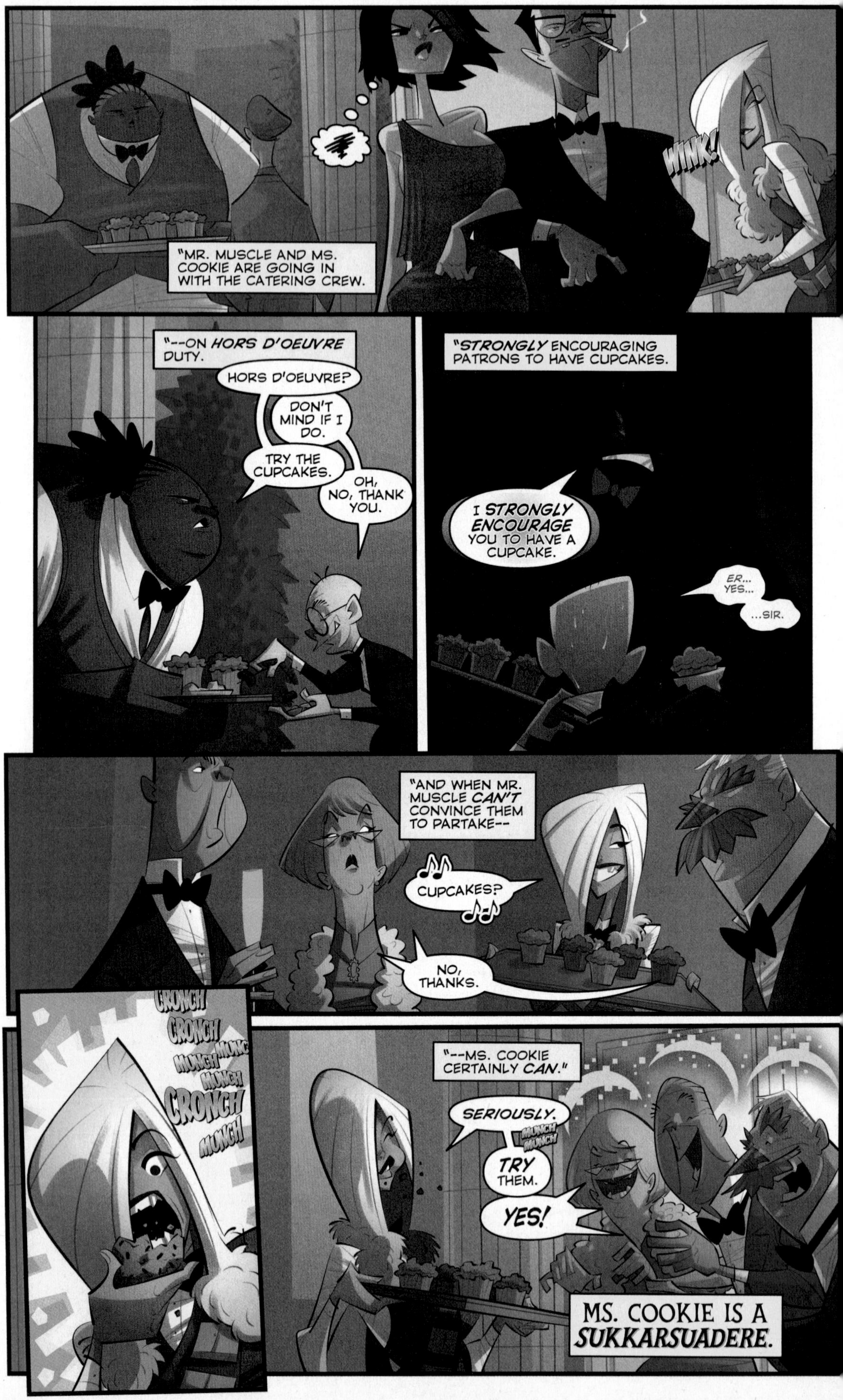
WINK!
"MR. MUSCLE AND MS. COOKIE ARE GOING IN WITH THE CATERING CREW.
"--ON HORS D'OEUVRE DUTY.
HORS D'OEUVRE?
DON'T MIND IF I DO.
TRY THE CUPCAKES.
OH, NO, THANK YOU.
"STRONGLY ENCOURAGING PATRONS TO HAVE CUPCAKES.
I STRONGLY ENCOURAGE YOU TO HAVE A CUPCAKE.
ER... YES...
...SIR.
"AND WHEN MR. MUSCLE CAN'T CONVINCE THEM TO PARTAKE--
CUPCAKES?
NO, THANKS.
CRONCH
CRONCH
MUNCH MUNCH
MUNCH
CRONCH
MUNCH
"--MS. COOKIE CERTAINLY CAN."
SERIOUSLY.
MUNCH MUNCH
TRY THEM.
YES!
MS. COOKIE IS A SUKKARSUADERE.

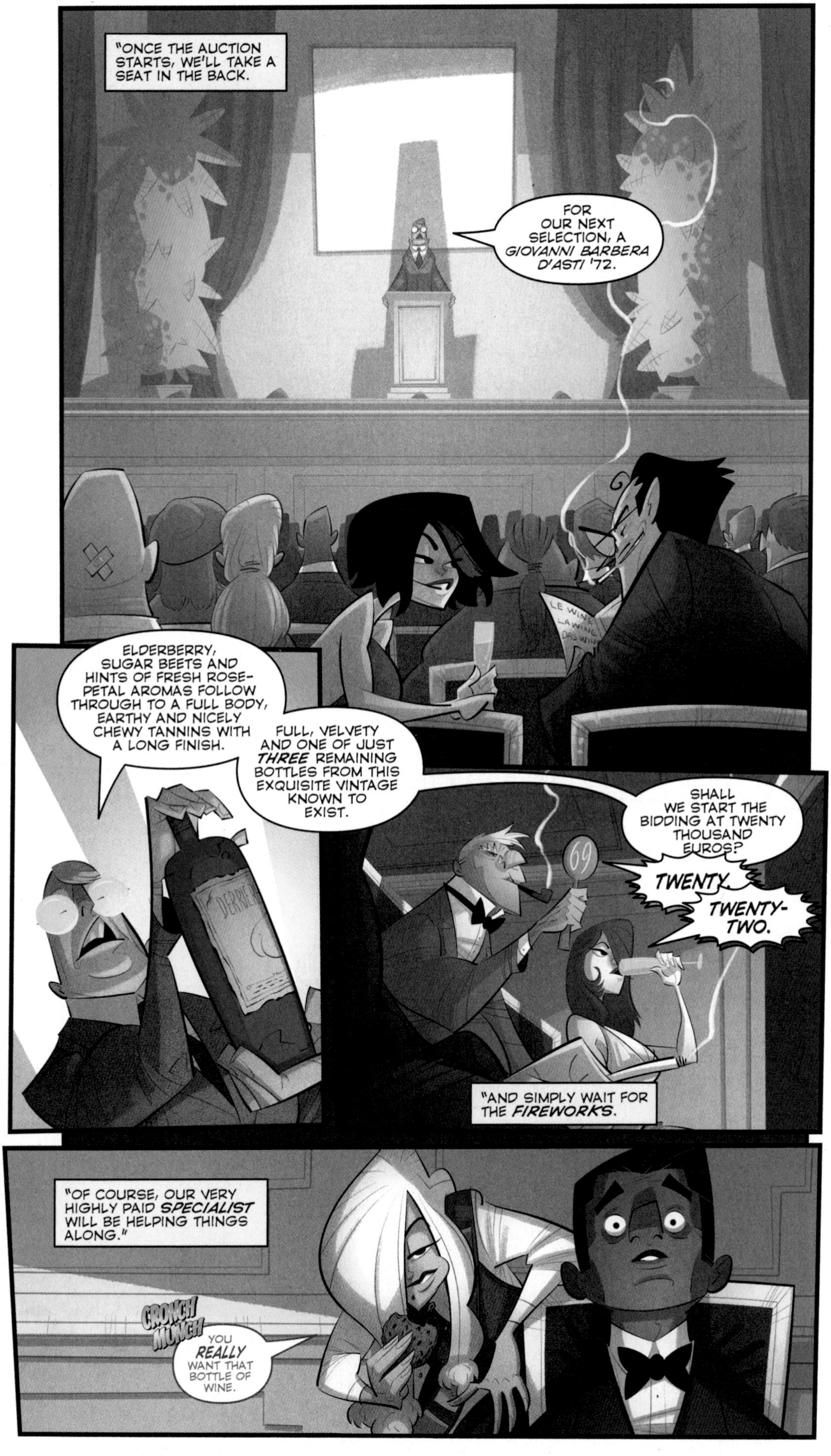
"ONCE THE AUCTION STARTS, WE'LL TAKE A SEAT IN THE BACK.
FOR OUR NEXT SELECTION, A *GIOVANNI BARBERA D'ASTI* '72.
LE WINE LA WINE DAS WINE
ELDERBERRY, SUGAR BEETS AND HINTS OF FRESH ROSE-PETAL AROMAS FOLLOW THROUGH TO A FULL BODY, EARTHY AND NICELY CHEWY TANNINS WITH A LONG FINISH.
FULL, VELVETY AND ONE OF JUST ***THREE*** REMAINING BOTTLES FROM THIS EXQUISITE VINTAGE KNOWN TO EXIST.
SHALL WE START THE BIDDING AT TWENTY THOUSAND EUROS?
69
TWENTY.
TWENTY-TWO.
"AND SIMPLY WAIT FOR THE ***FIREWORKS***.
"OF COURSE, OUR VERY HIGHLY PAID ***SPECIALIST*** WILL BE HELPING THINGS ALONG."
CRUNCH MUNCH
YOU ***REALLY*** WANT THAT BOTTLE OF WINE.

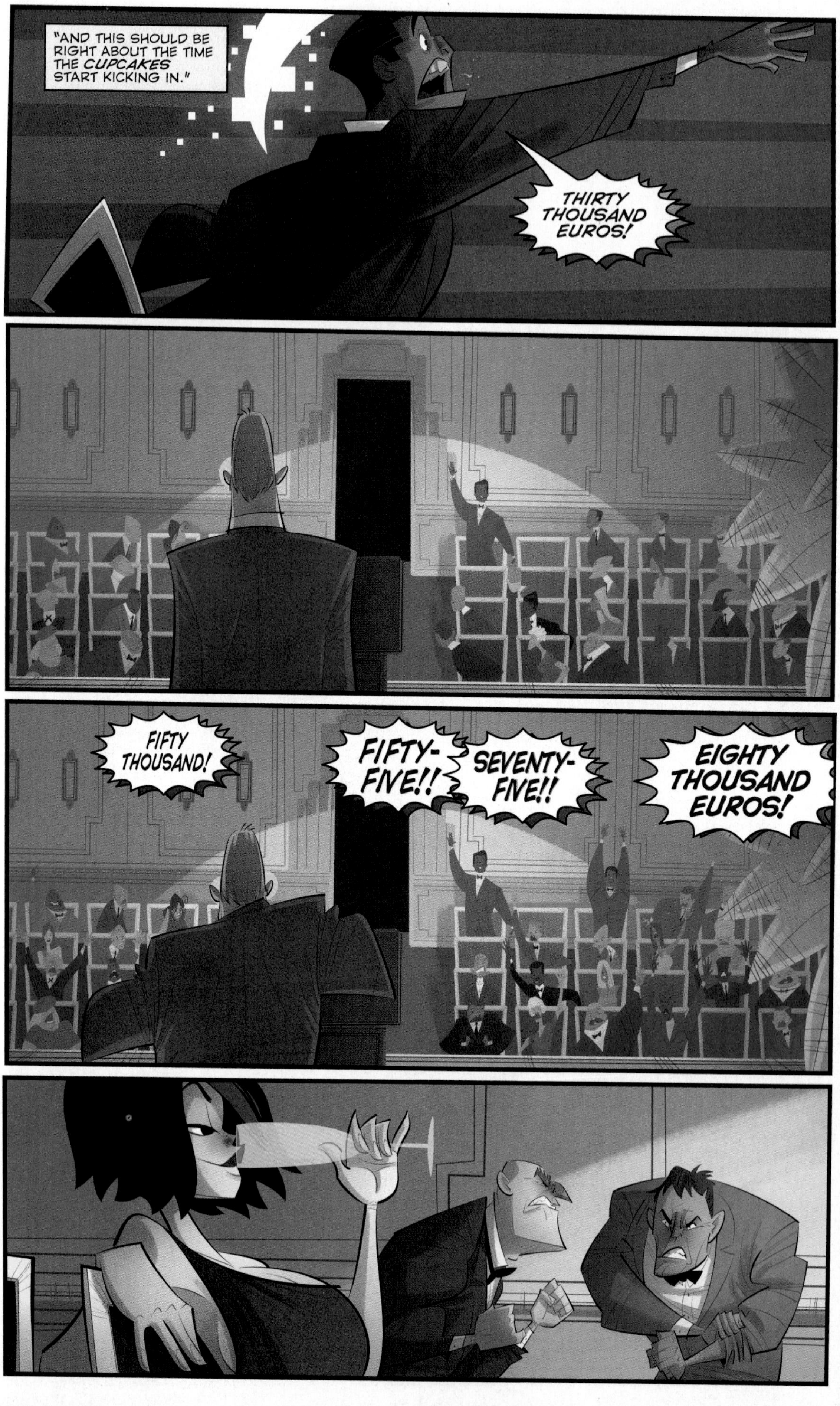
"AND THIS SHOULD BE RIGHT ABOUT THE TIME THE CUPCAKES START KICKING IN."
THIRTY THOUSAND EUROS!
FIFTY THOUSAND!
FIFTY-FIVE!!
SEVENTY-FIVE!!
EIGHTY THOUSAND EUROS!

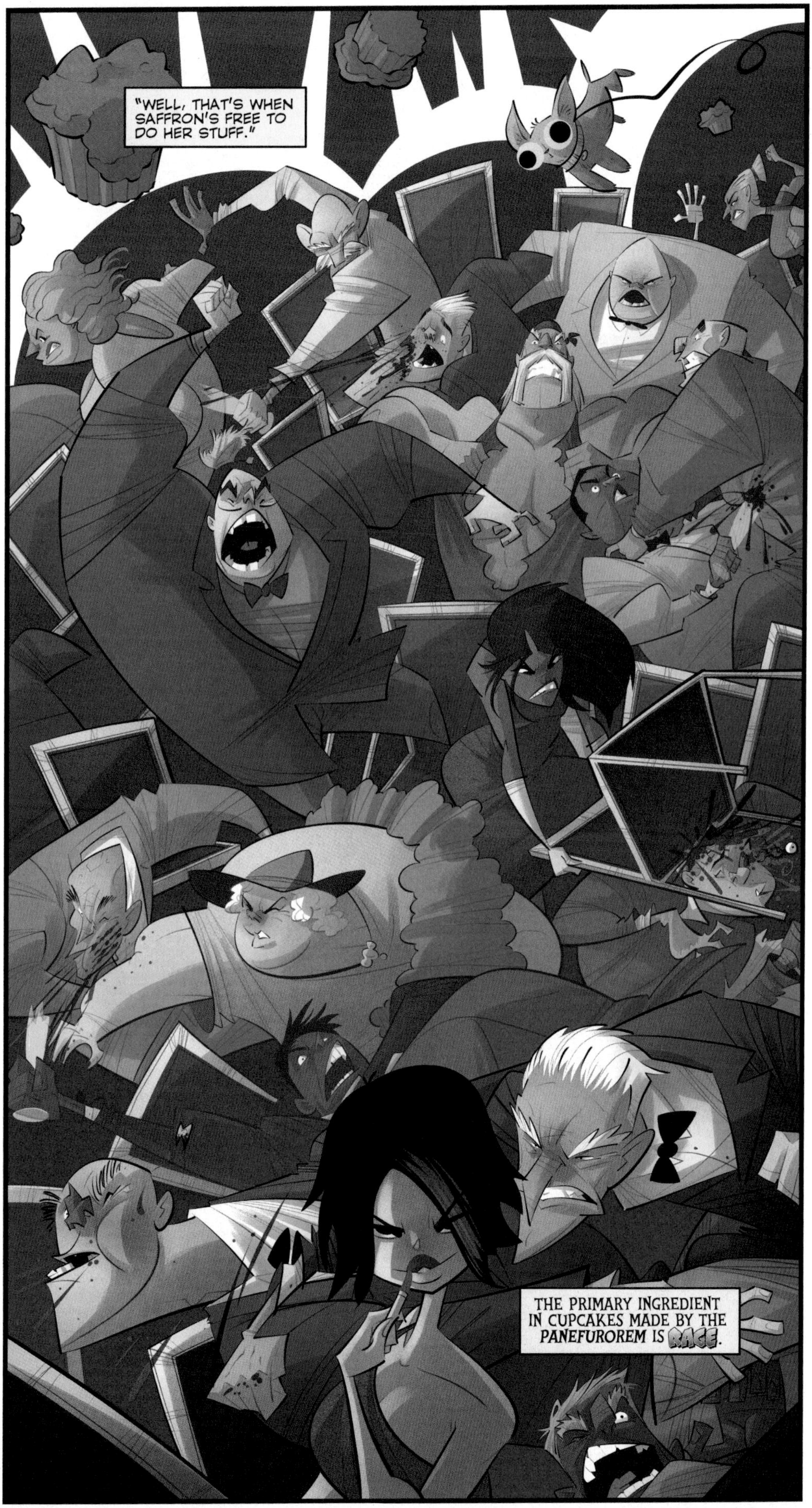
"WELL, THAT'S WHEN SAFFRON'S FREE TO DO HER STUFF."
THE PRIMARY INGREDIENT IN CUPCAKES MADE BY THE *PANEFURDREM* IS RAGE.

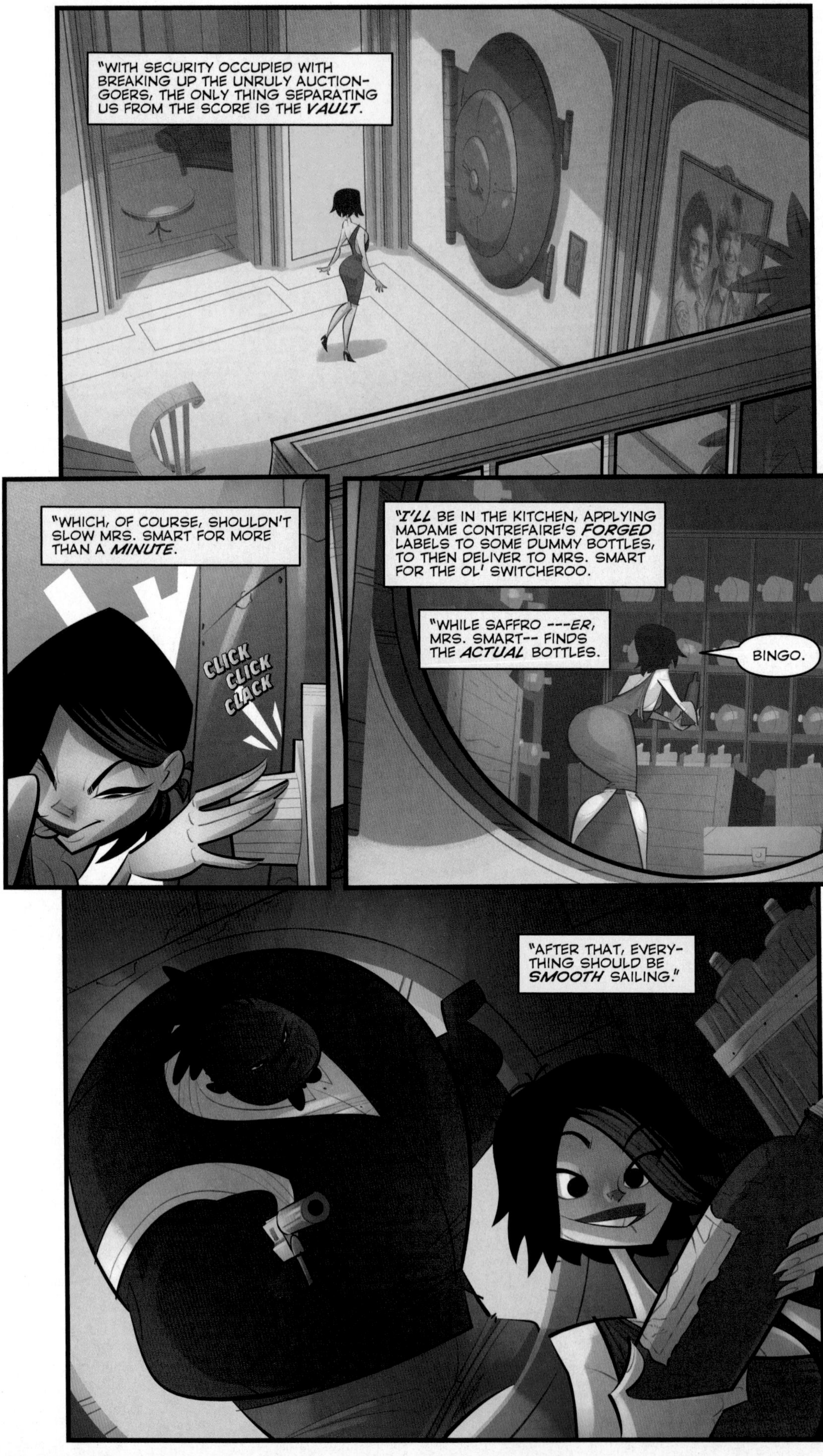
"WITH SECURITY OCCUPIED WITH BREAKING UP THE UNRULY AUCTION-GOERS, THE ONLY THING SEPARATING US FROM THE SCORE IS THE *VAULT*.
"WHICH, OF COURSE, SHOULDN'T SLOW MRS. SMART FOR MORE THAN A *MINUTE*.
CLICK CLICK CLACK
"*I'LL* BE IN THE KITCHEN, APPLYING MADAME CONTREFAIRE'S *FORGED* LABELS TO SOME DUMMY BOTTLES, TO THEN DELIVER TO MRS. SMART FOR THE OL' SWITCHEROO.
"WHILE SAFFRO ---*ER*, MRS. SMART-- FINDS THE *ACTUAL* BOTTLES.
BINGO.
"AFTER THAT, EVERY-THING SHOULD BE *SMOOTH* SAILING."

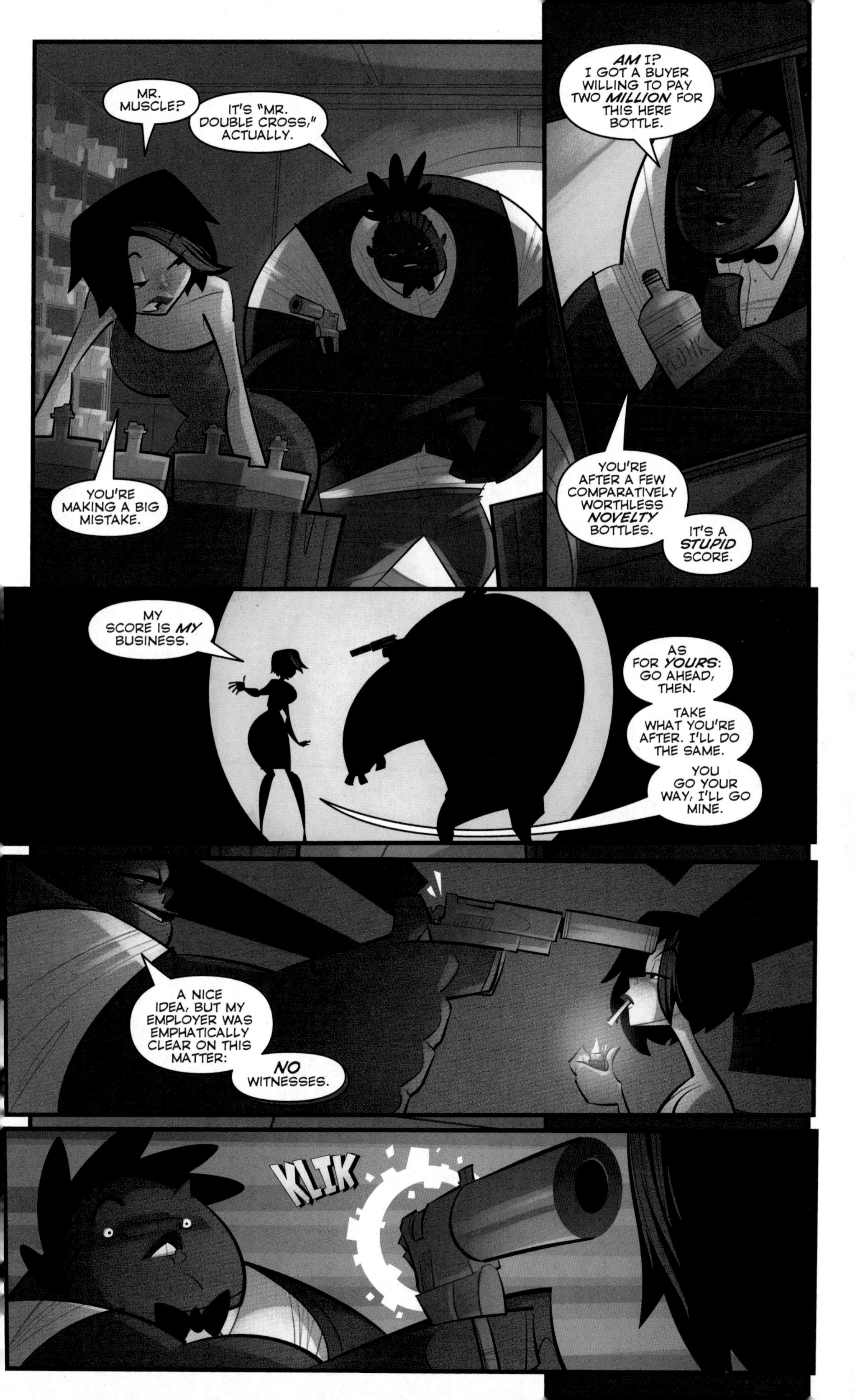
MR. MUSCLE?
IT'S "MR. DOUBLE CROSS," ACTUALLY.
YOU'RE MAKING A BIG MISTAKE.
AM I? I GOT A BUYER WILLING TO PAY TWO MILLION FOR THIS HERE BOTTLE.
YOU'RE AFTER A FEW COMPARATIVELY WORTHLESS NOVELTY BOTTLES.
IT'S A STUPID SCORE.
MY SCORE IS MY BUSINESS.
AS FOR YOURS: GO AHEAD, THEN.
TAKE WHAT YOU'RE AFTER. I'LL DO THE SAME.
YOU GO YOUR WAY, I'LL GO MINE.
A NICE IDEA, BUT MY EMPLOYER WAS EMPHATICALLY CLEAR ON THIS MATTER:
NO WITNESSES.
KLIK

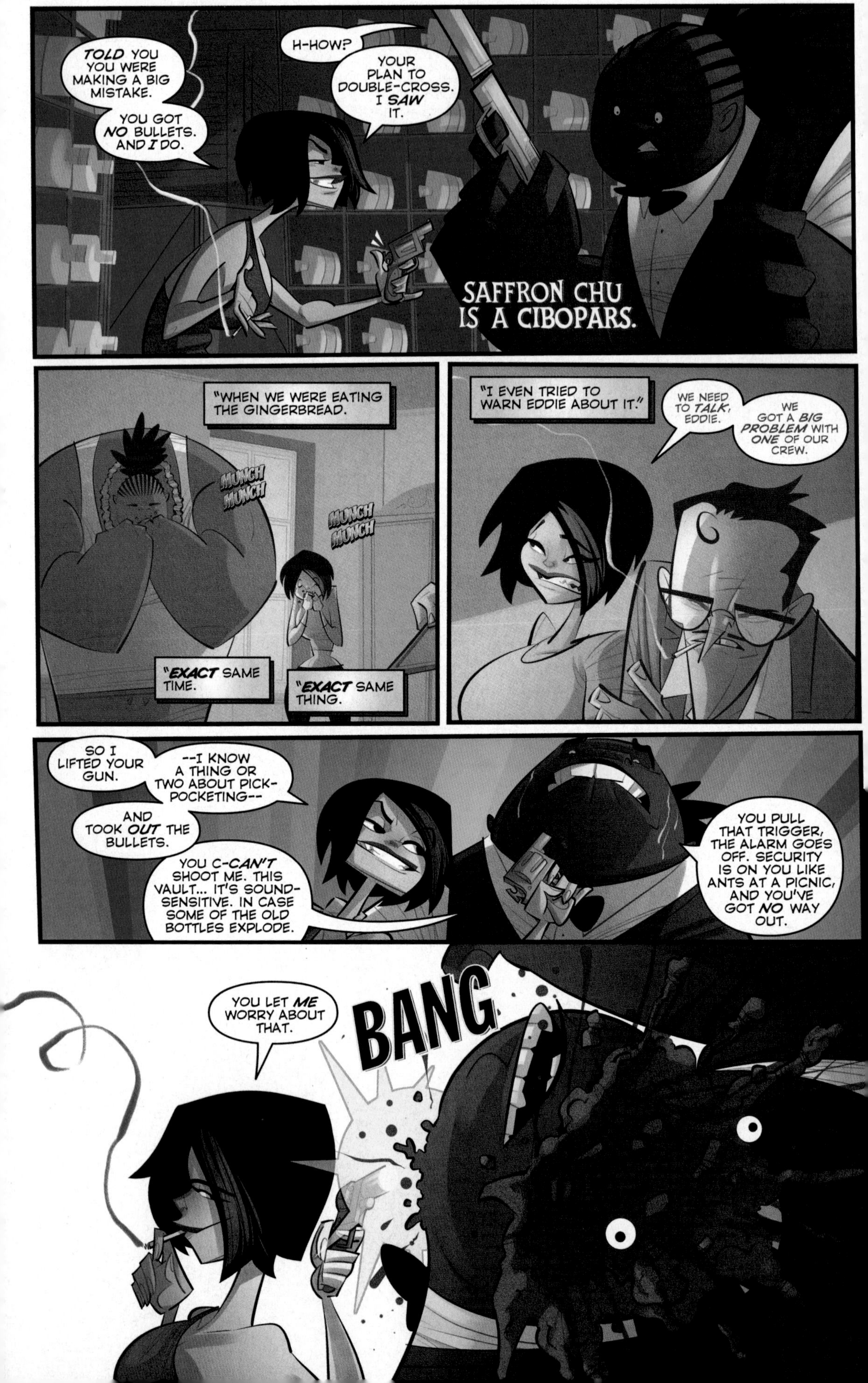
TOLD YOU YOU WERE MAKING A BIG MISTAKE.
YOU GOT NO BULLETS. AND I DO.
H-HOW?
YOUR PLAN TO DOUBLE-CROSS. I SAW IT.
SAFFRON CHU IS A CIBOPARS.
"WHEN WE WERE EATING THE GINGERBREAD.
MUNCH MUNCH
MUNCH MUNCH
"EXACT SAME TIME.
"EXACT SAME THING.
"I EVEN TRIED TO WARN EDDIE ABOUT IT."
WE NEED TO TALK, EDDIE.
WE GOT A BIG PROBLEM WITH ONE OF OUR CREW.
SO I LIFTED YOUR GUN.
--I KNOW A THING OR TWO ABOUT PICK-POCKETING--
AND TOOK OUT THE BULLETS.
YOU C-CAN'T SHOOT ME. THIS VAULT... IT'S SOUND-SENSITIVE. IN CASE SOME OF THE OLD BOTTLES EXPLODE.
YOU PULL THAT TRIGGER, THE ALARM GOES OFF. SECURITY IS ON YOU LIKE ANTS AT A PICNIC, AND YOU'VE GOT NO WAY OUT.
YOU LET ME WORRY ABOUT THAT.
BANG

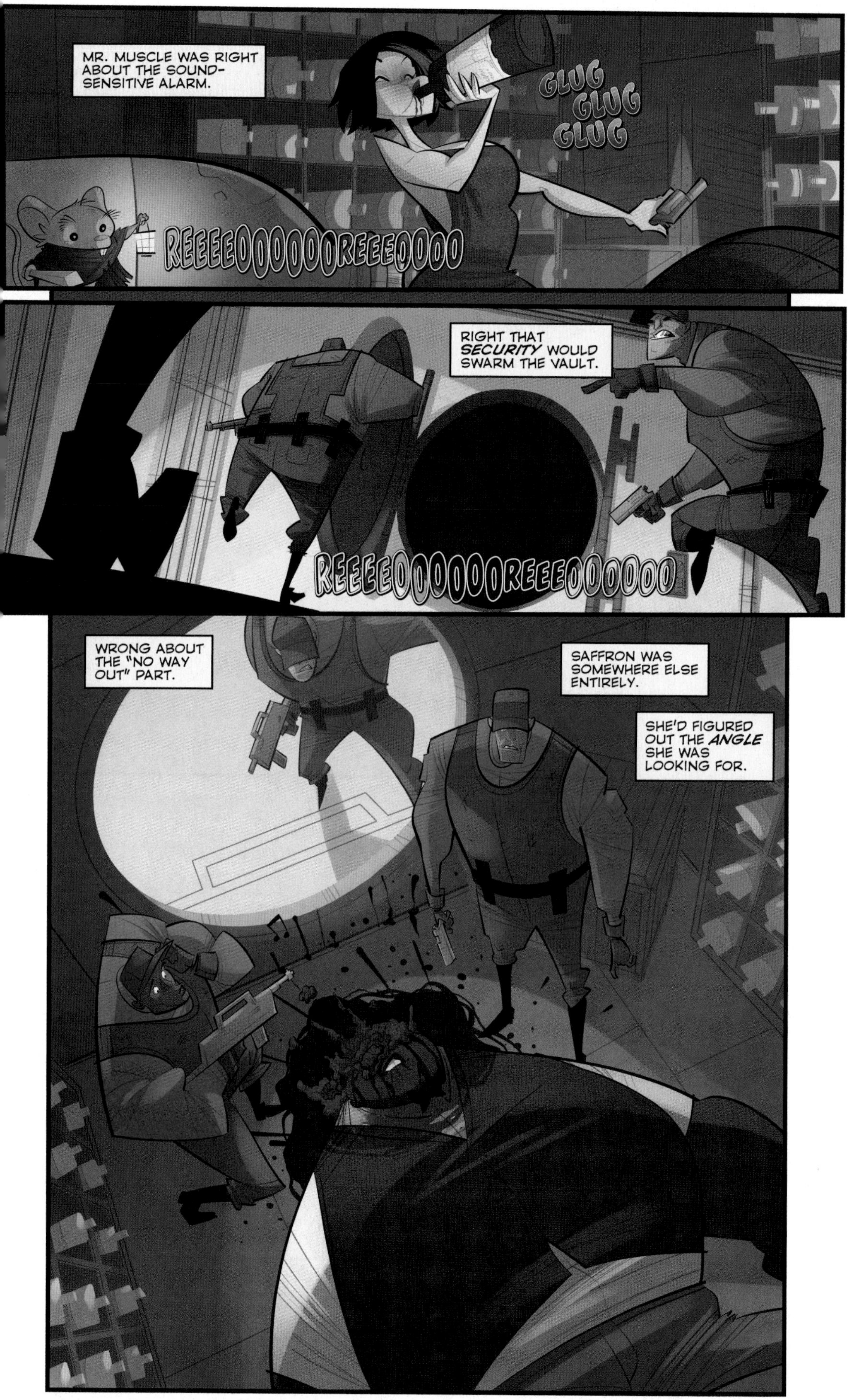
MR. MUSCLE WAS RIGHT ABOUT THE SOUND-SENSITIVE ALARM.
GLUG GLUG GLUG
REEEEOOOOOOREEEOOOO
RIGHT THAT *SECURITY* WOULD SWARM THE VAULT.
REEEEOOOOOOREEEOOOOOO
WRONG ABOUT THE "NO WAY OUT" PART.
SAFFRON WAS SOMEWHERE ELSE ENTIRELY.
SHE'D FIGURED OUT THE *ANGLE* SHE WAS LOOKING FOR.

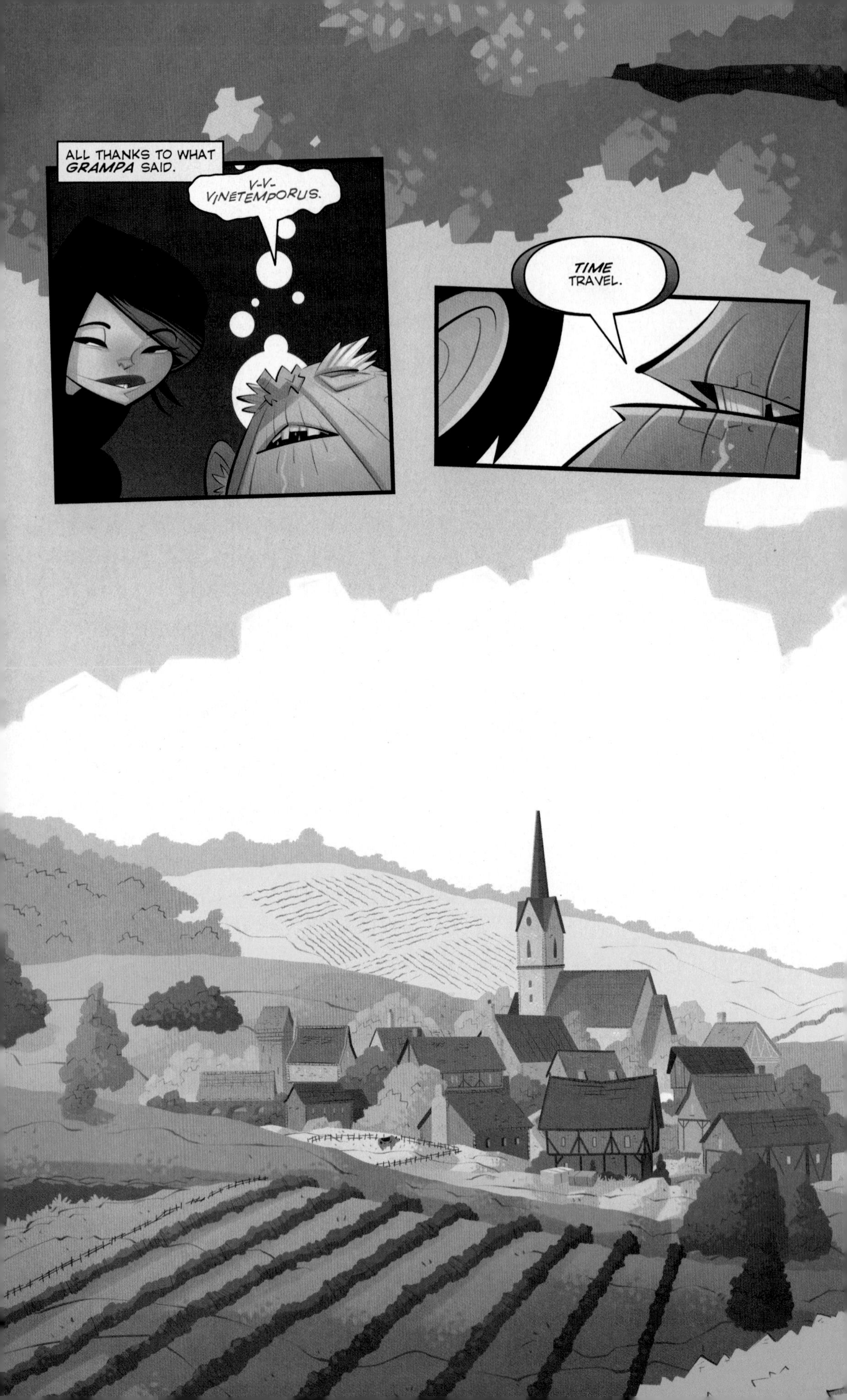
ALL THANKS TO WHAT *GRAMPA* SAID.
V-V- VINETEMPORUS.
TIME TRAVEL.

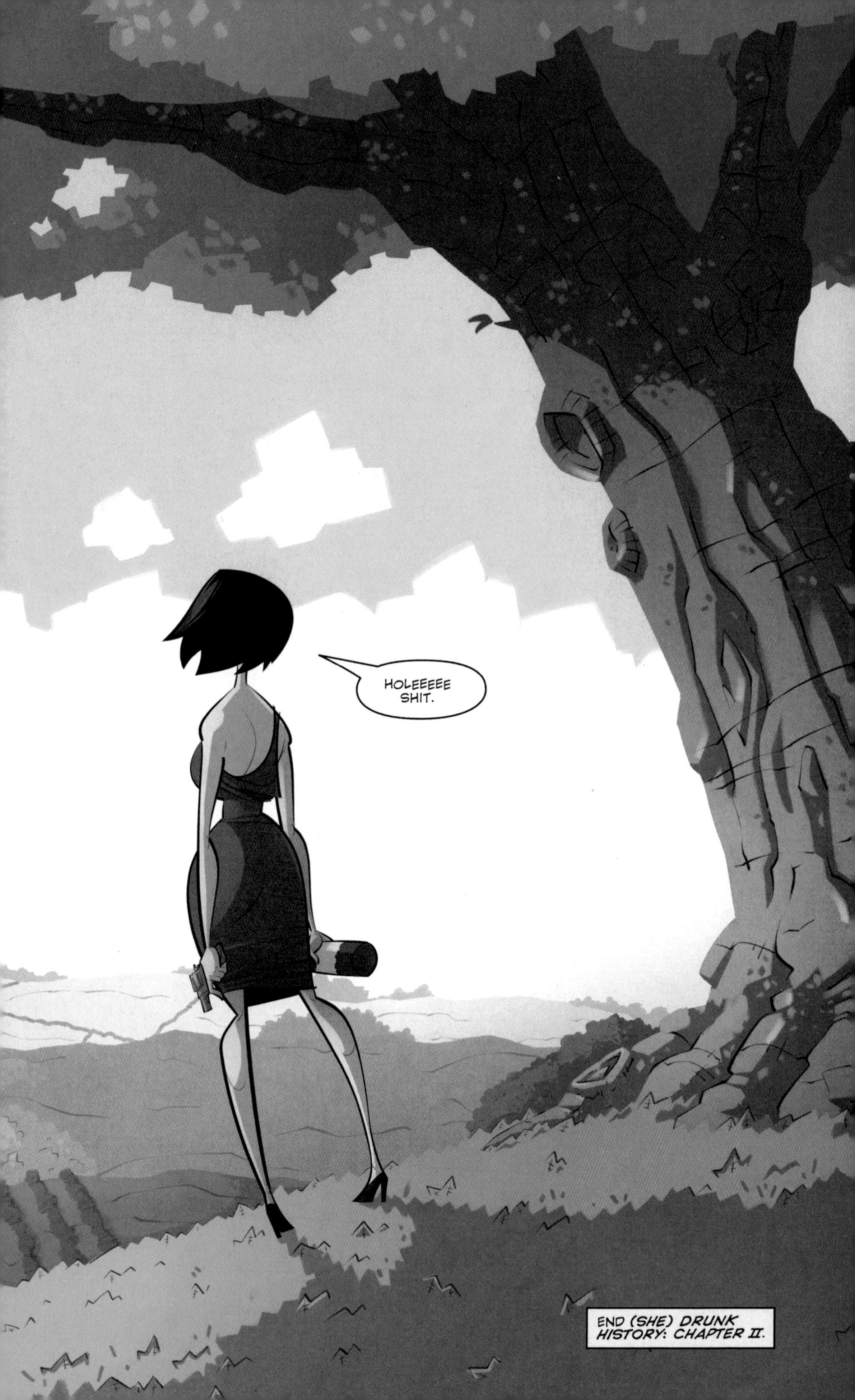
HOLEEEEE SHIT.
END (SHE) DRUNK HISTORY: CHAPTER II.

Chapter 3

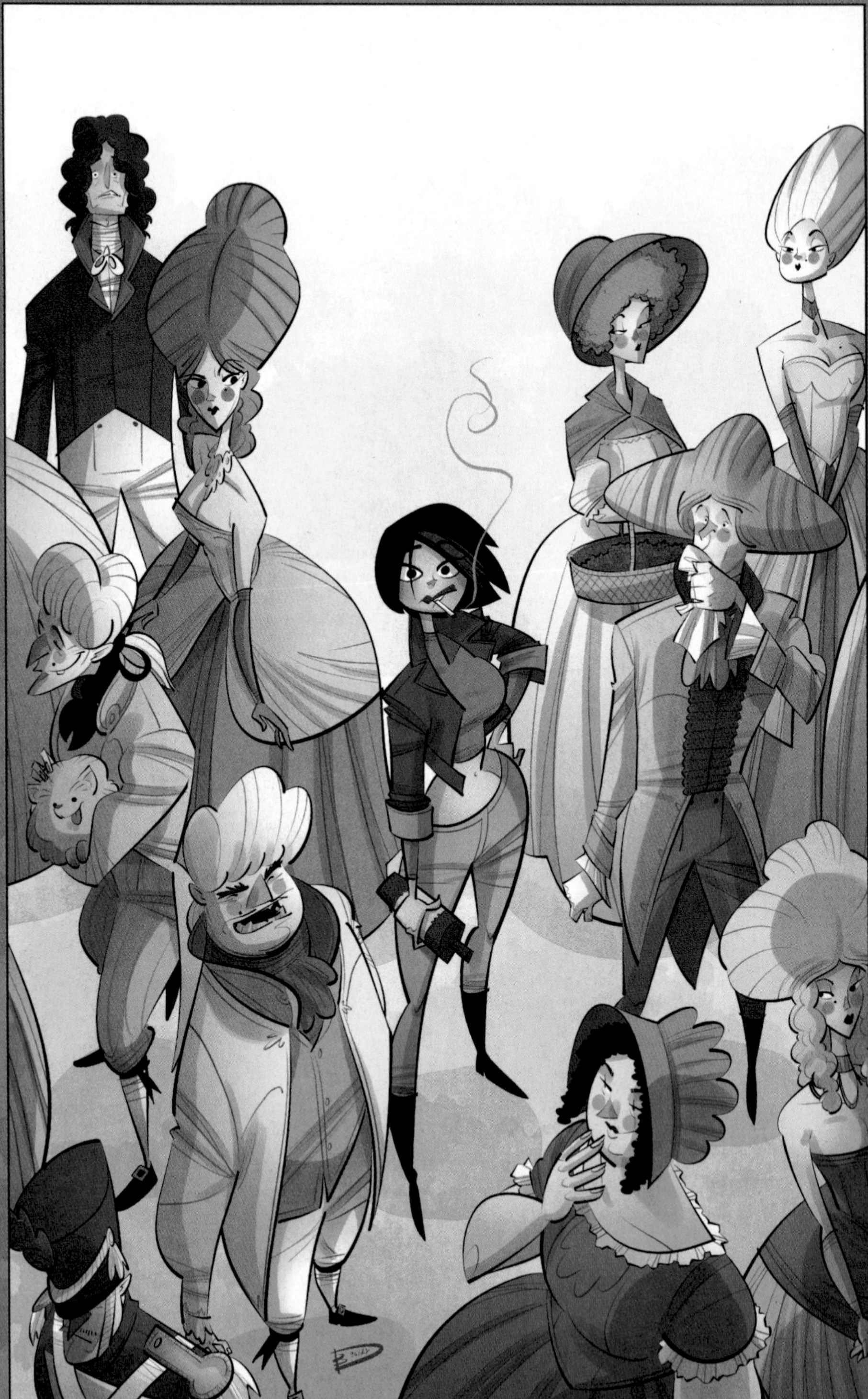

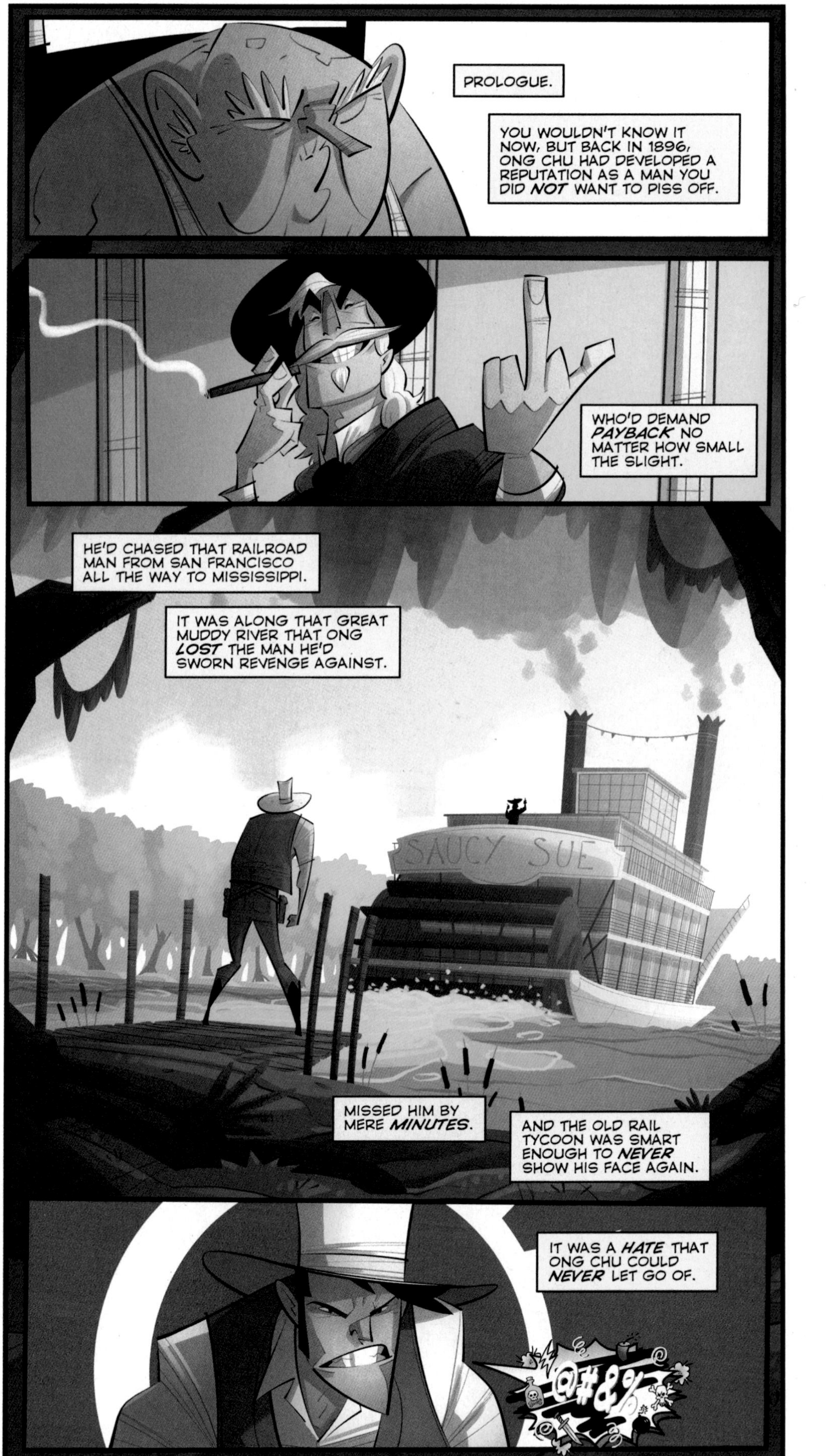
PROLOGUE.
YOU WOULDN'T KNOW IT NOW, BUT BACK IN 1896, ONG CHU HAD DEVELOPED A REPUTATION AS A MAN YOU DID NOT WANT TO PISS OFF.
WHO'D DEMAND PAYBACK NO MATTER HOW SMALL THE SLIGHT.
HE'D CHASED THAT RAILROAD MAN FROM SAN FRANCISCO ALL THE WAY TO MISSISSIPPI.
IT WAS ALONG THAT GREAT MUDDY RIVER THAT ONG LOST THE MAN HE'D SWORN REVENGE AGAINST.
SAUCY SUE
MISSED HIM BY MERE MINUTES.
AND THE OLD RAIL TYCOON WAS SMART ENOUGH TO NEVER SHOW HIS FACE AGAIN.
IT WAS A HATE THAT ONG CHU COULD NEVER LET GO OF.
@#&%

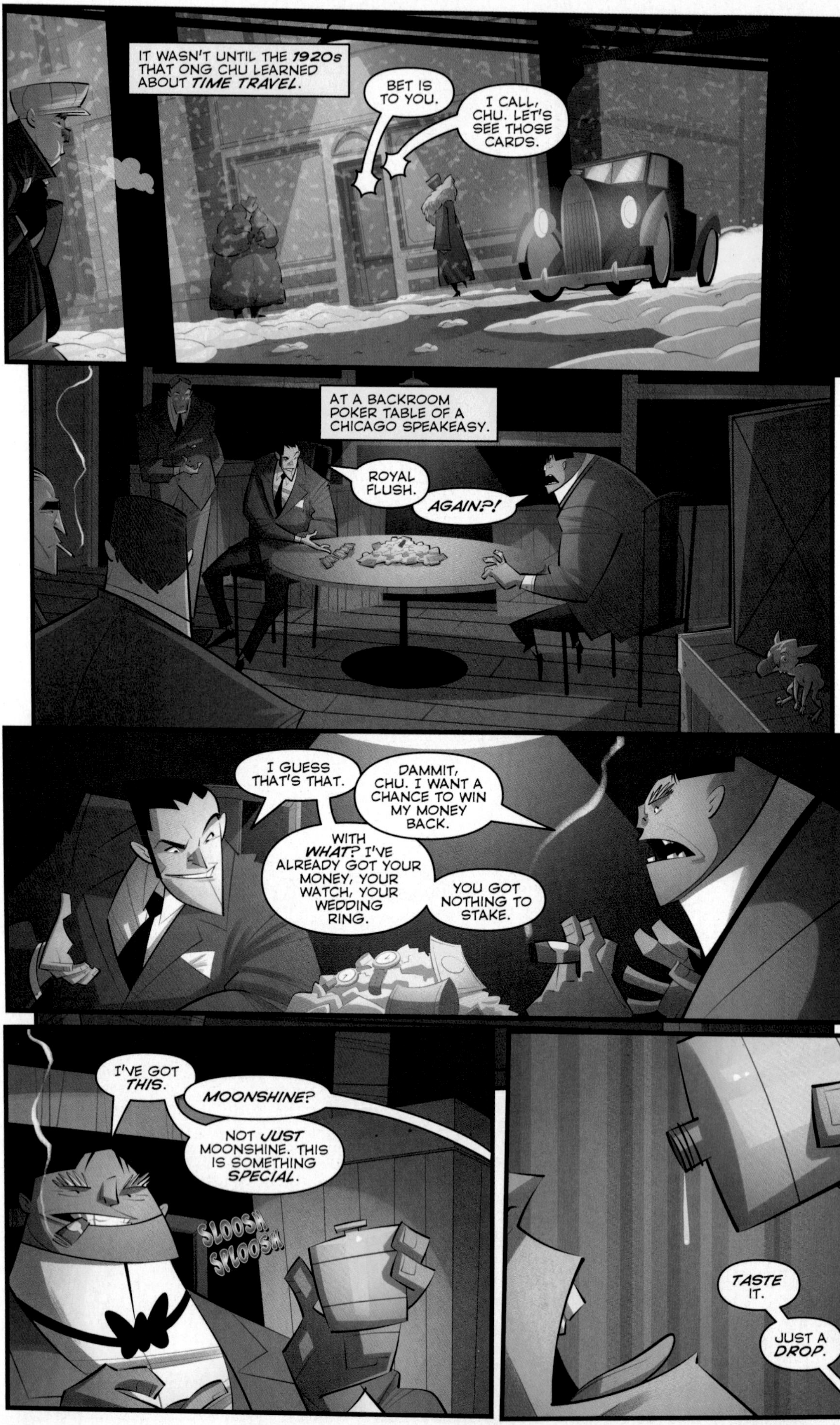
IT WASN'T UNTIL THE 1920s THAT ONG CHU LEARNED ABOUT TIME TRAVEL.
BET IS TO YOU.
I CALL, CHU. LET'S SEE THOSE CARDS.
AT A BACKROOM POKER TABLE OF A CHICAGO SPEAKEASY.
ROYAL FLUSH.
AGAIN?!
I GUESS THAT'S THAT.
DAMMIT, CHU. I WANT A CHANCE TO WIN MY MONEY BACK.
WITH WHAT? I'VE ALREADY GOT YOUR MONEY, YOUR WATCH, YOUR WEDDING RING.
YOU GOT NOTHING TO STAKE.
I'VE GOT THIS.
MOONSHINE?
NOT JUST MOONSHINE. THIS IS SOMETHING SPECIAL.
SLOOSH SPLOOSH
TASTE IT.
JUST A DROP.

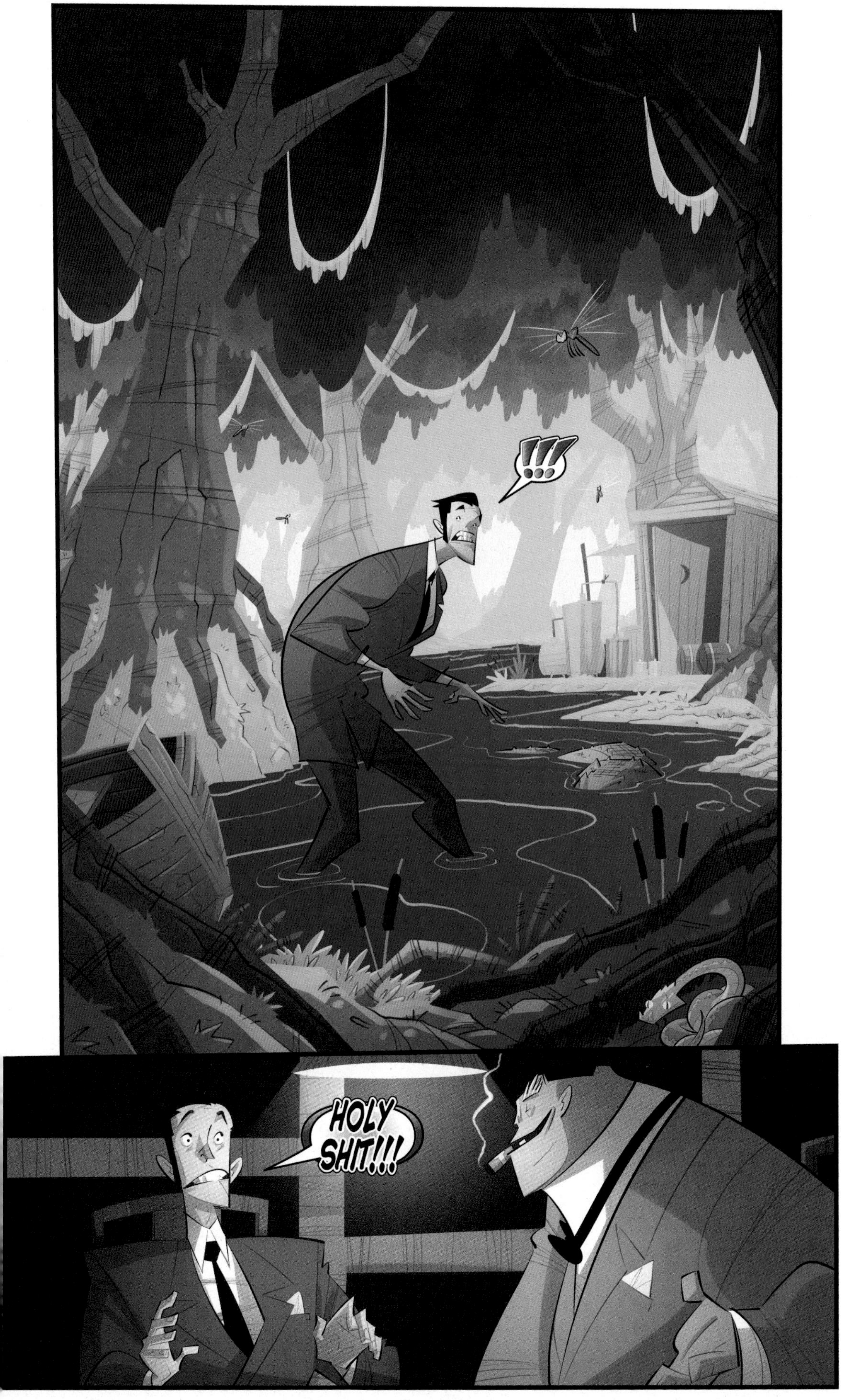
!!!
HOLY SHIT!!!

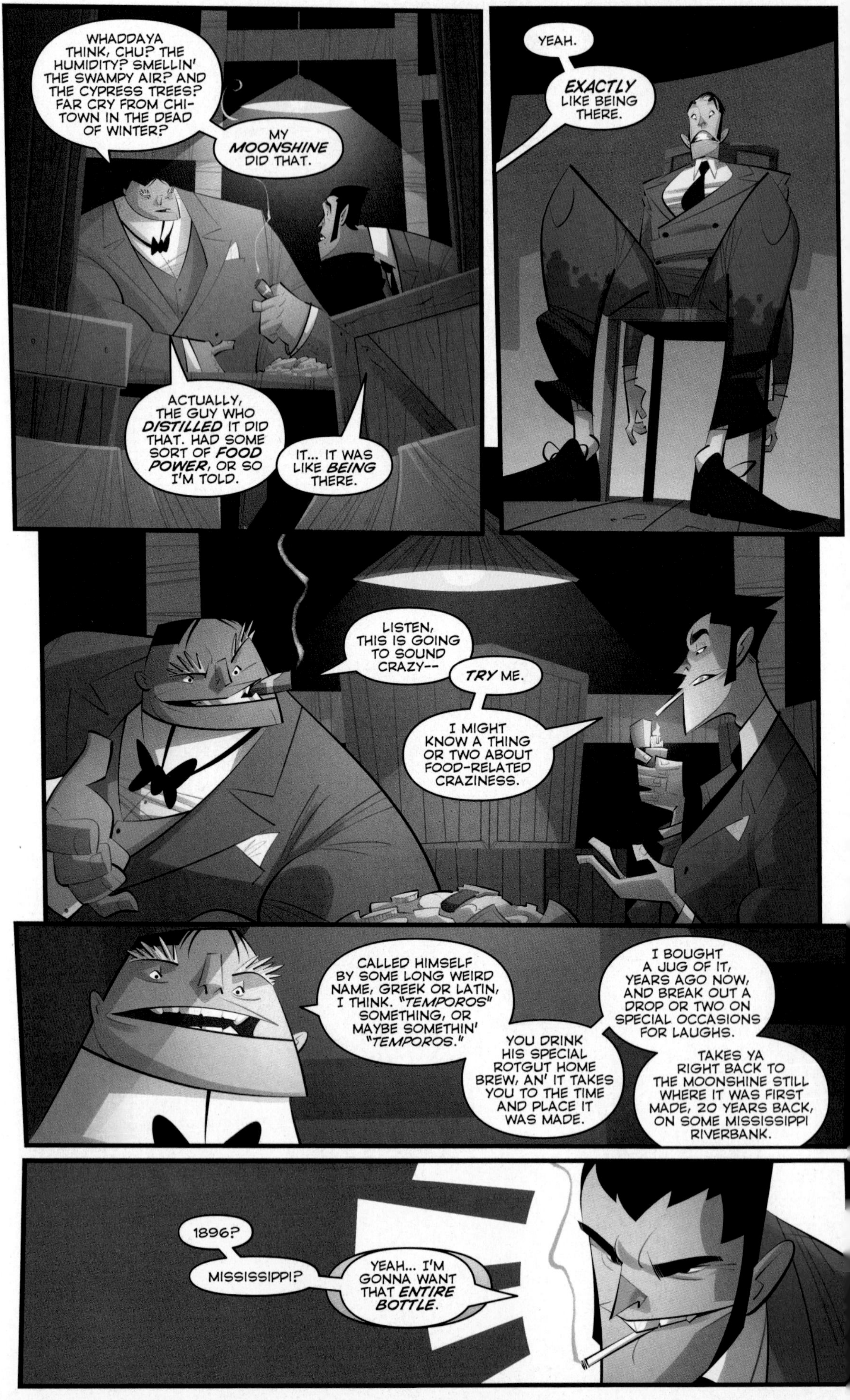
WHADDAYA THINK, CHU? THE HUMIDITY? SMELLIN' THE SWAMPY AIR? AND THE CYPRESS TREES? FAR CRY FROM CHI-TOWN IN THE DEAD OF WINTER?
MY MOONSHINE DID THAT.
ACTUALLY, THE GUY WHO DISTILLED IT DID THAT. HAD SOME SORT OF FOOD POWER, OR SO I'M TOLD.
IT... IT WAS LIKE BEING THERE.
YEAH.
EXACTLY LIKE BEING THERE.
LISTEN, THIS IS GOING TO SOUND CRAZY--
TRY ME.
I MIGHT KNOW A THING OR TWO ABOUT FOOD-RELATED CRAZINESS.
CALLED HIMSELF BY SOME LONG WEIRD NAME, GREEK OR LATIN, I THINK. "TEMPOROS" SOMETHING, OR MAYBE SOMETHIN' "TEMPOROS."
YOU DRINK HIS SPECIAL ROTGUT HOME BREW, AN' IT TAKES YOU TO THE TIME AND PLACE IT WAS MADE.
I BOUGHT A JUG OF IT, YEARS AGO NOW, AND BREAK OUT A DROP OR TWO ON SPECIAL OCCASIONS FOR LAUGHS.
TAKES YA RIGHT BACK TO THE MOONSHINE STILL WHERE IT WAS FIRST MADE, 20 YEARS BACK, ON SOME MISSISSIPPI RIVERBANK.
1896?
MISSISSIPPI?
YEAH... I'M GONNA WANT THAT ENTIRE BOTTLE.

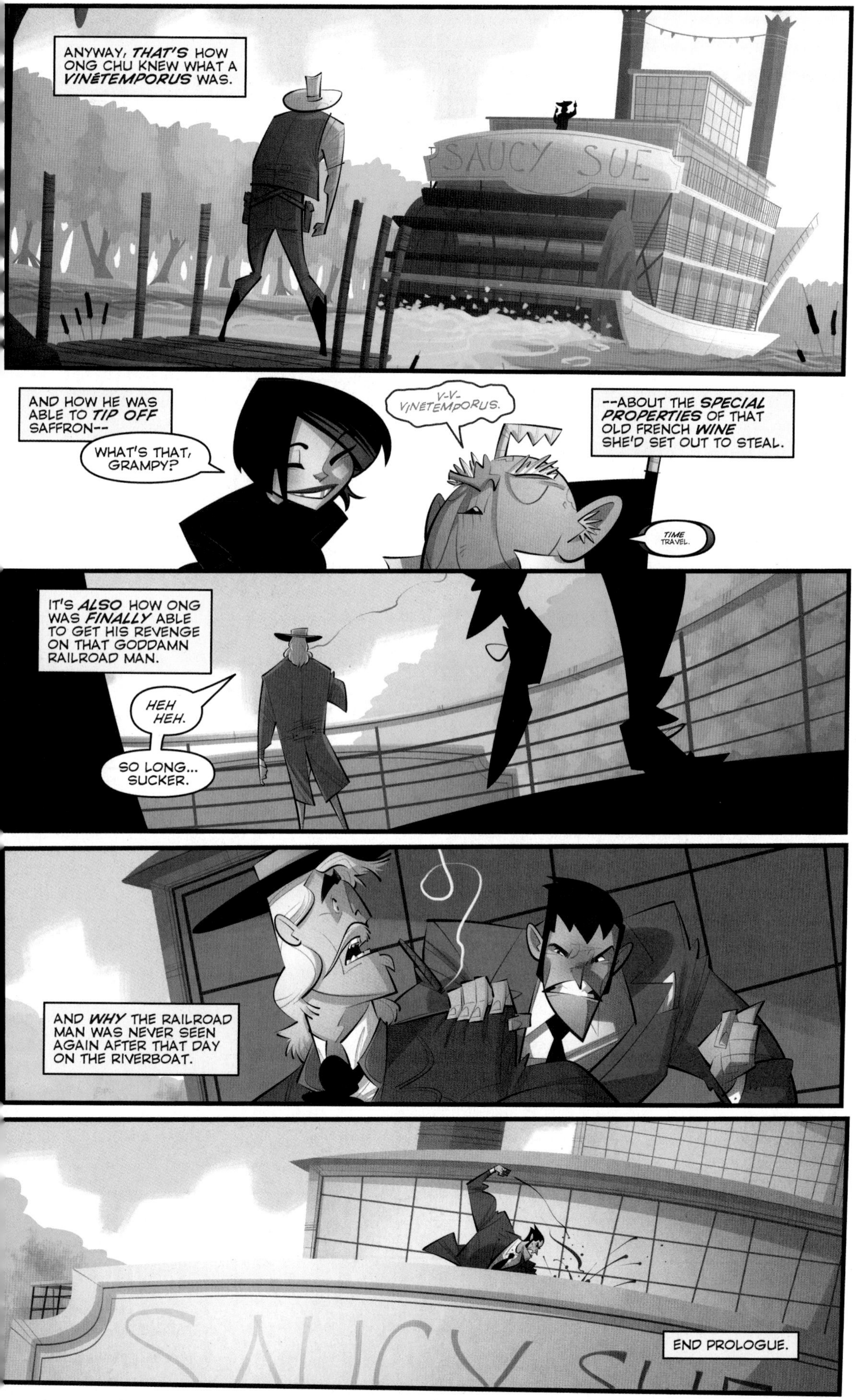
ANYWAY, THAT'S HOW ONG CHU KNEW WHAT A VINÉTEMPORUS WAS.
SAUCY SUE
AND HOW HE WAS ABLE TO TIP OFF SAFFRON--
WHAT'S THAT, GRAMPY?
V-V-VINETEMPORUS.
--ABOUT THE SPECIAL PROPERTIES OF THAT OLD FRENCH WINE SHE'D SET OUT TO STEAL.
TIME TRAVEL.
IT'S ALSO HOW ONG WAS FINALLY ABLE TO GET HIS REVENGE ON THAT GODDAMN RAILROAD MAN.
HEH HEH.
SO LONG... SUCKER.
AND WHY THE RAILROAD MAN WAS NEVER SEEN AGAIN AFTER THAT DAY ON THE RIVERBOAT.
END PROLOGUE.

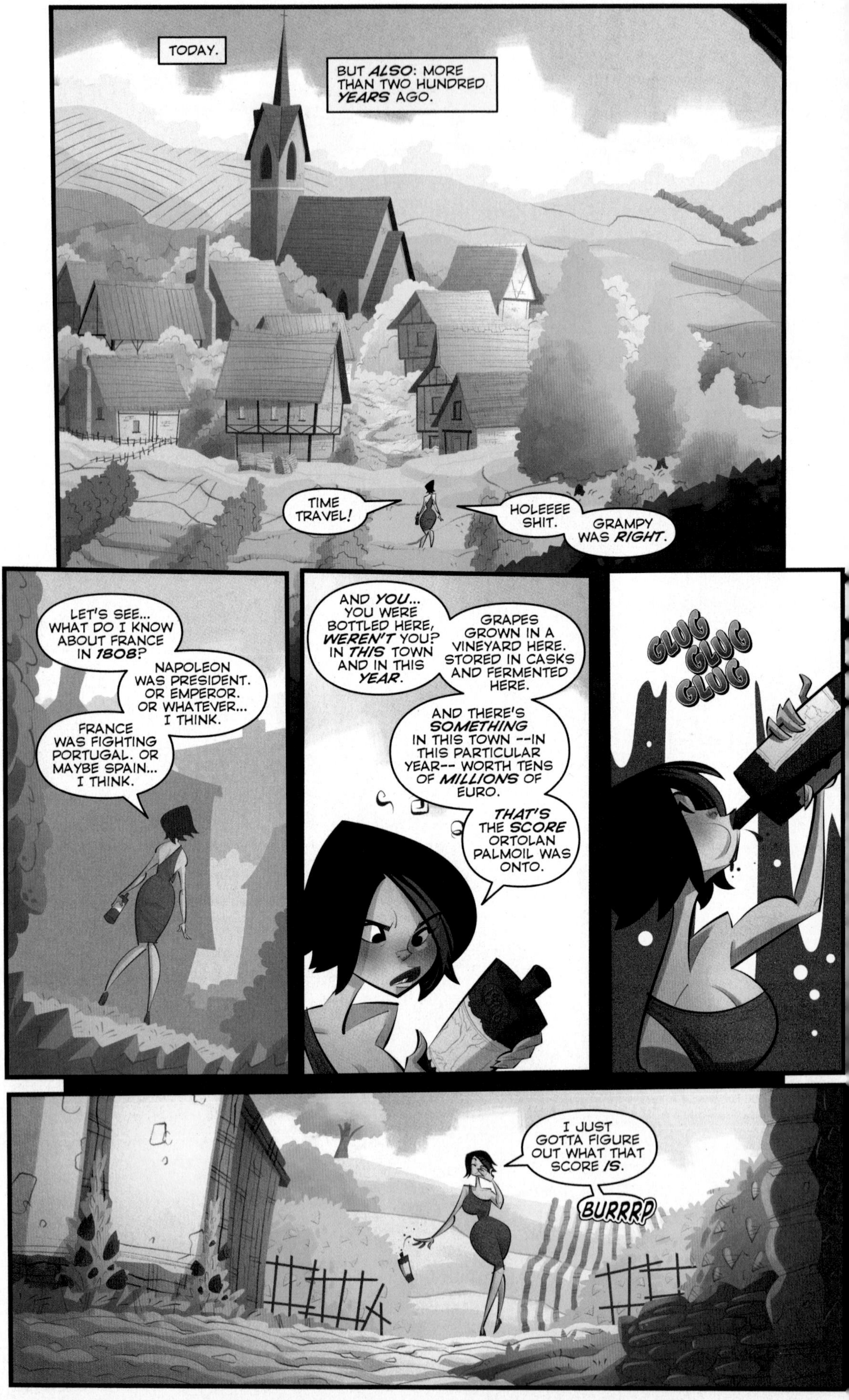
TODAY.
BUT ALSO: MORE THAN TWO HUNDRED YEARS AGO.
TIME TRAVEL!
HOLEEEE SHIT.
GRAMPY WAS RIGHT.
LET'S SEE... WHAT DO I KNOW ABOUT FRANCE IN 1808?
NAPOLEON WAS PRESIDENT. OR EMPEROR. OR WHATEVER... I THINK.
FRANCE WAS FIGHTING PORTUGAL. OR MAYBE SPAIN... I THINK.
AND YOU... YOU WERE BOTTLED HERE, WEREN'T YOU? IN THIS TOWN AND IN THIS YEAR.
GRAPES GROWN IN A VINEYARD HERE. STORED IN CASKS AND FERMENTED HERE.
AND THERE'S SOMETHING IN THIS TOWN --IN THIS PARTICULAR YEAR-- WORTH TENS OF MILLIONS OF EURO.
THAT'S THE SCORE ORTOLAN PALMOIL WAS ONTO.
GLUG GLUG GLUG
I JUST GOTTA FIGURE OUT WHAT THAT SCORE IS.
BURRRP

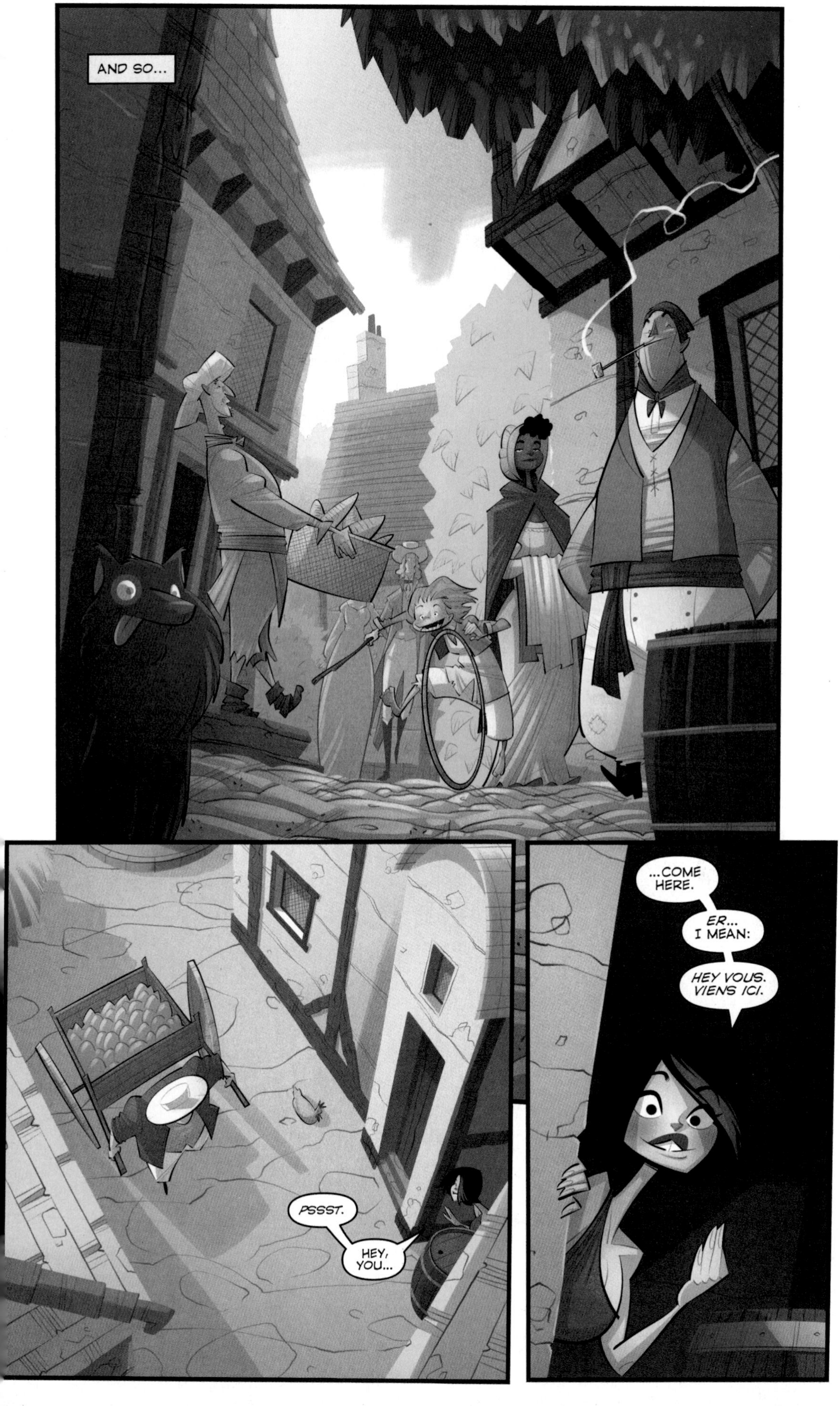
AND SO...
PSSST.
HEY, YOU...
...COME HERE.
ER... I MEAN:
HEY VOUS. VIENS ICI.

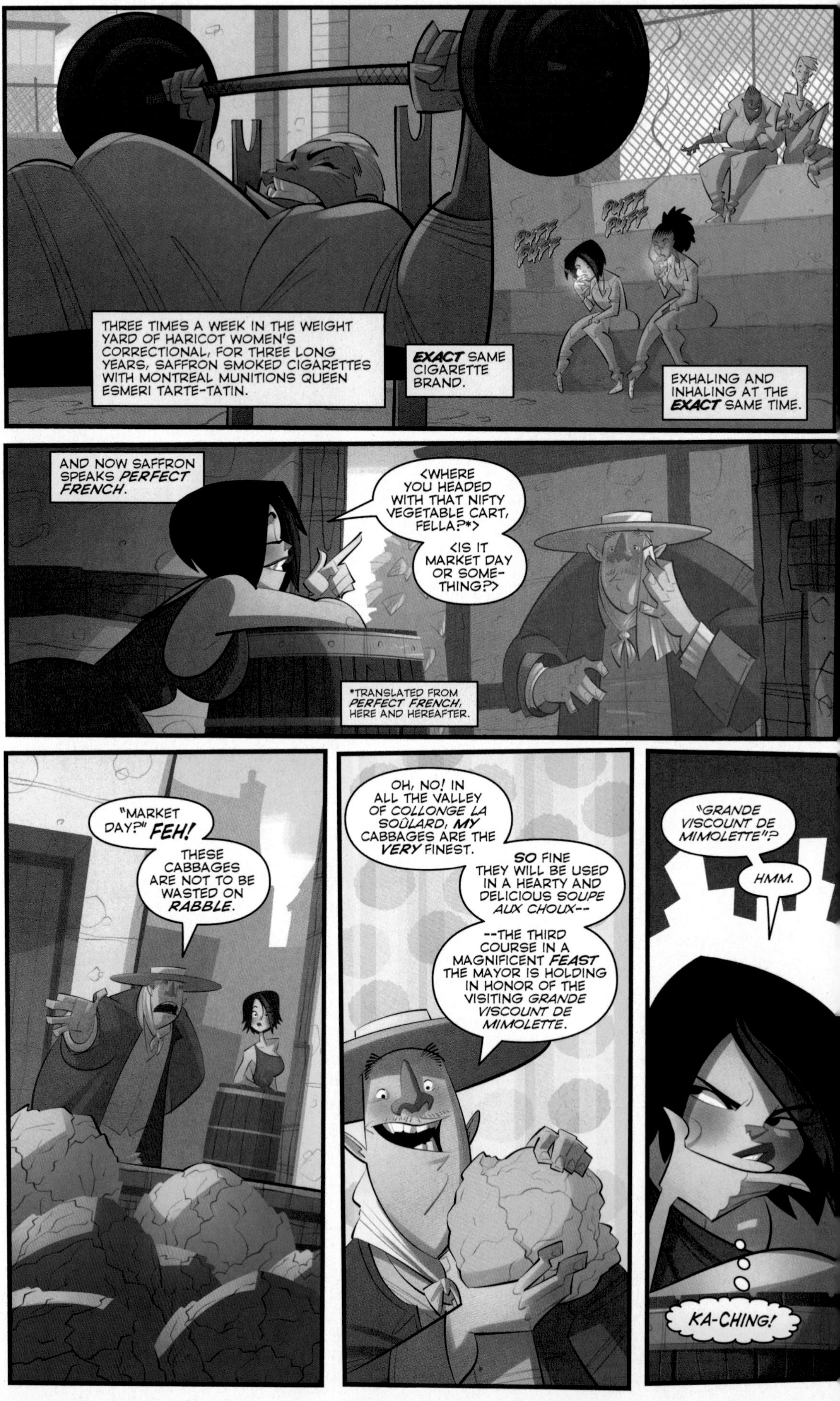
THREE TIMES A WEEK IN THE WEIGHT YARD OF HARICOT WOMEN'S CORRECTIONAL, FOR THREE LONG YEARS, SAFFRON SMOKED CIGARETTES WITH MONTREAL MUNITIONS QUEEN ESMERI TARTE-TATIN.
PUFF PUFF
PUFF PUFF
EXACT SAME CIGARETTE BRAND.
EXHALING AND INHALING AT THE EXACT SAME TIME.
AND NOW SAFFRON SPEAKS PERFECT FRENCH.
<WHERE YOU HEADED WITH THAT NIFTY VEGETABLE CART, FELLA?*>
<IS IT MARKET DAY OR SOME-THING?>
*TRANSLATED FROM PERFECT FRENCH, HERE AND HEREAFTER.
"MARKET DAY?" FEH!
THESE CABBAGES ARE NOT TO BE WASTED ON RABBLE.
OH, NO! IN ALL THE VALLEY OF COLLONGE LA SOÛLARD, MY CABBAGES ARE THE VERY FINEST.
SO FINE THEY WILL BE USED IN A HEARTY AND DELICIOUS SOUPE AUX CHOUX--
--THE THIRD COURSE IN A MAGNIFICENT FEAST THE MAYOR IS HOLDING IN HONOR OF THE VISITING GRANDE VISCOUNT DE MIMOLETTE.
"GRANDE VISCOUNT DE MIMOLETTE"?
HMM.
KA-CHING!

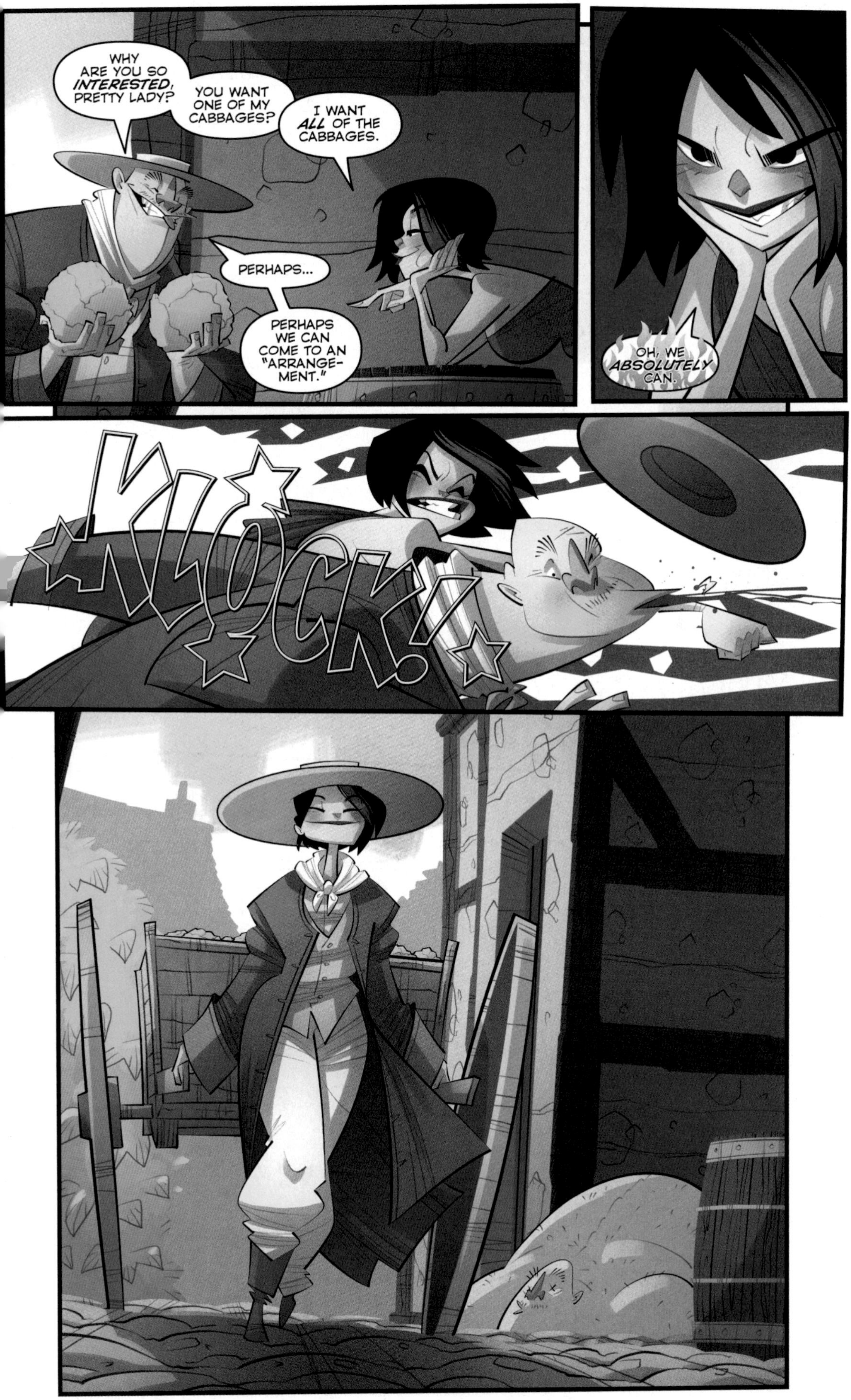
WHY ARE YOU SO INTERESTED, PRETTY LADY?
YOU WANT ONE OF MY CABBAGES?
I WANT ALL OF THE CABBAGES.
PERHAPS...
PERHAPS WE CAN COME TO AN "ARRANGE-MENT."
OH, WE ABSOLUTELY CAN.
KLOCK!!

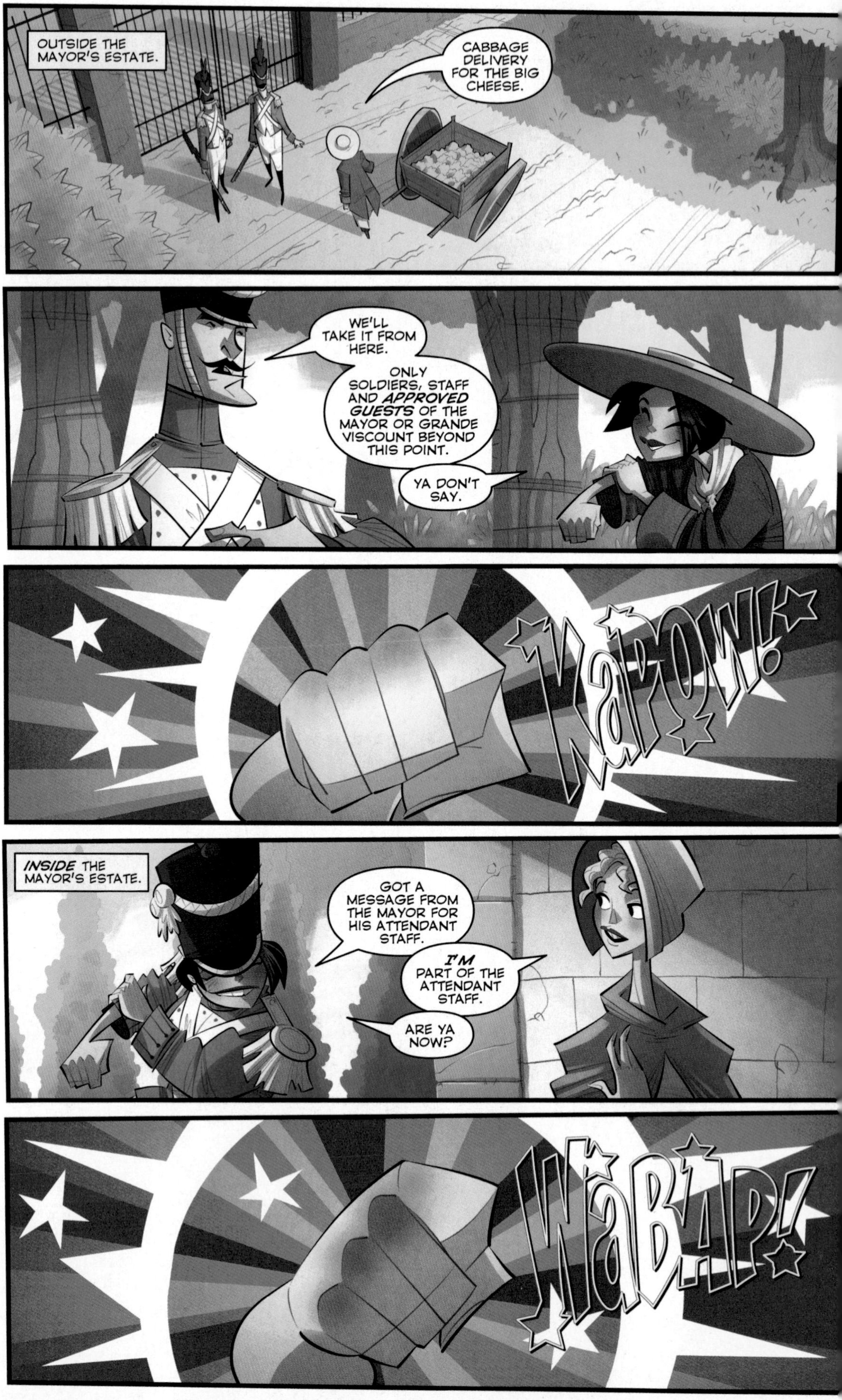
OUTSIDE THE MAYOR'S ESTATE.
CABBAGE DELIVERY FOR THE BIG CHEESE.
WE'LL TAKE IT FROM HERE.
ONLY SOLDIERS, STAFF AND APPROVED GUESTS OF THE MAYOR OR GRANDE VISCOUNT BEYOND THIS POINT.
YA DON'T SAY.
KAPOW!
INSIDE THE MAYOR'S ESTATE.
GOT A MESSAGE FROM THE MAYOR FOR HIS ATTENDANT STAFF.
I'M PART OF THE ATTENDANT STAFF.
ARE YA NOW?
WABAP!

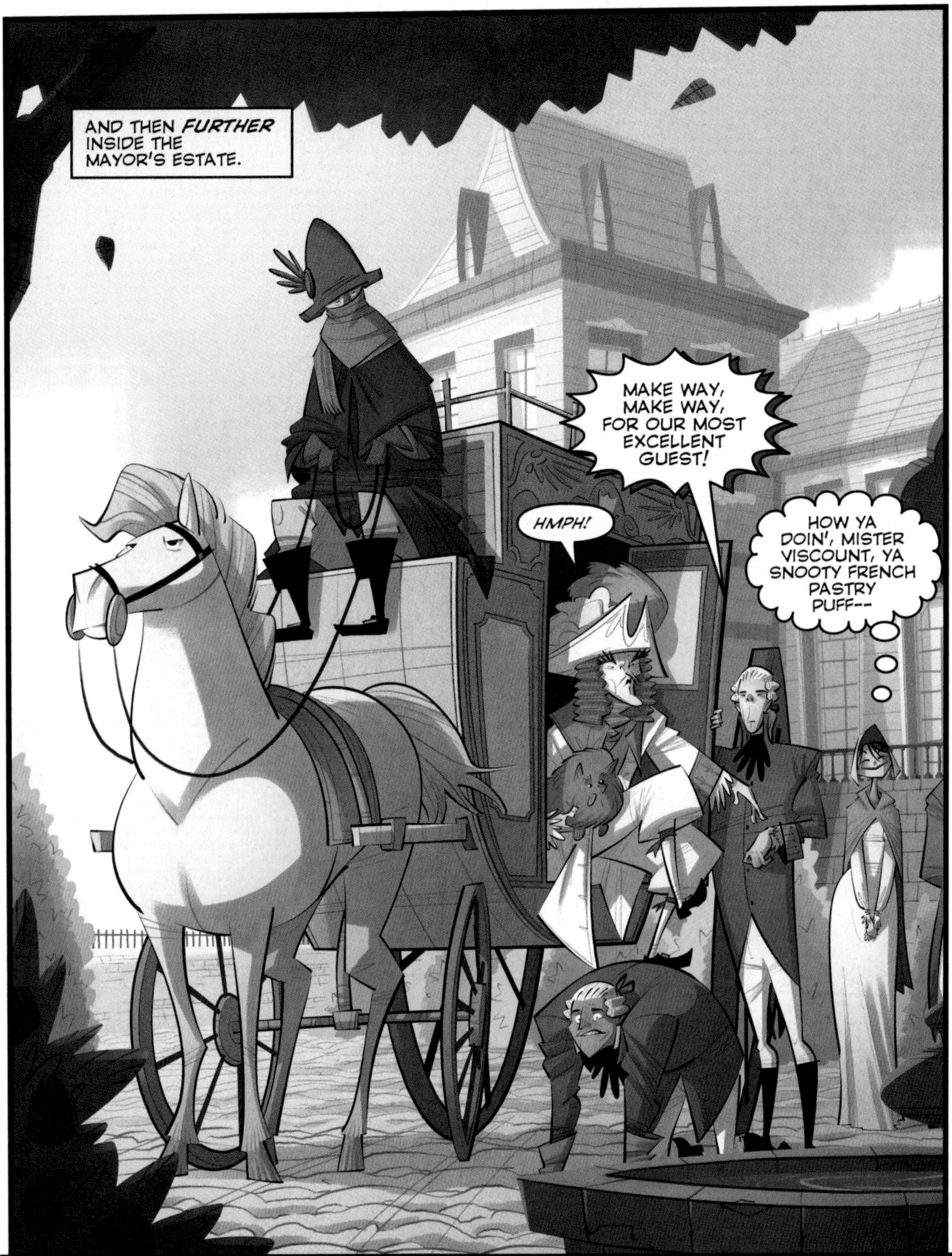
AND THEN *FURTHER* INSIDE THE MAYOR'S ESTATE.
MAKE WAY, MAKE WAY, FOR OUR MOST EXCELLENT GUEST!
HMPH!
HOW YA DOIN', MISTER VISCOUNT, YA SNOOTY FRENCH PASTRY PUFF--

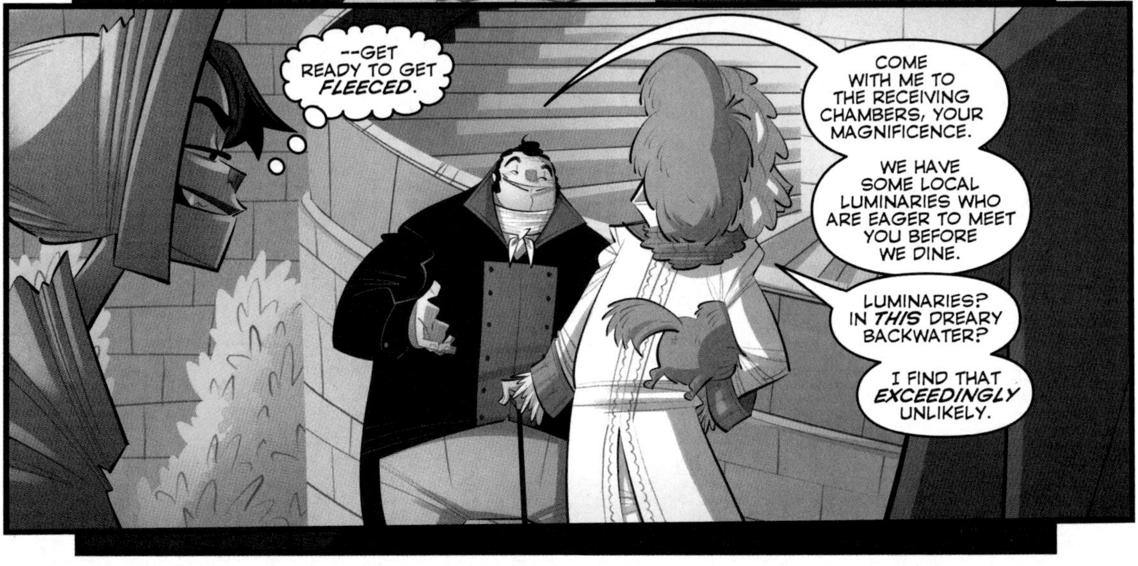
--GET READY TO GET *FLEECED*.
COME WITH ME TO THE RECEIVING CHAMBERS, YOUR MAGNIFICENCE.
WE HAVE SOME LOCAL LUMINARIES WHO ARE EAGER TO MEET YOU BEFORE WE DINE.
LUMINARIES? IN *THIS* DREARY BACKWATER?
I FIND THAT *EXCEEDINGLY* UNLIKELY.

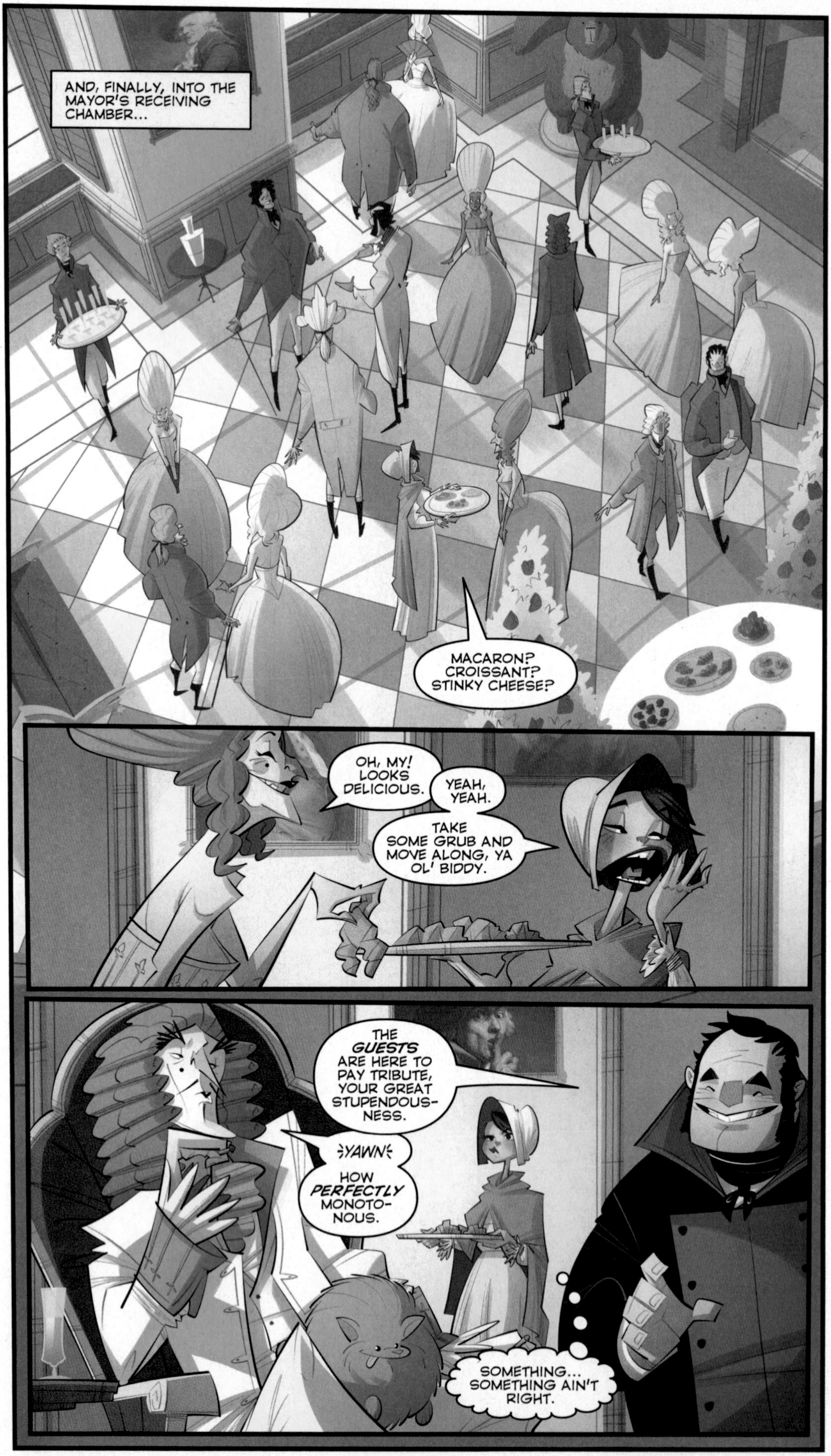
AND, FINALLY, INTO THE MAYOR'S RECEIVING CHAMBER...
MACARON? CROISSANT? STINKY CHEESE?
OH, MY! LOOKS DELICIOUS.
YEAH, YEAH.
TAKE SOME GRUB AND MOVE ALONG, YA OL' BIDDY.
THE GUESTS ARE HERE TO PAY TRIBUTE, YOUR GREAT STUPENDOUSNESS.
YAWN
HOW PERFECTLY MONOTONOUS.
SOMETHING... SOMETHING AIN'T RIGHT.

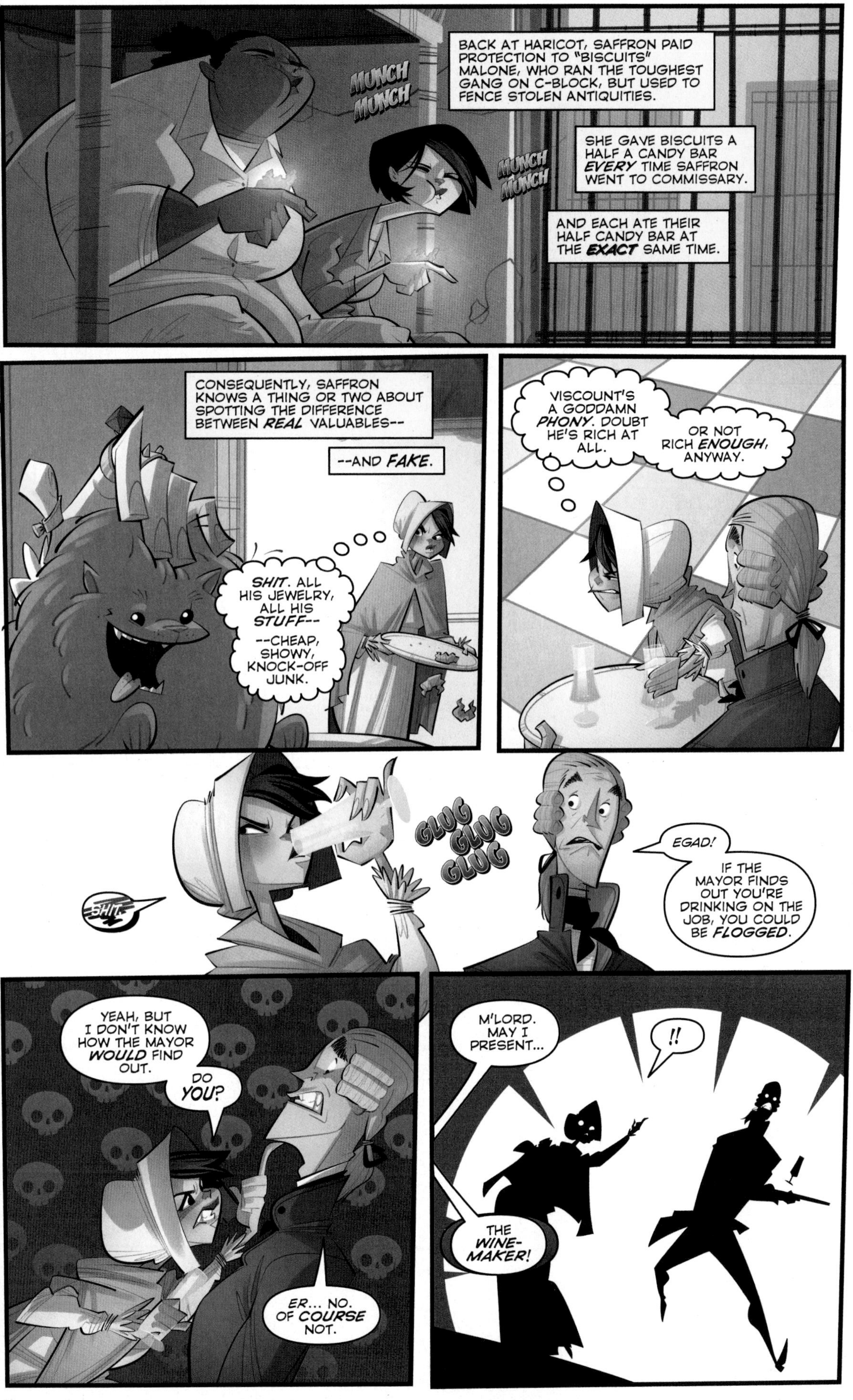
BACK AT HARICOT, SAFFRON PAID PROTECTION TO "BISCUITS" MALONE, WHO RAN THE TOUGHEST GANG ON C-BLOCK, BUT USED TO FENCE STOLEN ANTIQUITIES.
MUNCH MUNCH
MUNCH MUNCH
SHE GAVE BISCUITS A HALF A CANDY BAR EVERY TIME SAFFRON WENT TO COMMISSARY.
AND EACH ATE THEIR HALF CANDY BAR AT THE EXACT SAME TIME.
CONSEQUENTLY, SAFFRON KNOWS A THING OR TWO ABOUT SPOTTING THE DIFFERENCE BETWEEN REAL VALUABLES--
--AND FAKE.
SHIT. ALL HIS JEWELRY, ALL HIS STUFF--
--CHEAP, SHOWY, KNOCK-OFF JUNK.
VISCOUNT'S A GODDAMN PHONY. DOUBT HE'S RICH AT ALL.
OR NOT RICH ENOUGH, ANYWAY.
SHIT.
GLUG GLUG GLUG
EGAD!
IF THE MAYOR FINDS OUT YOU'RE DRINKING ON THE JOB, YOU COULD BE FLOGGED.
YEAH, BUT I DON'T KNOW HOW THE MAYOR WOULD FIND OUT.
DO YOU?
ER... NO. OF COURSE NOT.
M'LORD. MAY I PRESENT...
!!
THE WINE-MAKER!

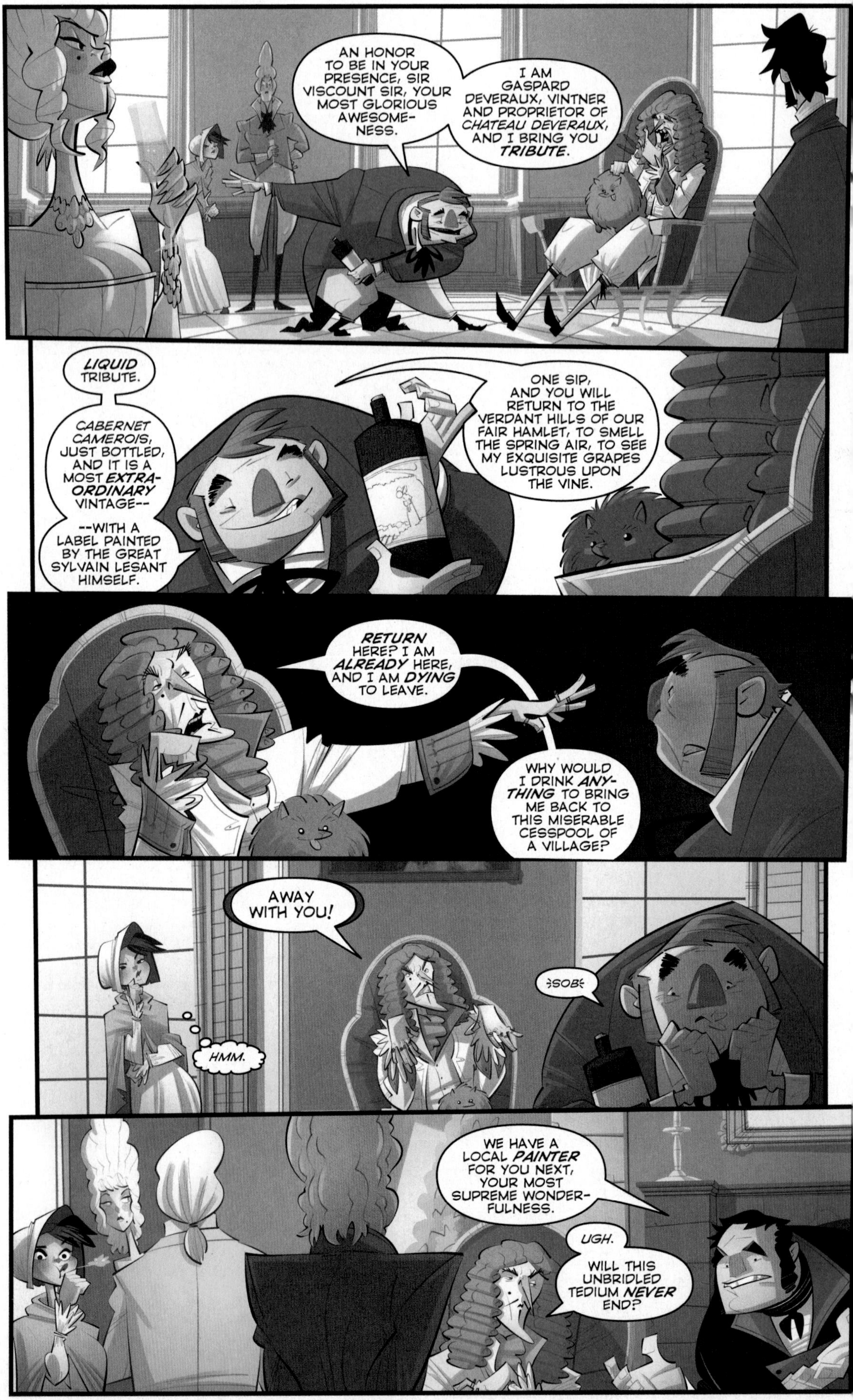
AN HONOR TO BE IN YOUR PRESENCE, SIR VISCOUNT SIR, YOUR MOST GLORIOUS AWESOME-NESS.
I AM GASPARD DEVERAUX, VINTNER AND PROPRIETOR OF *CHATEAU DEVERAUX*, AND I BRING YOU ***TRIBUTE***.
LIQUID TRIBUTE.
CABERNET CAMEROIS, JUST BOTTLED, AND IT IS A MOST ***EXTRA-ORDINARY*** VINTAGE--
--WITH A LABEL PAINTED BY THE GREAT SYLVAIN LESANT HIMSELF.
ONE SIP, AND YOU WILL RETURN TO THE VERDANT HILLS OF OUR FAIR HAMLET, TO SMELL THE SPRING AIR, TO SEE MY EXQUISITE GRAPES LUSTROUS UPON THE VINE.
RETURN HERE? I AM ***ALREADY*** HERE, AND I AM ***DYING*** TO LEAVE.
WHY WOULD I DRINK ***ANY-THING*** TO BRING ME BACK TO THIS MISERABLE CESSPOOL OF A VILLAGE?
AWAY WITH YOU!
SOB
HMM.
WE HAVE A LOCAL ***PAINTER*** FOR YOU NEXT, YOUR MOST SUPREME WONDER-FULNESS.
UGH.
WILL THIS UNBRIDLED TEDIUM ***NEVER*** END?

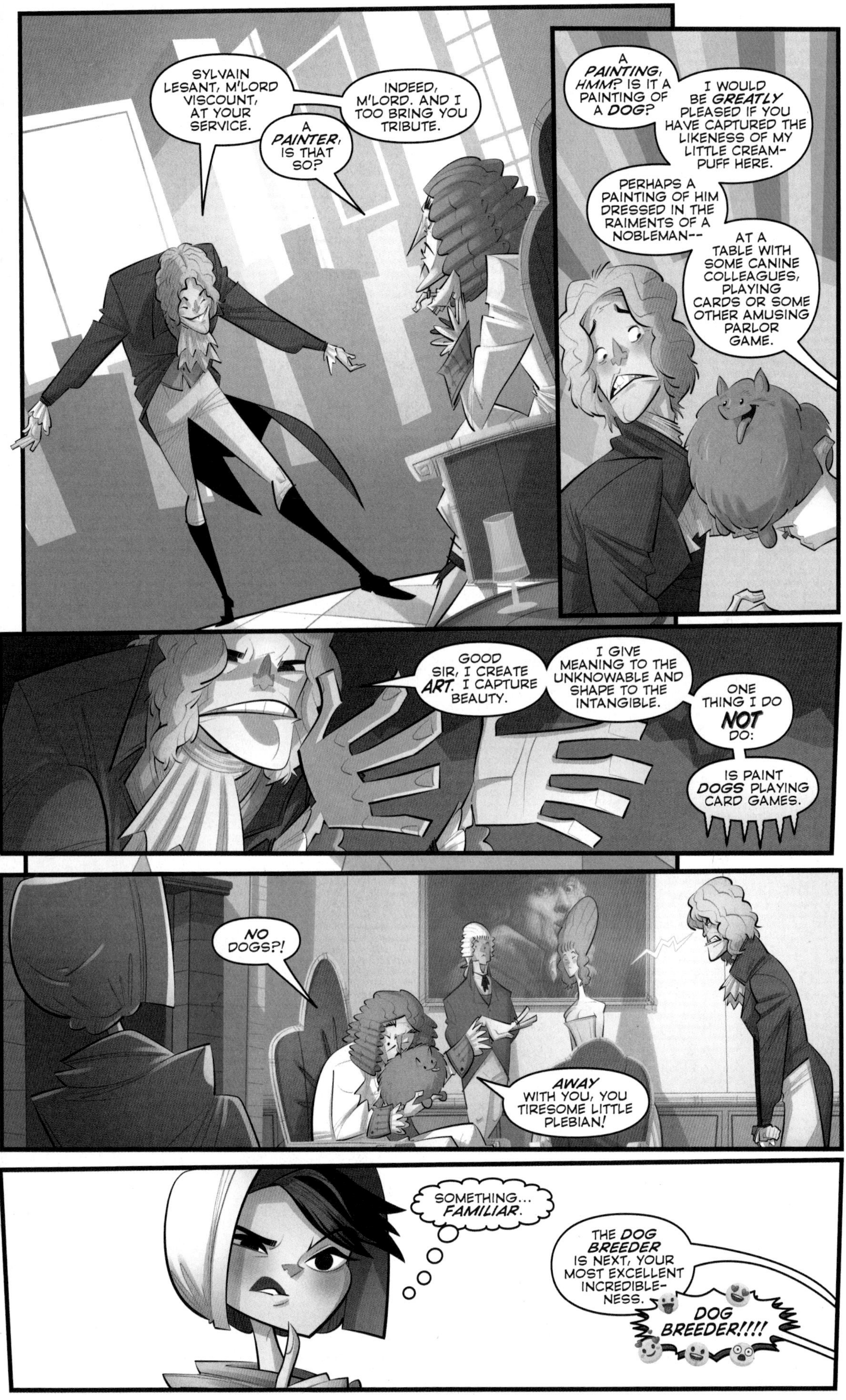
SYLVAIN LESANT, M'LORD VISCOUNT, AT YOUR SERVICE.
A *PAINTER*, IS THAT SO?
INDEED, M'LORD. AND I TOO BRING YOU TRIBUTE.
A *PAINTING*, *HMM?* IS IT A PAINTING OF A *DOG*?
I WOULD BE *GREATLY* PLEASED IF YOU HAVE CAPTURED THE LIKENESS OF MY LITTLE CREAM-PUFF HERE.
PERHAPS A PAINTING OF HIM DRESSED IN THE RAIMENTS OF A NOBLEMAN--
AT A TABLE WITH SOME CANINE COLLEAGUES, PLAYING CARDS OR SOME OTHER AMUSING PARLOR GAME.
GOOD SIR, I CREATE *ART*. I CAPTURE BEAUTY.
I GIVE MEANING TO THE UNKNOWABLE AND SHAPE TO THE INTANGIBLE.
ONE THING I DO *NOT* DO:
IS PAINT *DOGS* PLAYING CARD GAMES.
NO DOGS?!
AWAY WITH YOU, YOU TIRESOME LITTLE PLEBIAN!
SOMETHING... *FAMILIAR*.
THE *DOG BREEDER* IS NEXT, YOUR MOST EXCELLENT INCREDIBLE-NESS.
DOG BREEDER!!!!

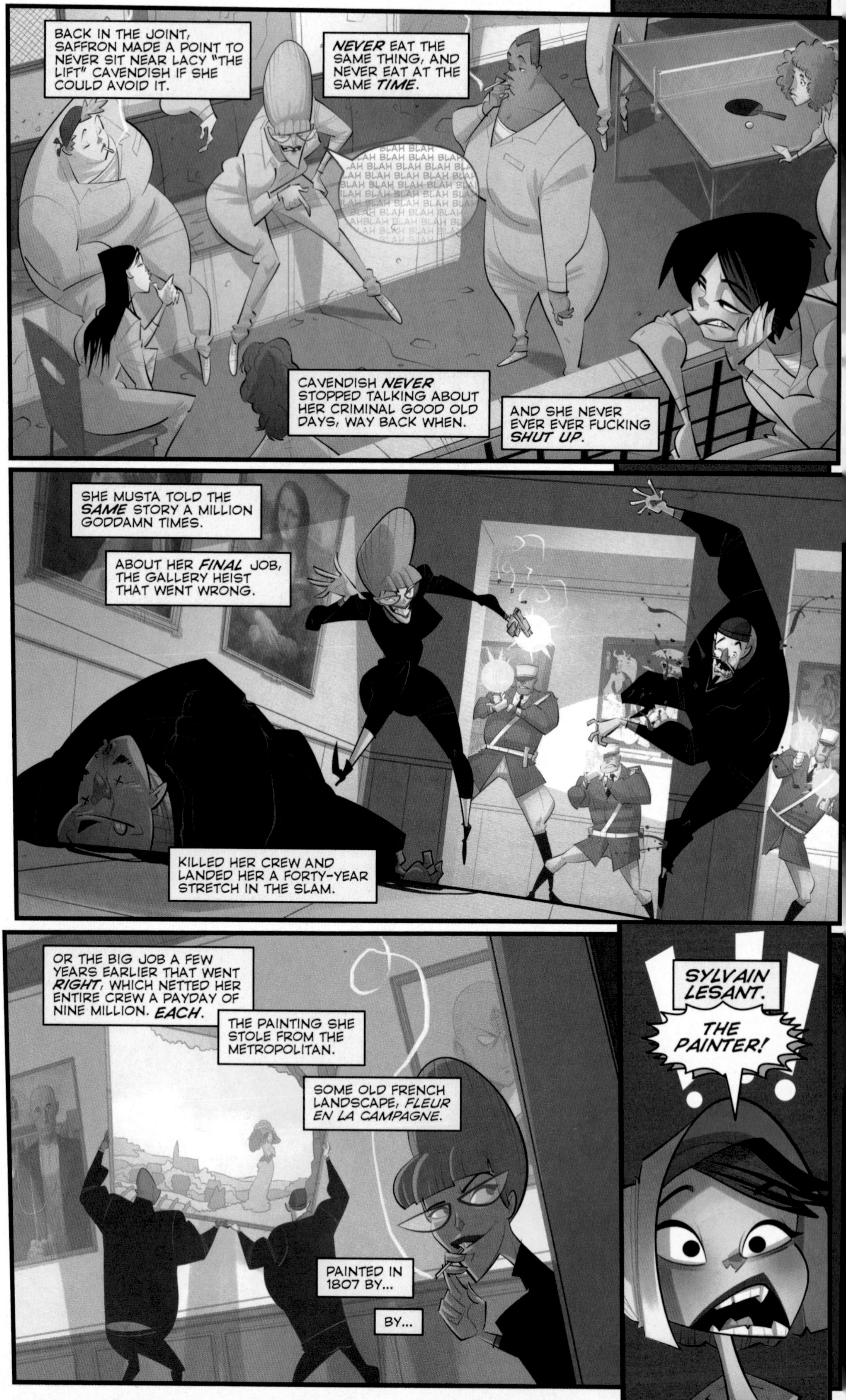

BACK IN THE JOINT, SAFFRON MADE A POINT TO NEVER SIT NEAR LACY "THE LIFT" CAVENDISH IF SHE COULD AVOID IT.
NEVER EAT THE SAME THING, AND NEVER EAT AT THE SAME TIME.
CAVENDISH NEVER STOPPED TALKING ABOUT HER CRIMINAL GOOD OLD DAYS, WAY BACK WHEN.
AND SHE NEVER EVER EVER FUCKING SHUT UP.
SHE MUSTA TOLD THE SAME STORY A MILLION GODDAMN TIMES.
ABOUT HER FINAL JOB, THE GALLERY HEIST THAT WENT WRONG.
KILLED HER CREW AND LANDED HER A FORTY-YEAR STRETCH IN THE SLAM.
OR THE BIG JOB A FEW YEARS EARLIER THAT WENT RIGHT, WHICH NETTED HER ENTIRE CREW A PAYDAY OF NINE MILLION. EACH.
THE PAINTING SHE STOLE FROM THE METROPOLITAN.
SOME OLD FRENCH LANDSCAPE, FLEUR EN LA CAMPAGNE.
PAINTED IN 1807 BY...
BY...
SYLVAIN LESANT.
THE PAINTER!

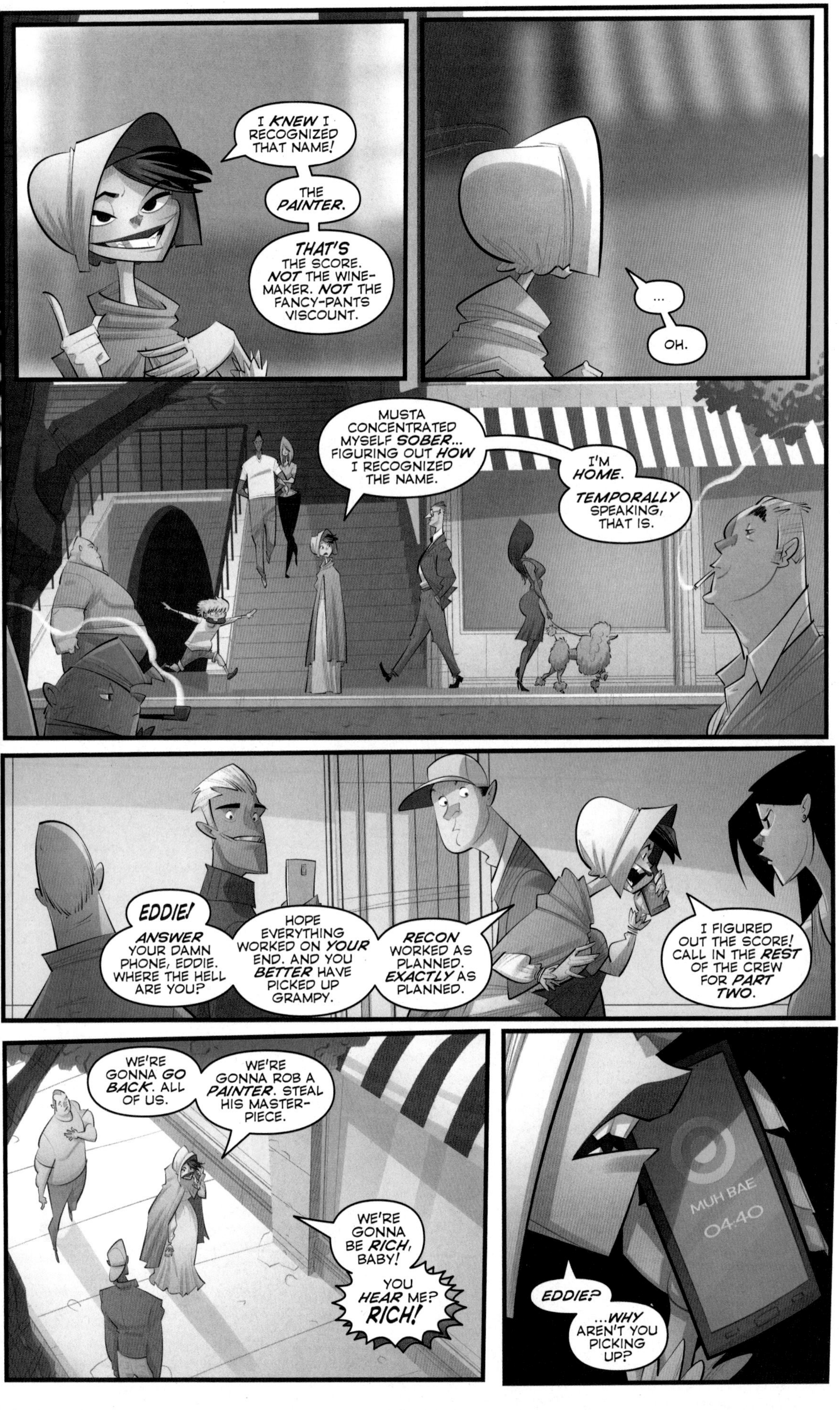
I KNEW I RECOGNIZED THAT NAME!
THE PAINTER.
THAT'S THE SCORE. NOT THE WINE-MAKER. NOT THE FANCY-PANTS VISCOUNT.
...
OH.
MUSTA CONCENTRATED MYSELF SOBER... FIGURING OUT HOW I RECOGNIZED THE NAME.
I'M HOME.
TEMPORALLY SPEAKING, THAT IS.
EDDIE!
ANSWER YOUR DAMN PHONE, EDDIE. WHERE THE HELL ARE YOU?
HOPE EVERYTHING WORKED ON YOUR END. AND YOU BETTER HAVE PICKED UP GRAMPY.
RECON WORKED AS PLANNED. EXACTLY AS PLANNED.
I FIGURED OUT THE SCORE! CALL IN THE REST OF THE CREW FOR PART TWO.
WE'RE GONNA GO BACK. ALL OF US.
WE'RE GONNA ROB A PAINTER. STEAL HIS MASTER-PIECE.
WE'RE GONNA BE RICH, BABY!
YOU HEAR ME? RICH!
MUH BAE
04:40
EDDIE?
...WHY AREN'T YOU PICKING UP?

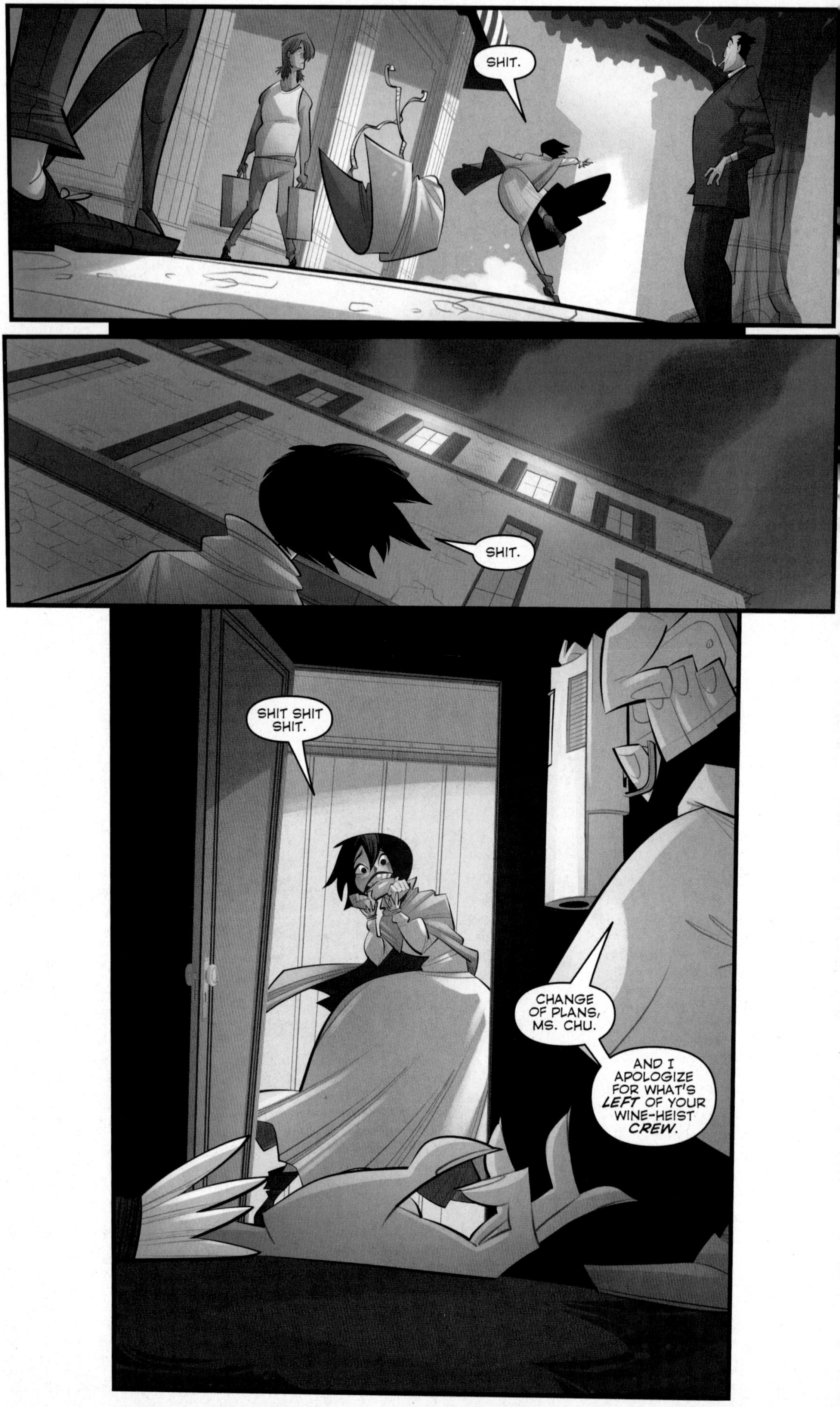
SHIT.
SHIT.
SHIT SHIT SHIT.
CHANGE OF PLANS, MS. CHU.
AND I APOLOGIZE FOR WHAT'S *LEFT* OF YOUR WINE-HEIST *CREW*.

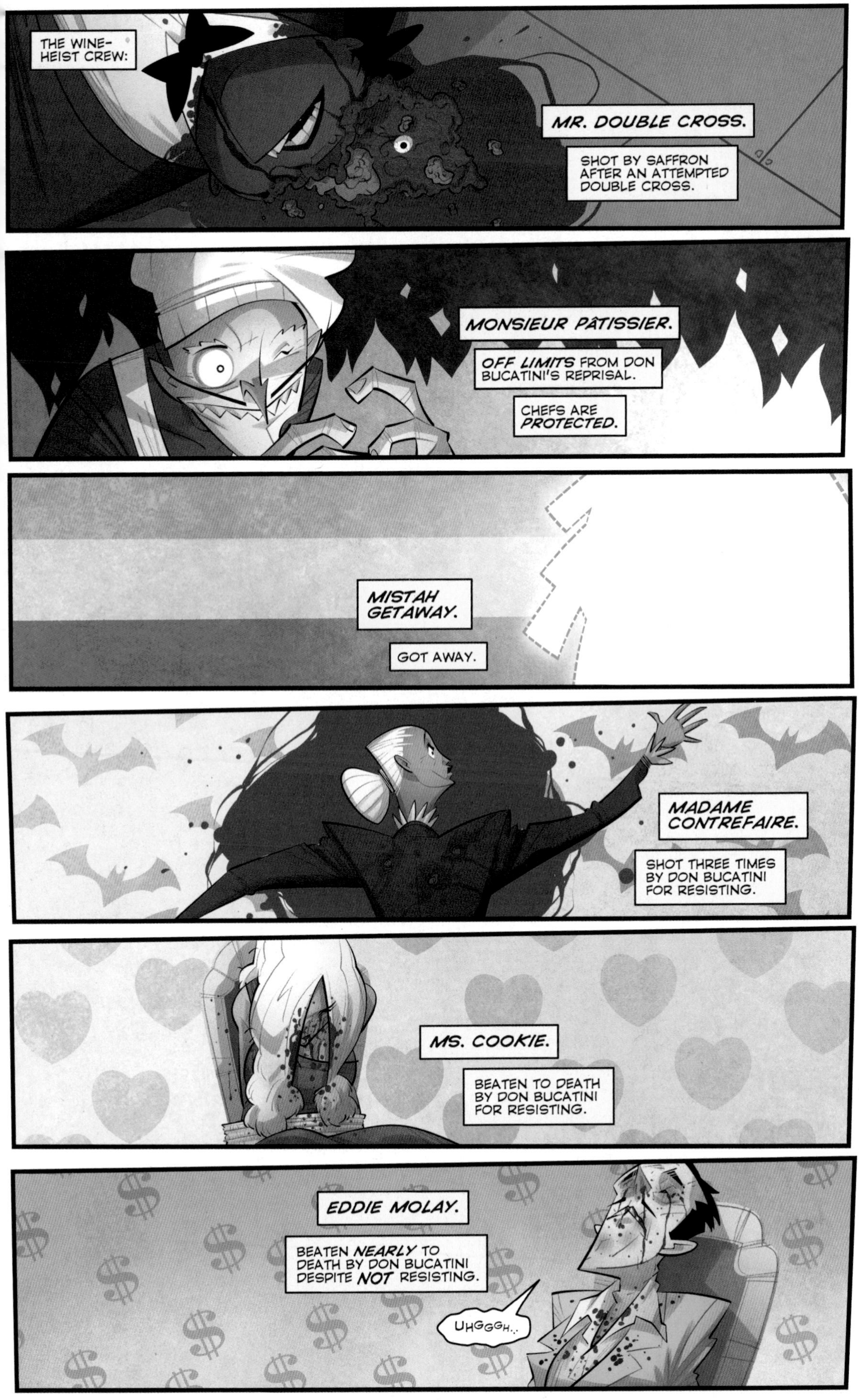
THE WINE-HEIST CREW:
MR. DOUBLE CROSS.
SHOT BY SAFFRON AFTER AN ATTEMPTED DOUBLE CROSS.
MONSIEUR PÂTISSIER.
OFF LIMITS FROM DON BUCATINI'S REPRISAL.
CHEFS ARE PROTECTED.
MISTAH GETAWAY.
GOT AWAY.
MADAME CONTREFAIRE.
SHOT THREE TIMES BY DON BUCATINI FOR RESISTING.
MS. COOKIE.
BEATEN TO DEATH BY DON BUCATINI FOR RESISTING.
EDDIE MOLAY.
BEATEN NEARLY TO DEATH BY DON BUCATINI DESPITE NOT RESISTING.
UHGGGH...

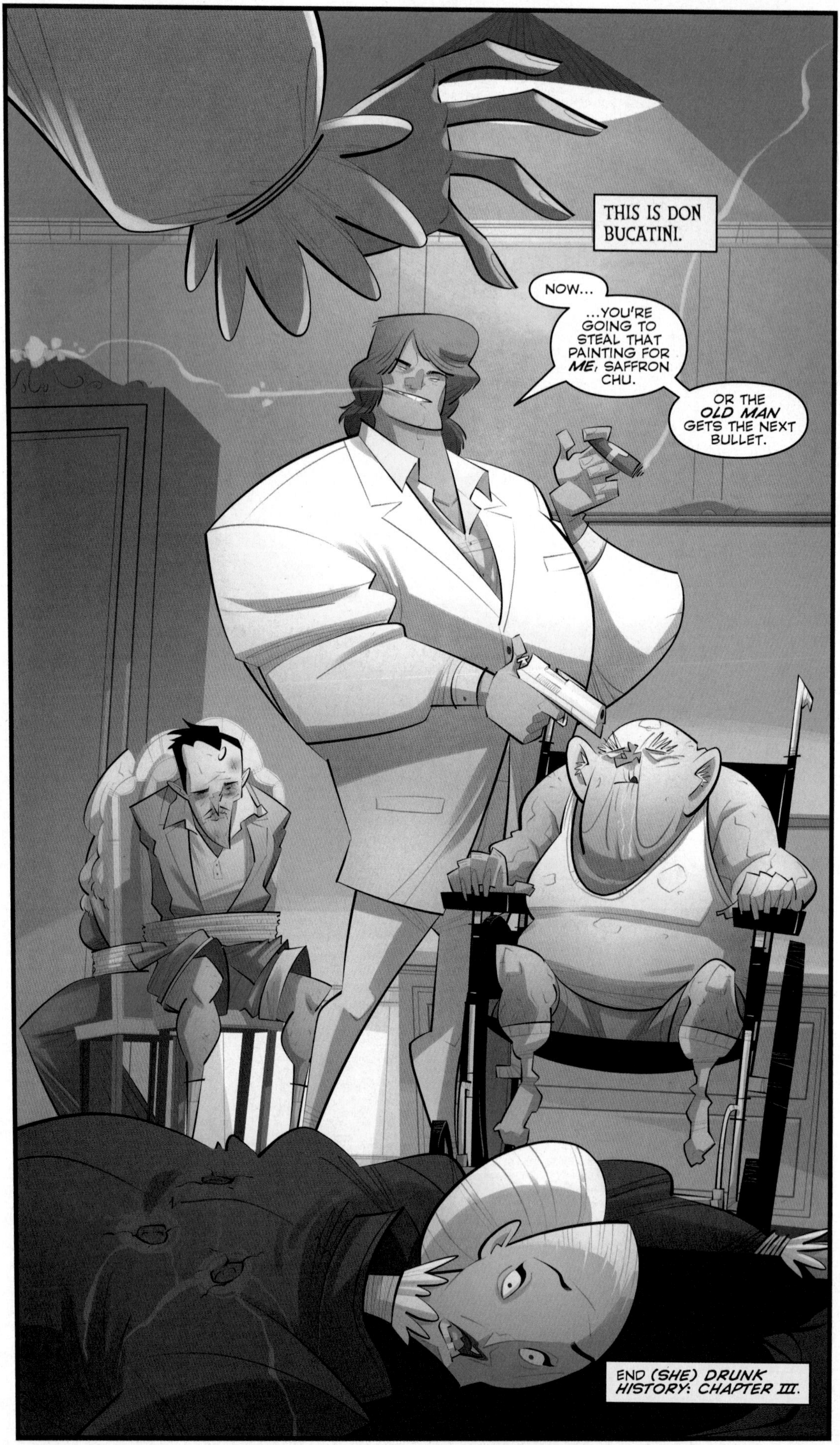
THIS IS DON BUCATINI.
NOW...
...YOU'RE GOING TO STEAL THAT PAINTING FOR ME, SAFFRON CHU.
OR THE OLD MAN GETS THE NEXT BULLET.
END (SHE) DRUNK HISTORY: CHAPTER III.

Chapter 4

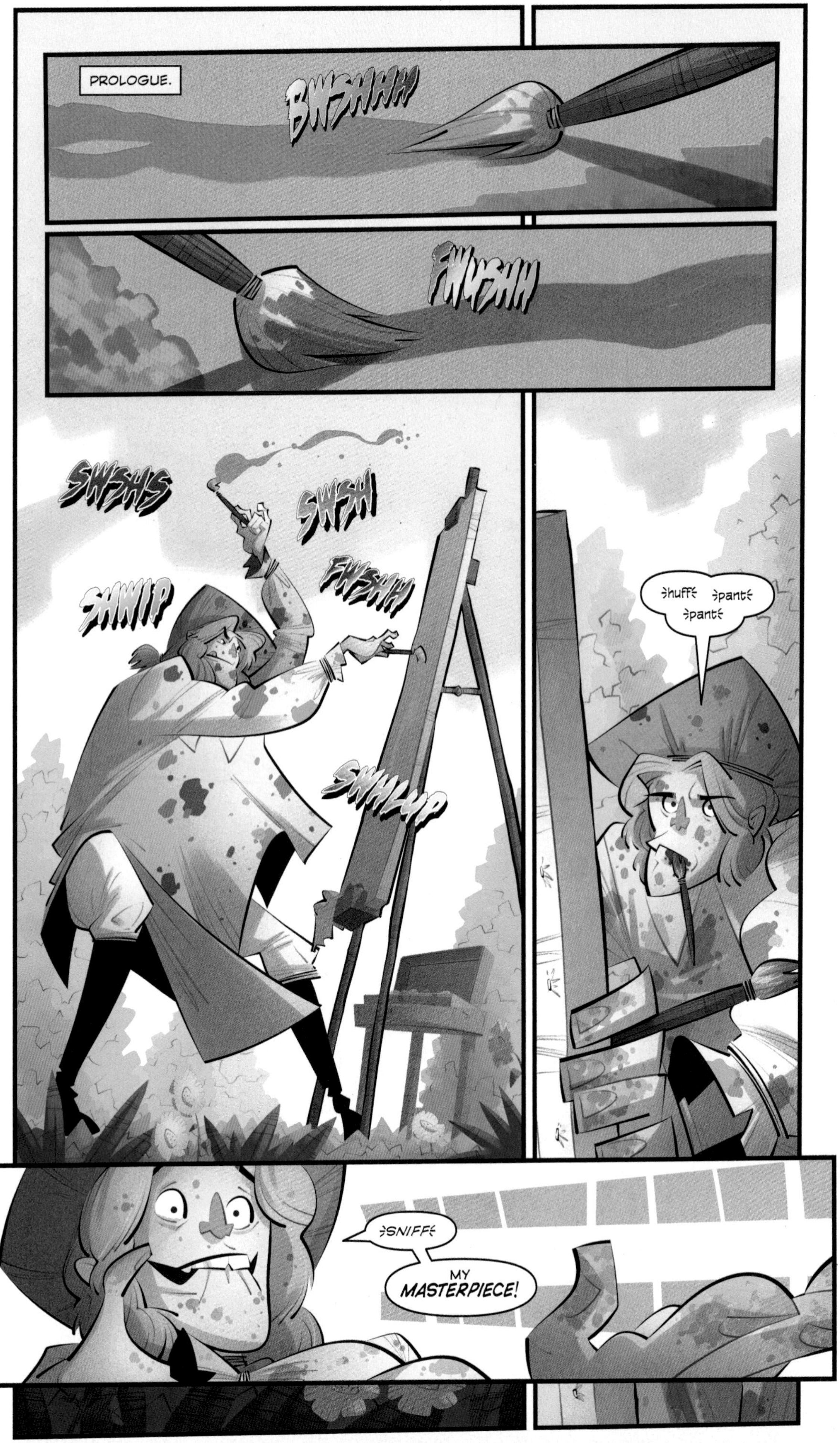
PROLOGUE.
BWSHHH
FWUSHH
SWSHS
SWSH
FWSHH
SHWIP
SWHLUP
huff pant pant
SNIFF
MY MASTERPIECE!

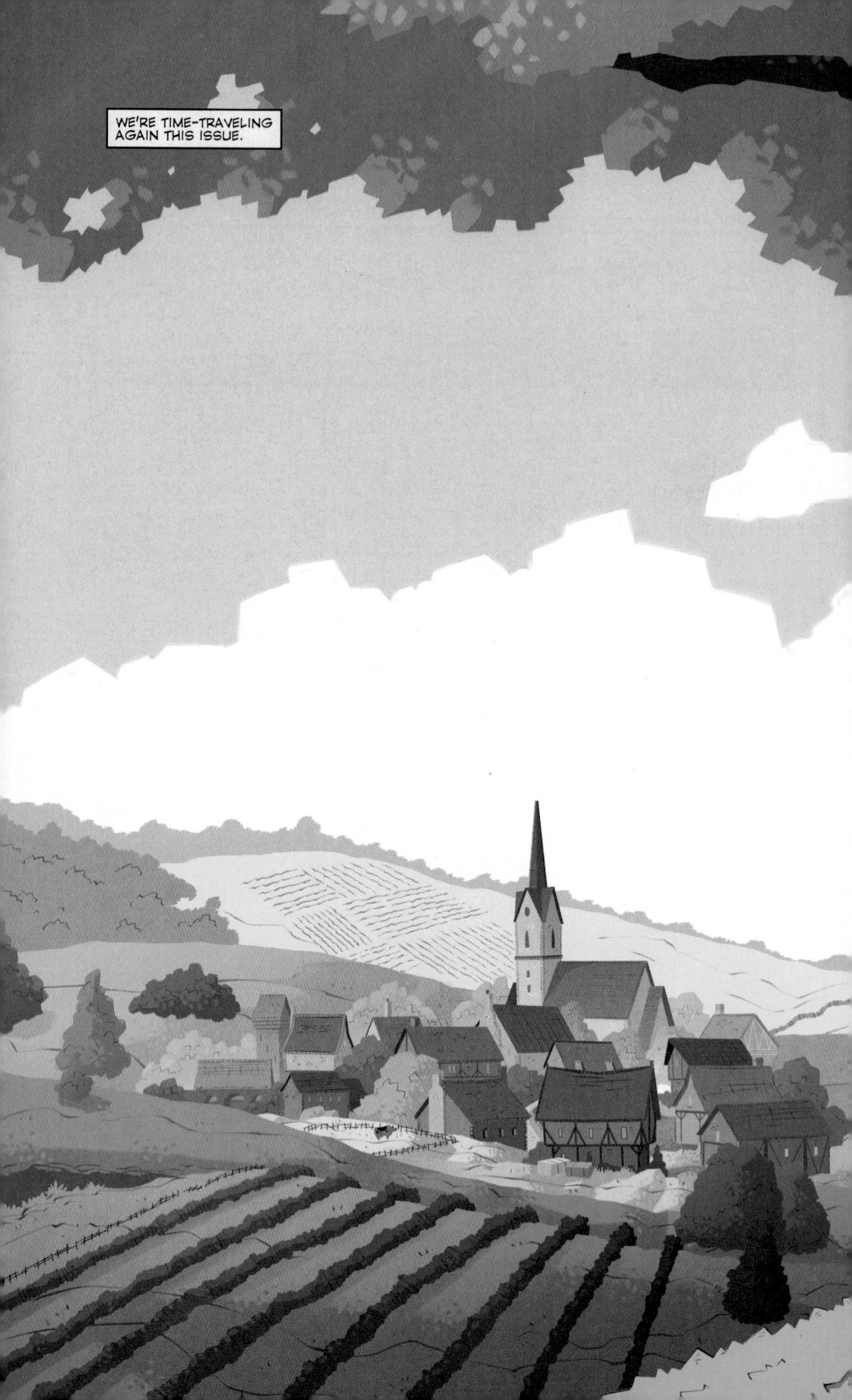
WE'RE TIME-TRAVELING AGAIN THIS ISSUE.

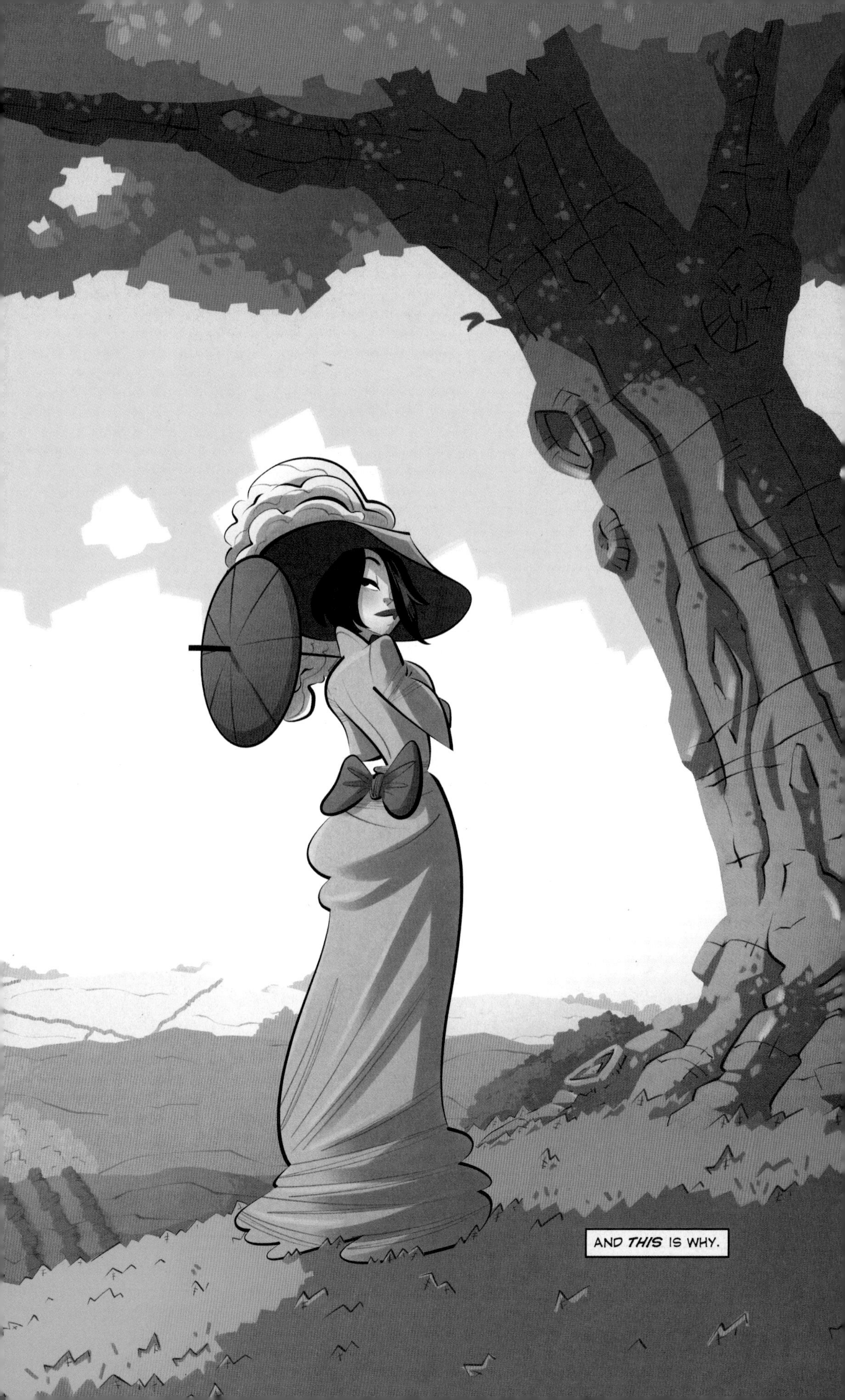
AND *THIS* IS WHY.

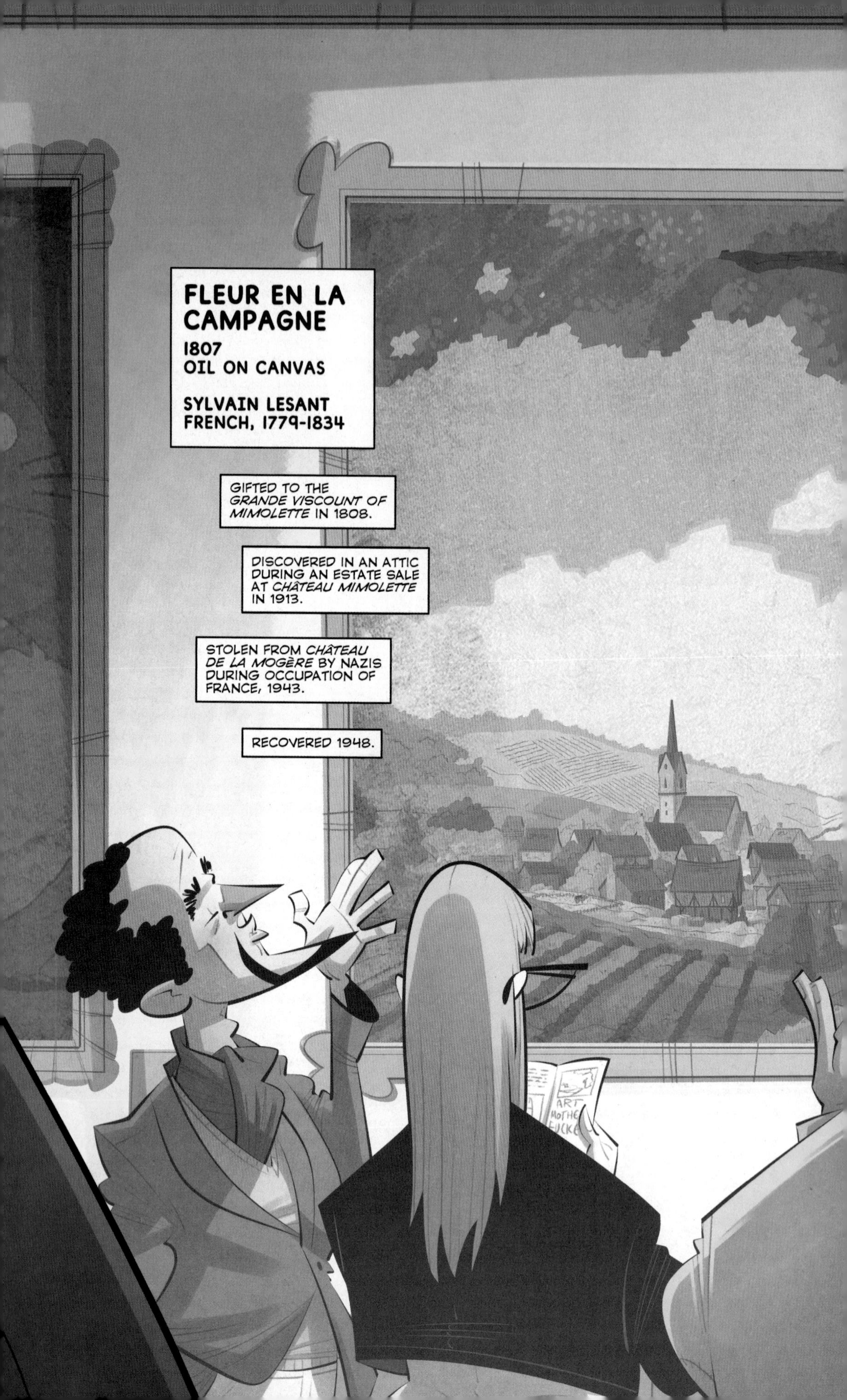
FLEUR EN LA CAMPAGNE
1807
OIL ON CANVAS
SYLVAIN LESANT
FRENCH, 1779-1834
GIFTED TO THE *GRANDE VISCOUNT OF MIMOLETTE* IN 1808.
DISCOVERED IN AN ATTIC DURING AN ESTATE SALE AT *CHÂTEAU MIMOLETTE* IN 1913.
STOLEN FROM *CHÂTEAU DE LA MOGÈRE* BY NAZIS DURING OCCUPATION OF FRANCE, 1943.
RECOVERED 1948.

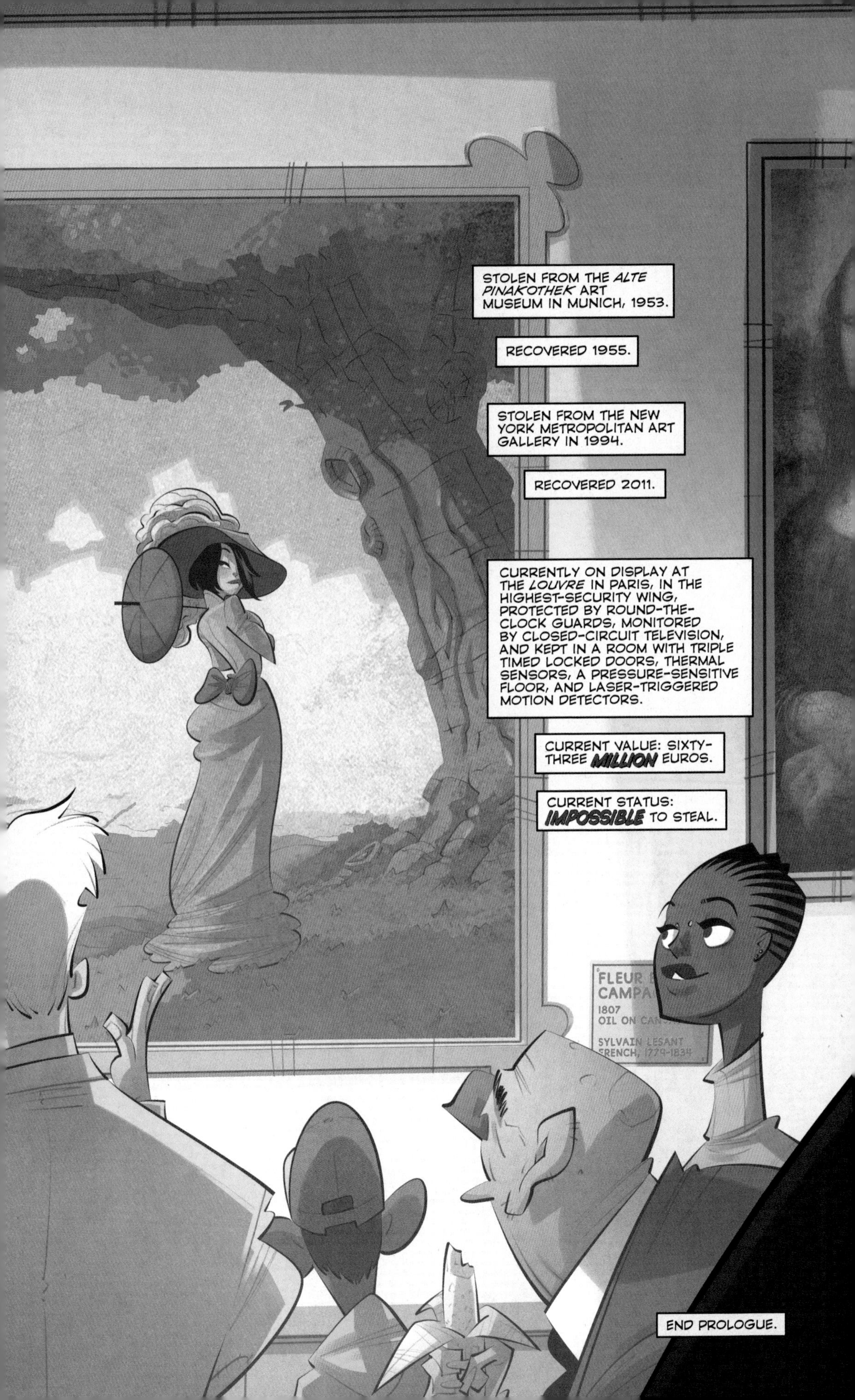
STOLEN FROM THE *ALTE PINAKOTHEK* ART MUSEUM IN MUNICH, 1953.
RECOVERED 1955.
STOLEN FROM THE NEW YORK METROPOLITAN ART GALLERY IN 1994.
RECOVERED 2011.
CURRENTLY ON DISPLAY AT THE *LOUVRE* IN PARIS, IN THE HIGHEST-SECURITY WING, PROTECTED BY ROUND-THE-CLOCK GUARDS, MONITORED BY CLOSED-CIRCUIT TELEVISION, AND KEPT IN A ROOM WITH TRIPLE TIMED LOCKED DOORS, THERMAL SENSORS, A PRESSURE-SENSITIVE FLOOR, AND LASER-TRIGGERED MOTION DETECTORS.
CURRENT VALUE: SIXTY-THREE **MILLION** EUROS.
CURRENT STATUS: **IMPOSSIBLE** TO STEAL.
FLEUR
1807
SYLVAIN LESANT
FRENCH, 1779-1834
END PROLOGUE.

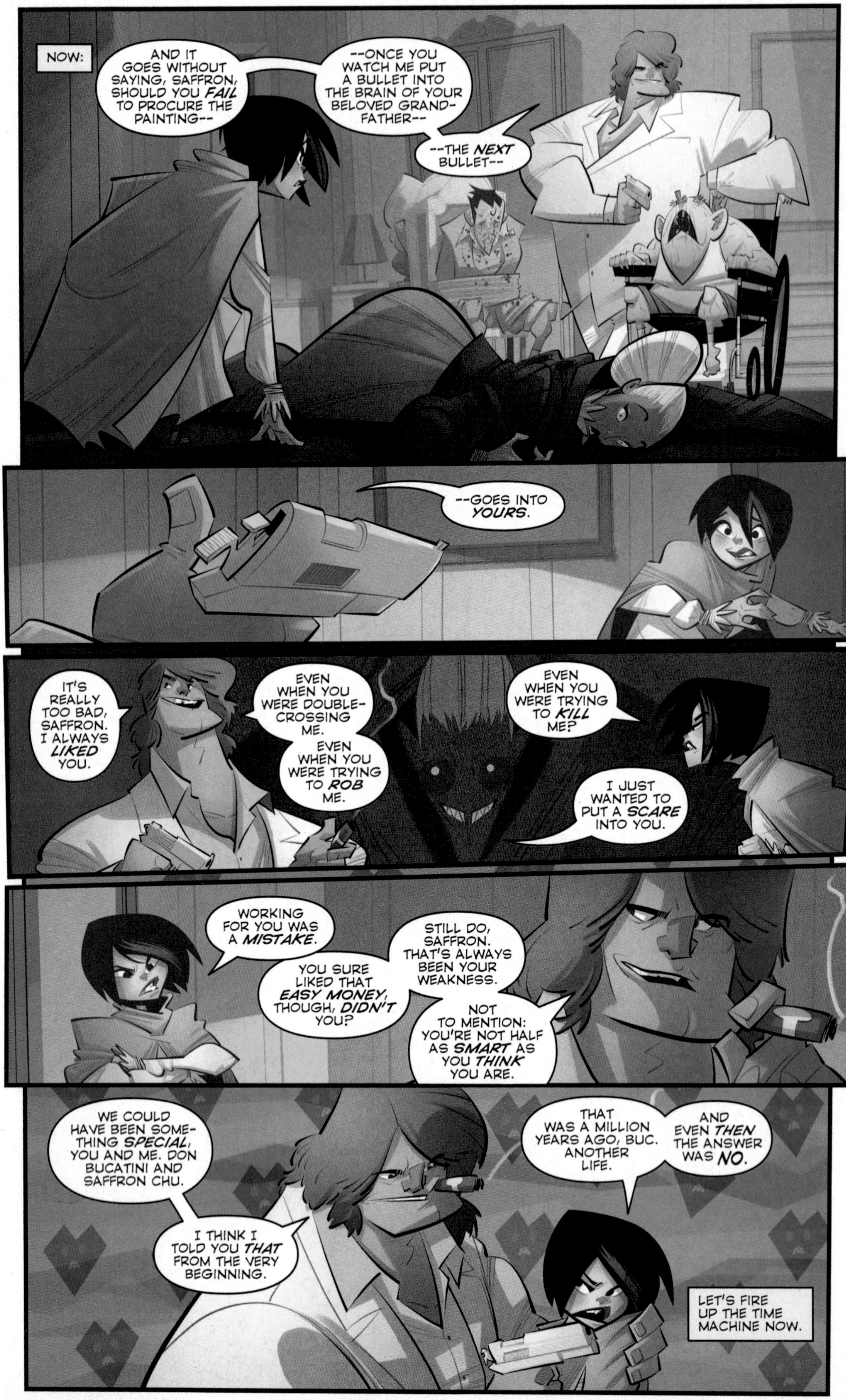
NOW:
AND IT GOES WITHOUT SAYING, SAFFRON, SHOULD YOU FAIL TO PROCURE THE PAINTING--
--ONCE YOU WATCH ME PUT A BULLET INTO THE BRAIN OF YOUR BELOVED GRAND-FATHER--
--THE NEXT BULLET--
--GOES INTO YOURS.
IT'S REALLY TOO BAD, SAFFRON. I ALWAYS LIKED YOU.
EVEN WHEN YOU WERE DOUBLE-CROSSING ME.
EVEN WHEN YOU WERE TRYING TO ROB ME.
EVEN WHEN YOU WERE TRYING TO KILL ME?
I JUST WANTED TO PUT A SCARE INTO YOU.
WORKING FOR YOU WAS A MISTAKE.
YOU SURE LIKED THAT EASY MONEY, THOUGH, DIDN'T YOU?
STILL DO, SAFFRON. THAT'S ALWAYS BEEN YOUR WEAKNESS.
NOT TO MENTION: YOU'RE NOT HALF AS SMART AS YOU THINK YOU ARE.
WE COULD HAVE BEEN SOME-THING SPECIAL, YOU AND ME. DON BUCATINI AND SAFFRON CHU.
I THINK I TOLD YOU THAT FROM THE VERY BEGINNING.
THAT WAS A MILLION YEARS AGO, BUC. ANOTHER LIFE.
AND EVEN THEN THE ANSWER WAS NO.
LET'S FIRE UP THE TIME MACHINE NOW.

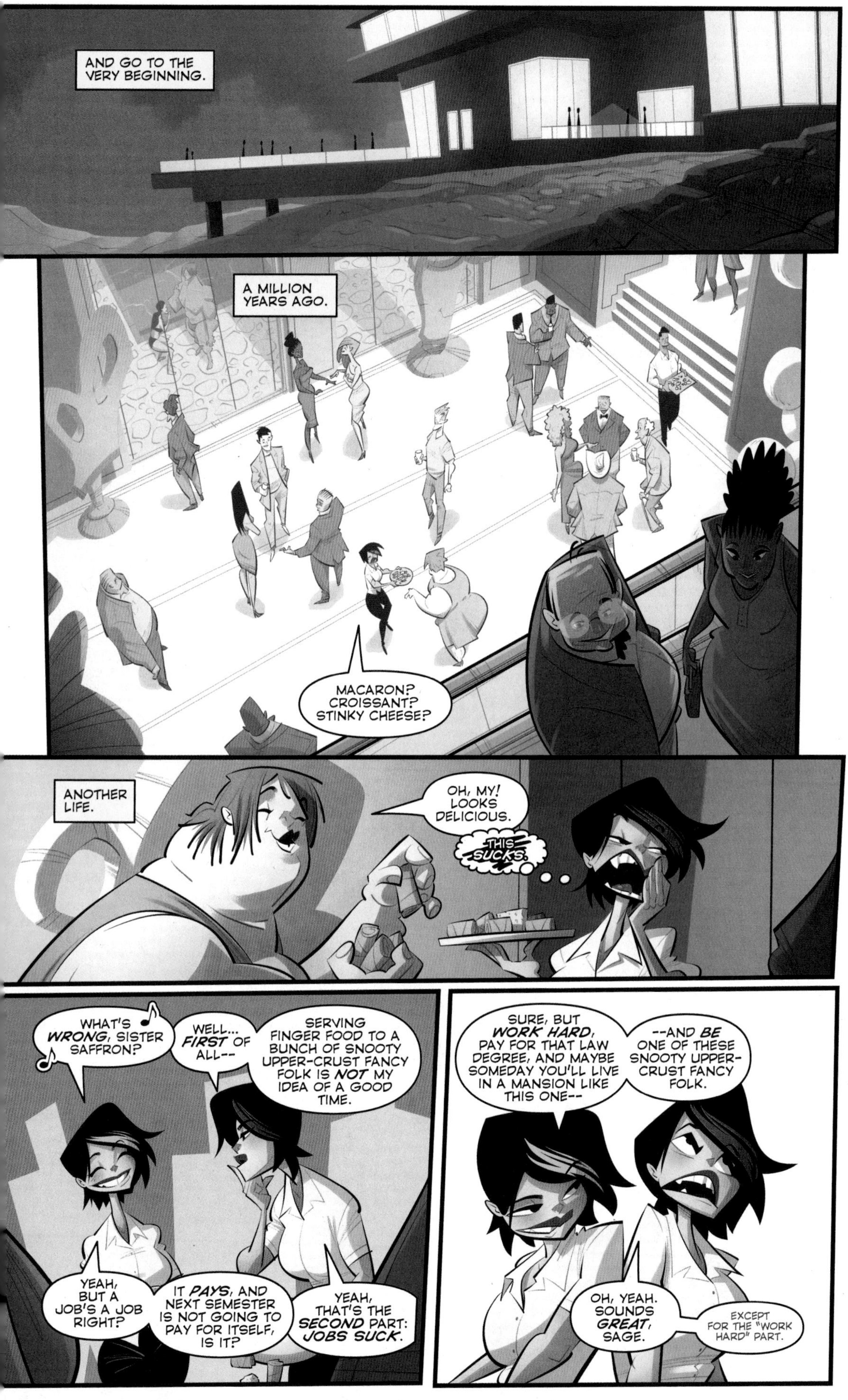
AND GO TO THE VERY BEGINNING.
A MILLION YEARS AGO.
MACARON? CROISSANT? STINKY CHEESE?
ANOTHER LIFE.
OH, MY! LOOKS DELICIOUS.
THIS SUCKS.
WHAT'S WRONG, SISTER SAFFRON?
WELL... FIRST OF ALL--
SERVING FINGER FOOD TO A BUNCH OF SNOOTY UPPER-CRUST FANCY FOLK IS NOT MY IDEA OF A GOOD TIME.
YEAH, BUT A JOB'S A JOB RIGHT?
IT PAYS, AND NEXT SEMESTER IS NOT GOING TO PAY FOR ITSELF, IS IT?
YEAH, THAT'S THE SECOND PART: JOBS SUCK.
SURE, BUT WORK HARD, PAY FOR THAT LAW DEGREE, AND MAYBE SOMEDAY YOU'LL LIVE IN A MANSION LIKE THIS ONE--
--AND BE ONE OF THESE SNOOTY UPPER-CRUST FANCY FOLK.
OH, YEAH. SOUNDS GREAT, SAGE.
EXCEPT FOR THE "WORK HARD" PART.

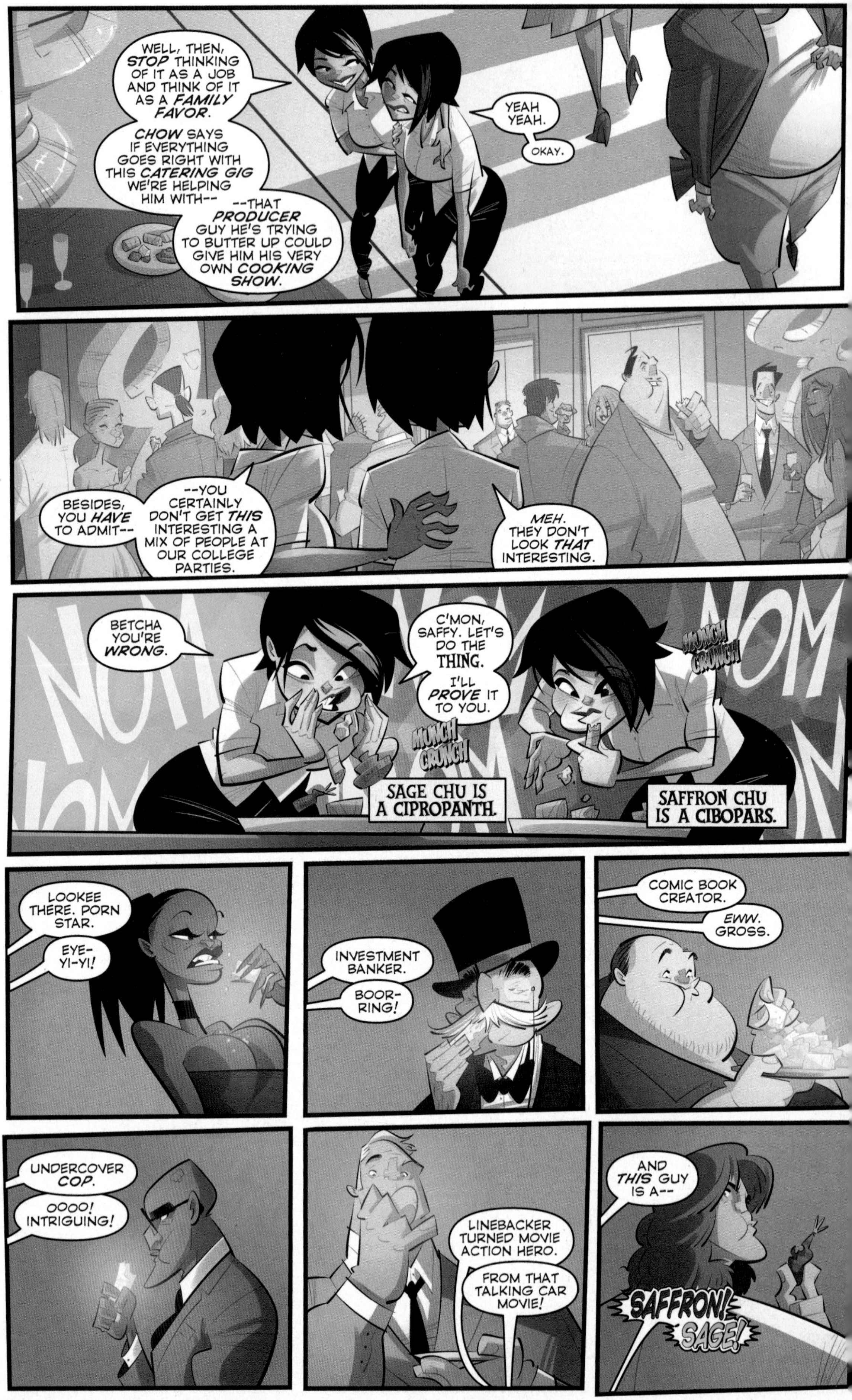
WELL, THEN, STOP THINKING OF IT AS A JOB AND THINK OF IT AS A FAMILY FAVOR.
CHOW SAYS IF EVERYTHING GOES RIGHT WITH THIS CATERING GIG WE'RE HELPING HIM WITH--
--THAT PRODUCER GUY HE'S TRYING TO BUTTER UP COULD GIVE HIM HIS VERY OWN COOKING SHOW.
YEAH YEAH.
OKAY.
BESIDES, YOU HAVE TO ADMIT--
--YOU CERTAINLY DON'T GET THIS INTERESTING A MIX OF PEOPLE AT OUR COLLEGE PARTIES.
MEH. THEY DON'T LOOK THAT INTERESTING.
BETCHA YOU'RE WRONG.
C'MON, SAFFY. LET'S DO THE THING.
I'LL PROVE IT TO YOU.
NOM NOM NOM NOM
MUNCH CRUNCH
MUNCH CRUNCH
SAGE CHU IS A CIPROPANTH.
SAFFRON CHU IS A CIBOPARS.
LOOKEE THERE. PORN STAR.
EYE-YI-YI!
INVESTMENT BANKER.
BOOR-RING!
COMIC BOOK CREATOR.
EWW. GROSS.
UNDERCOVER COP.
OOOO! INTRIGUING!
LINEBACKER TURNED MOVIE ACTION HERO.
FROM THAT TALKING CAR MOVIE!
AND THIS GUY IS A--
SAFFRON!
SAGE!

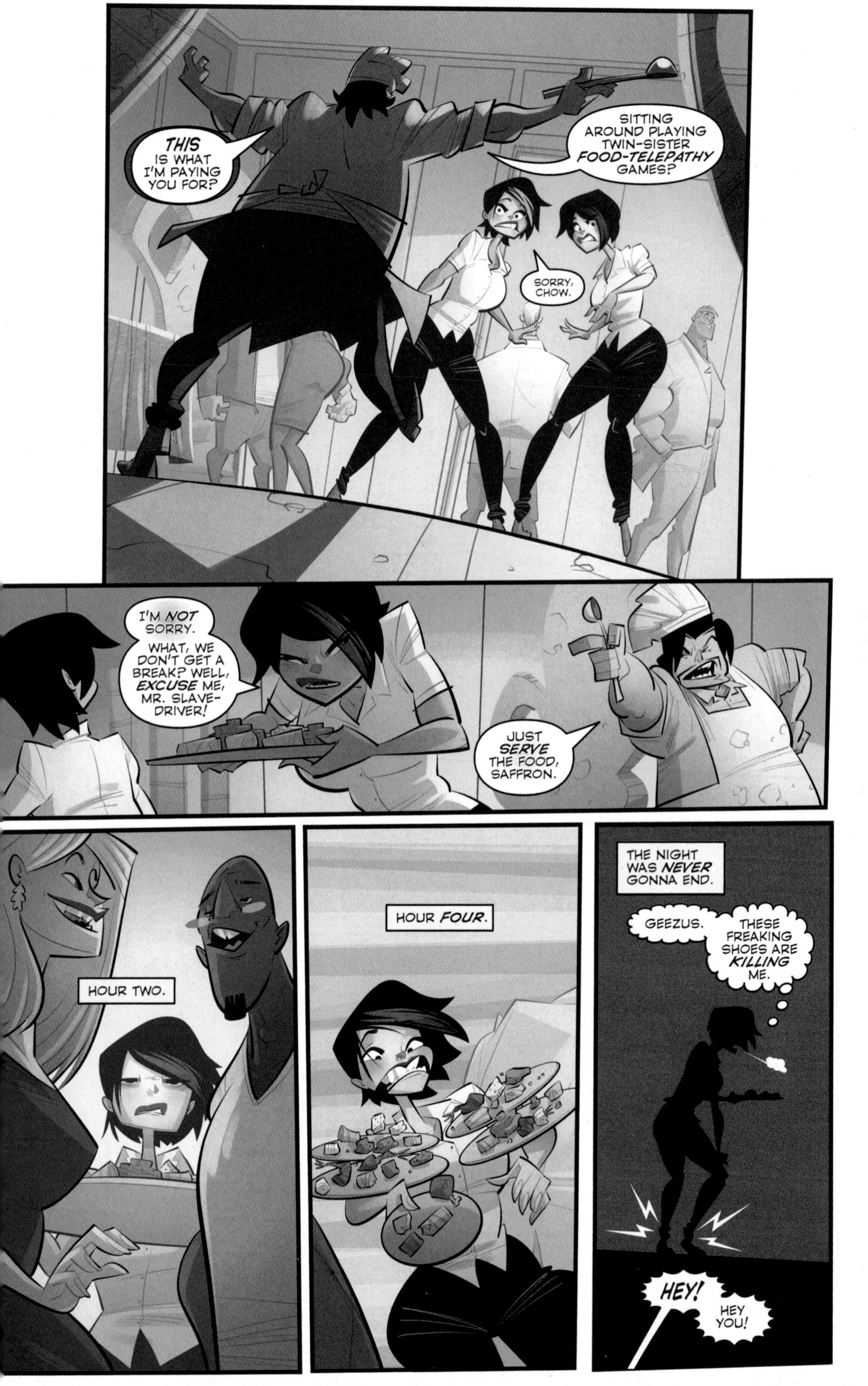

THIS IS WHAT I'M PAYING YOU FOR?
SITTING AROUND PLAYING TWIN-SISTER FOOD-TELEPATHY GAMES?
SORRY, CHOW.
I'M NOT SORRY.
WHAT, WE DON'T GET A BREAK? WELL, EXCUSE ME, MR. SLAVE-DRIVER!
JUST SERVE THE FOOD, SAFFRON.
HOUR TWO.
HOUR FOUR.
THE NIGHT WAS NEVER GONNA END.
GEEZUS.
THESE FREAKING SHOES ARE KILLING ME.
HEY!
HEY YOU!

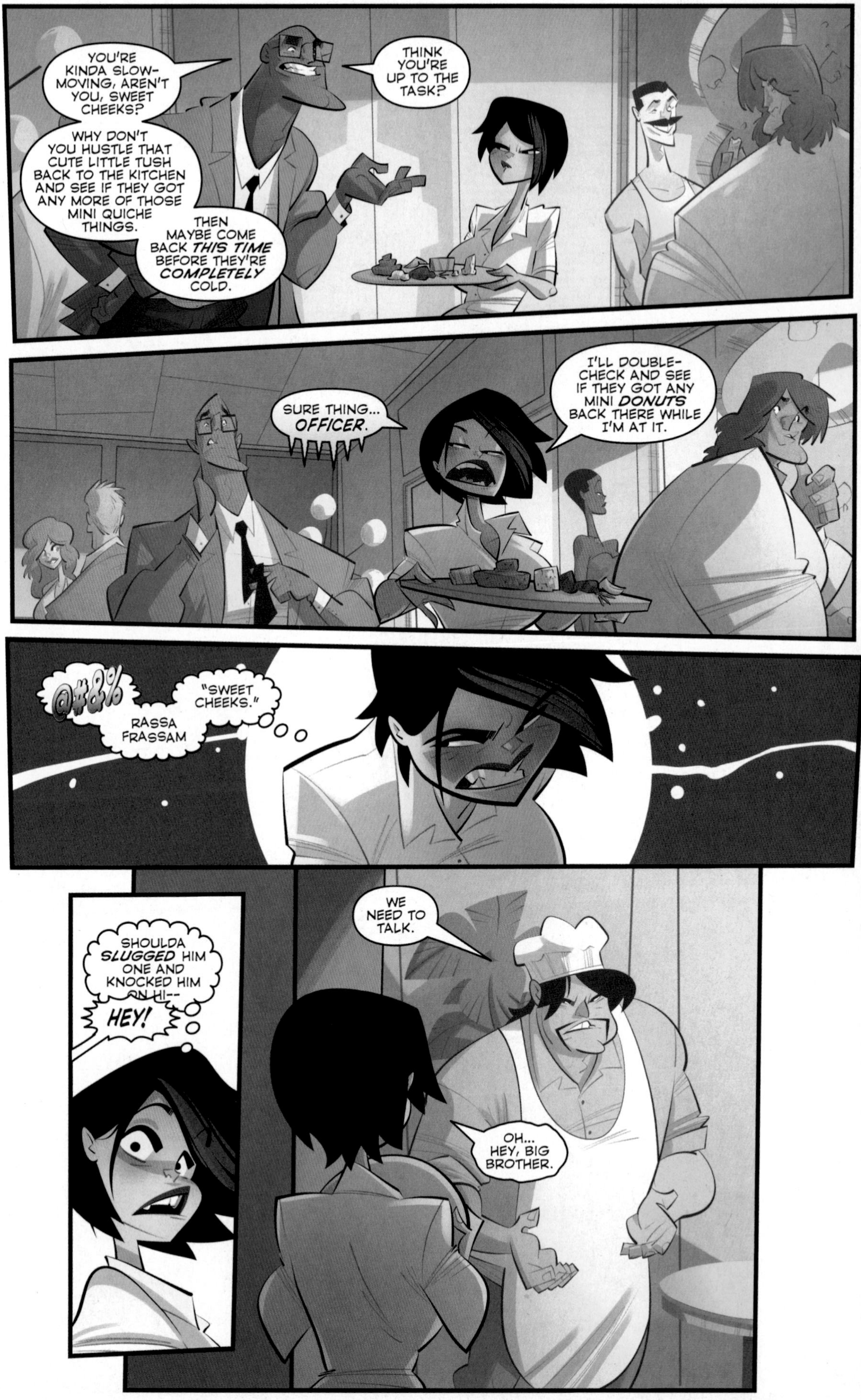
YOU'RE KINDA SLOW-MOVING, AREN'T YOU, SWEET CHEEKS?
WHY DON'T YOU HUSTLE THAT CUTE LITTLE TUSH BACK TO THE KITCHEN AND SEE IF THEY GOT ANY MORE OF THOSE MINI QUICHE THINGS.
THEN MAYBE COME BACK *THIS TIME* BEFORE THEY'RE *COMPLETELY* COLD.
THINK YOU'RE UP TO THE TASK?
SURE THING... *OFFICER*.
I'LL DOUBLE-CHECK AND SEE IF THEY GOT ANY MINI *DONUTS* BACK THERE WHILE I'M AT IT.
@#&%
RASSA FRASSAM
"SWEET CHEEKS."
SHOULDA *SLUGGED* HIM ONE AND KNOCKED HIM ON HI--
HEY!
WE NEED TO TALK.
OH... HEY, BIG BROTHER.

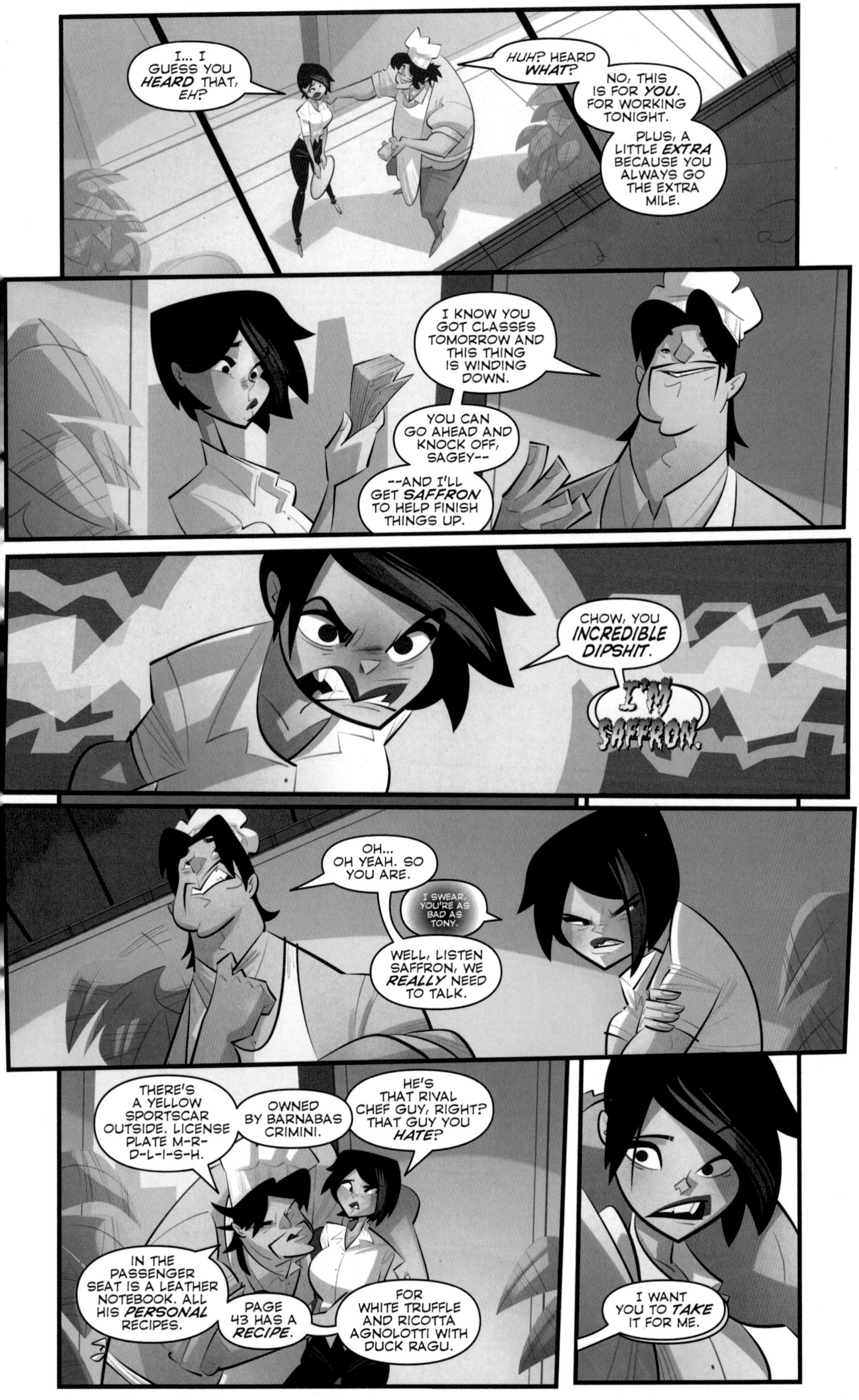
I... I GUESS YOU HEARD THAT, EH?
HUH? HEARD WHAT?
NO, THIS IS FOR YOU. FOR WORKING TONIGHT.
PLUS, A LITTLE EXTRA BECAUSE YOU ALWAYS GO THE EXTRA MILE.
I KNOW YOU GOT CLASSES TOMORROW AND THIS THING IS WINDING DOWN.
YOU CAN GO AHEAD AND KNOCK OFF, SAGEY--
--AND I'LL GET SAFFRON TO HELP FINISH THINGS UP.
CHOW, YOU INCREDIBLE DIPSHIT.
I'M SAFFRON.
OH... OH YEAH. SO YOU ARE.
I SWEAR, YOU'RE AS BAD AS TONY.
WELL, LISTEN SAFFRON, WE REALLY NEED TO TALK.
THERE'S A YELLOW SPORTSCAR OUTSIDE. LICENSE PLATE M-R-D-L-I-S-H.
OWNED BY BARNABAS CRIMINI.
HE'S THAT RIVAL CHEF GUY, RIGHT? THAT GUY YOU HATE?
IN THE PASSENGER SEAT IS A LEATHER NOTEBOOK. ALL HIS PERSONAL RECIPES.
PAGE 43 HAS A RECIPE.
FOR WHITE TRUFFLE AND RICOTTA AGNOLOTTI WITH DUCK RAGU.
I WANT YOU TO TAKE IT FOR ME.

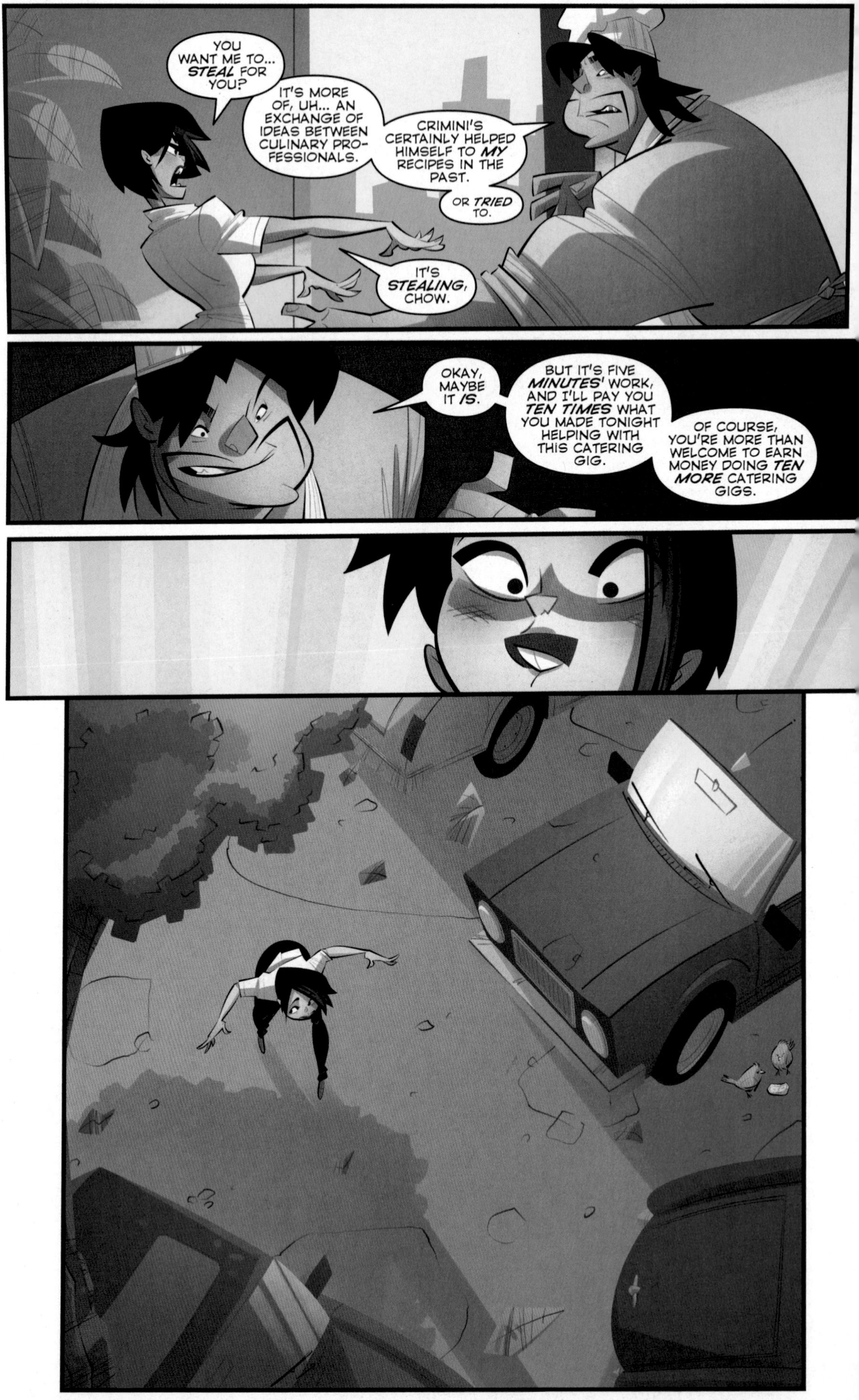
YOU WANT ME TO... STEAL FOR YOU?
IT'S MORE OF, UH... AN EXCHANGE OF IDEAS BETWEEN CULINARY PRO-FESSIONALS.
CRIMINI'S CERTAINLY HELPED HIMSELF TO MY RECIPES IN THE PAST.
OR TRIED TO.
IT'S STEALING, CHOW.
OKAY, MAYBE IT IS.
BUT IT'S FIVE MINUTES' WORK, AND I'LL PAY YOU TEN TIMES WHAT YOU MADE TONIGHT HELPING WITH THIS CATERING GIG.
OF COURSE, YOU'RE MORE THAN WELCOME TO EARN MONEY DOING TEN MORE CATERING GIGS.

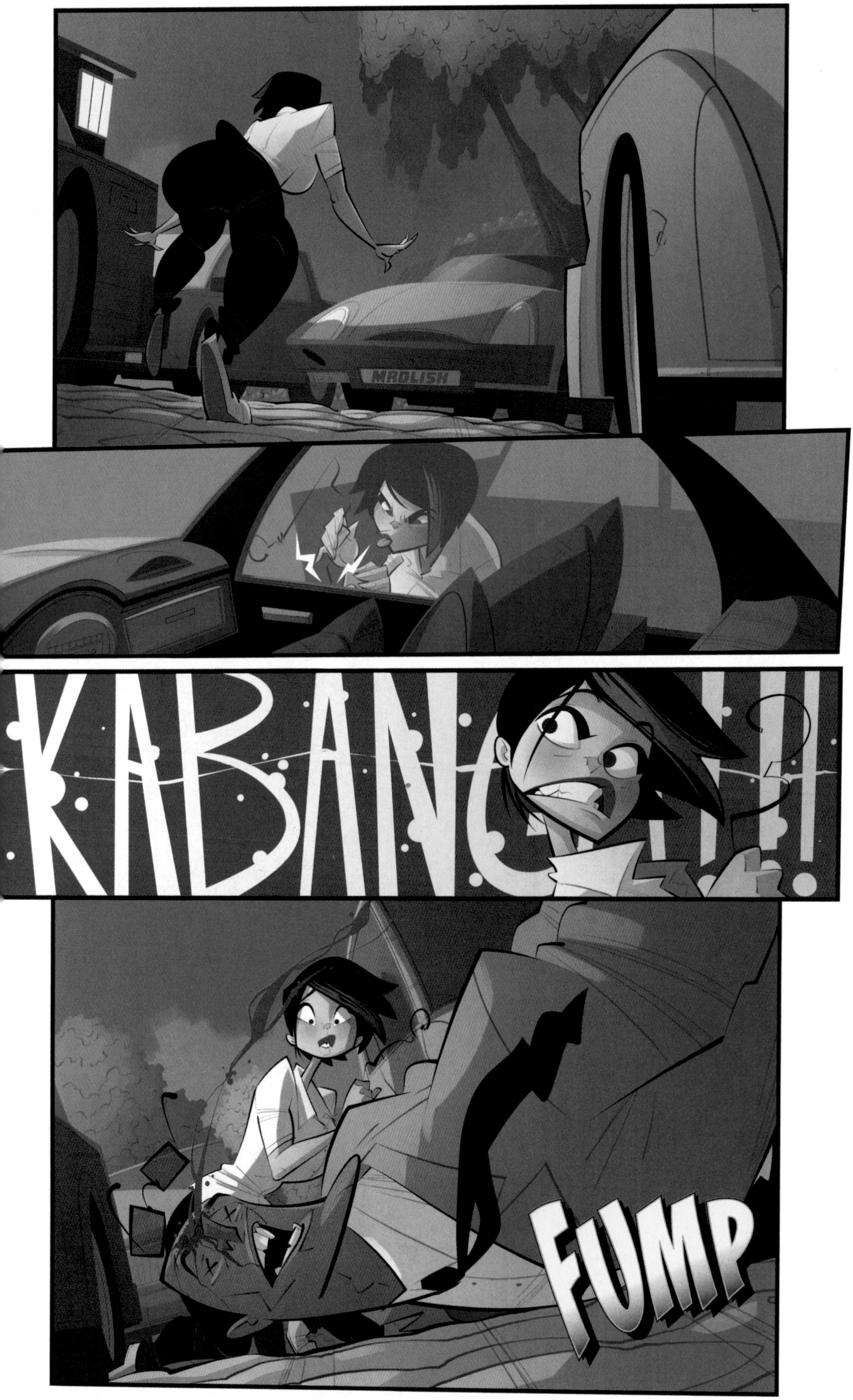
MADLISH
KABANG!!!
FUMP

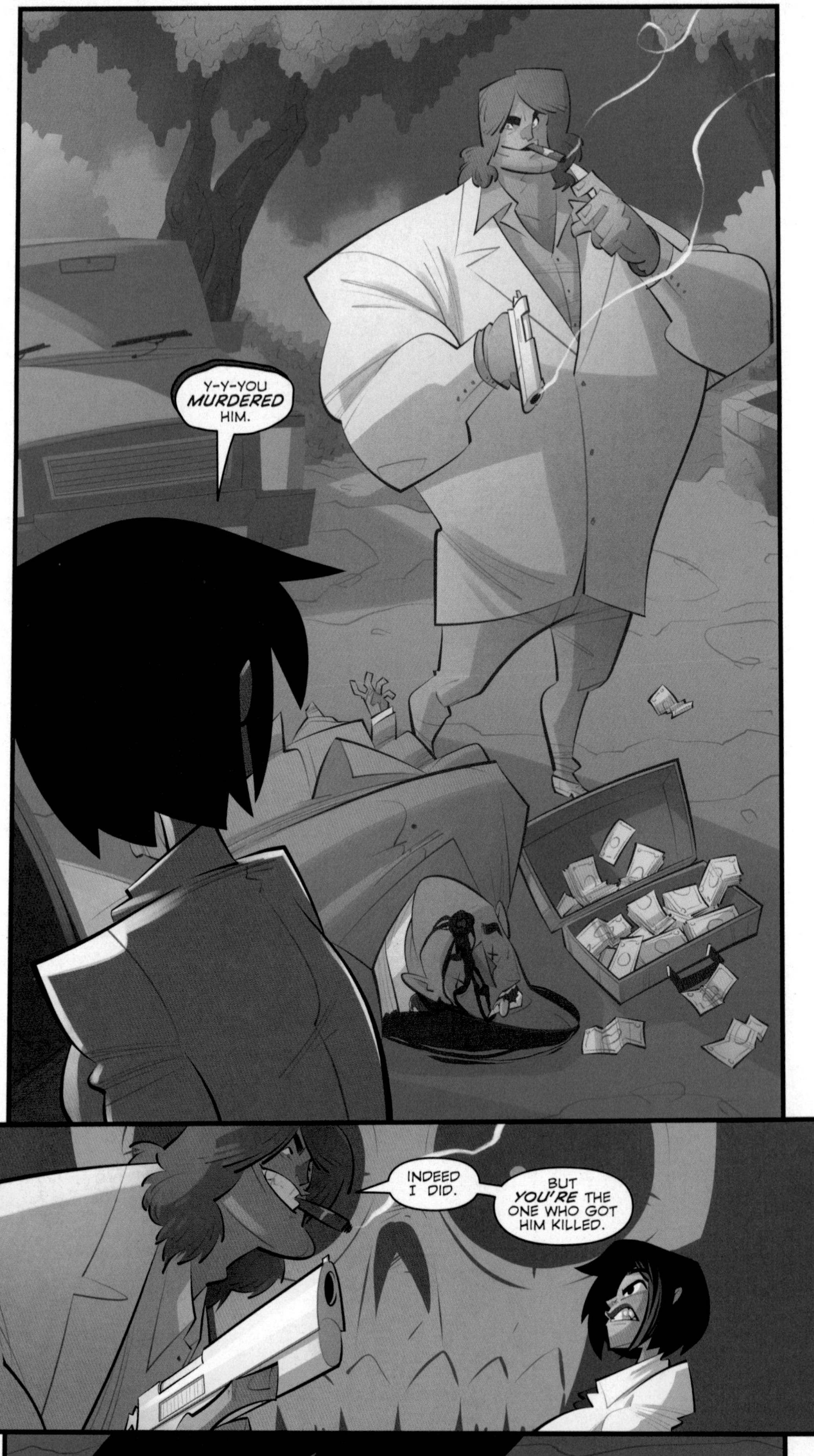
Y-Y-YOU *MURDERED* HIM.
INDEED I DID.
BUT *YOU'RE* THE ONE WHO GOT HIM KILLED.

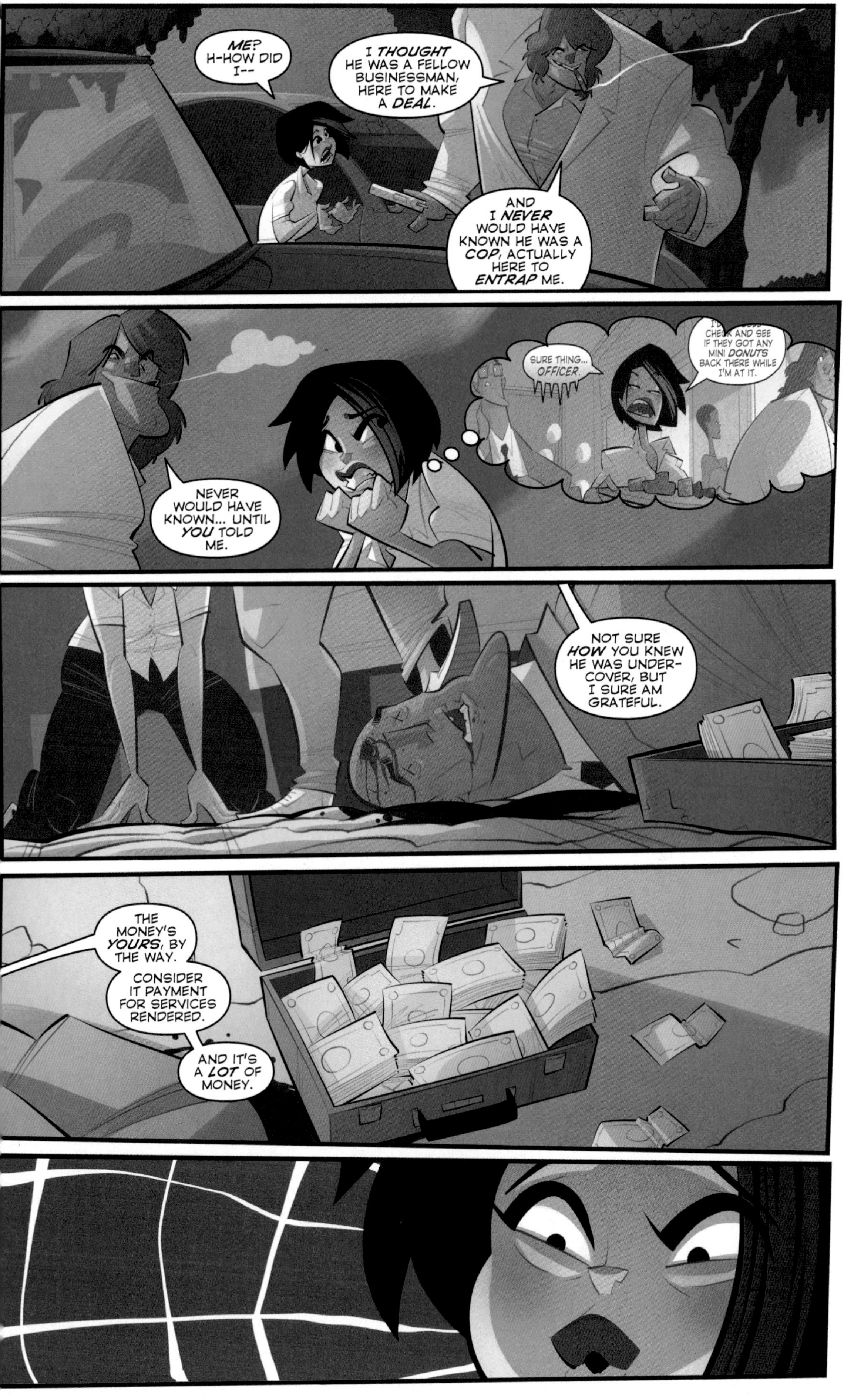

ME? H-HOW DID I--
I THOUGHT HE WAS A FELLOW BUSINESSMAN, HERE TO MAKE A DEAL.
AND I NEVER WOULD HAVE KNOWN HE WAS A COP, ACTUALLY HERE TO ENTRAP ME.
NEVER WOULD HAVE KNOWN... UNTIL YOU TOLD ME.
SURE THING... OFFICER.
AND SEE IF THEY GOT ANY MINI DONUTS BACK THERE WHILE I'M AT IT.
NOT SURE HOW YOU KNEW HE WAS UNDER-COVER, BUT I SURE AM GRATEFUL.
THE MONEY'S YOURS, BY THE WAY.
CONSIDER IT PAYMENT FOR SERVICES RENDERED.
AND IT'S A LOT OF MONEY.

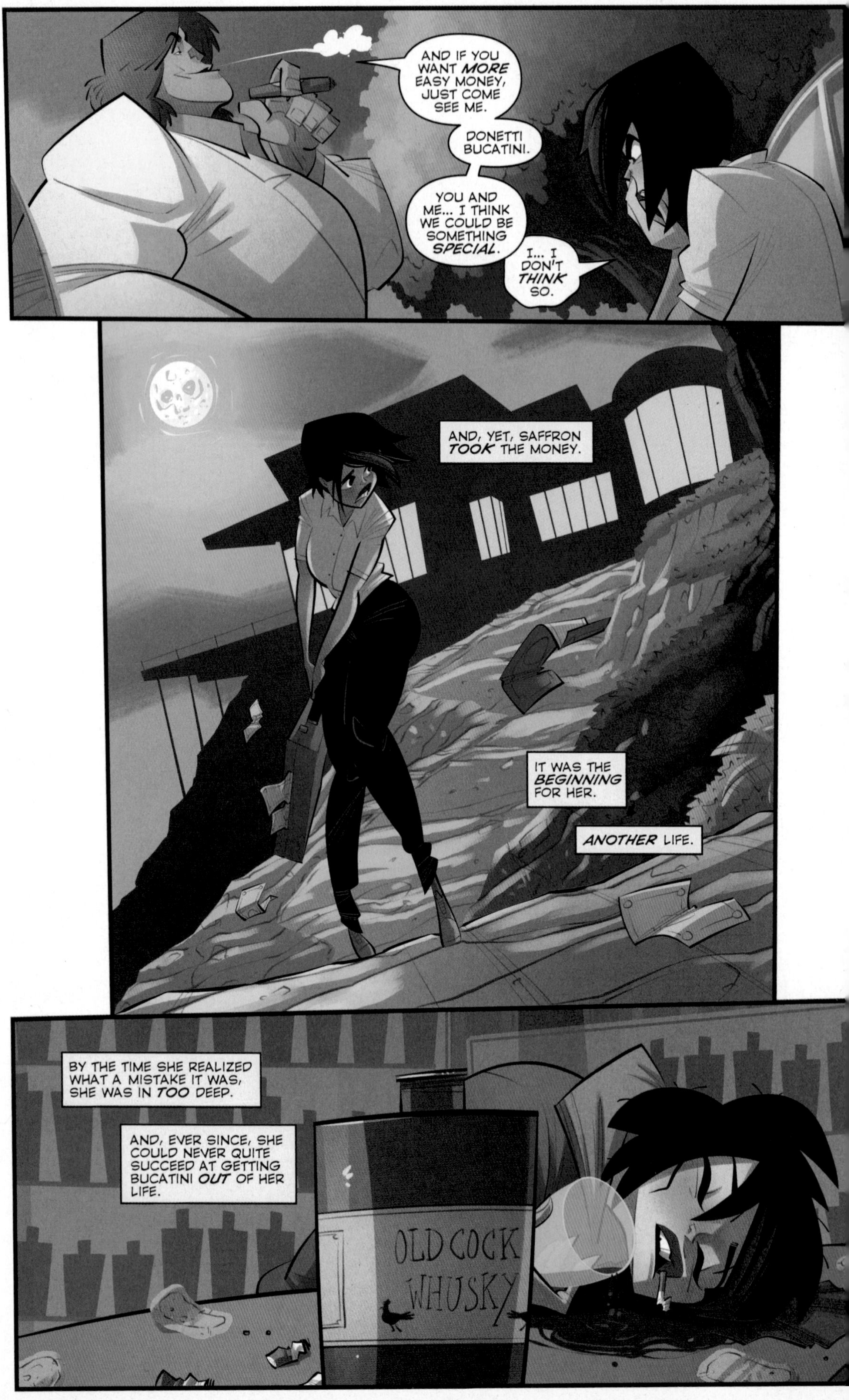
AND IF YOU WANT MORE EASY MONEY, JUST COME SEE ME.
DONETTI BUCATINI.
YOU AND ME... I THINK WE COULD BE SOMETHING SPECIAL.
I... I DON'T THINK SO.
AND, YET, SAFFRON TOOK THE MONEY.
IT WAS THE BEGINNING FOR HER.
ANOTHER LIFE.
BY THE TIME SHE REALIZED WHAT A MISTAKE IT WAS, SHE WAS IN TOO DEEP.
AND, EVER SINCE, SHE COULD NEVER QUITE SUCCEED AT GETTING BUCATINI OUT OF HER LIFE.
OLD COCK WHUSKY

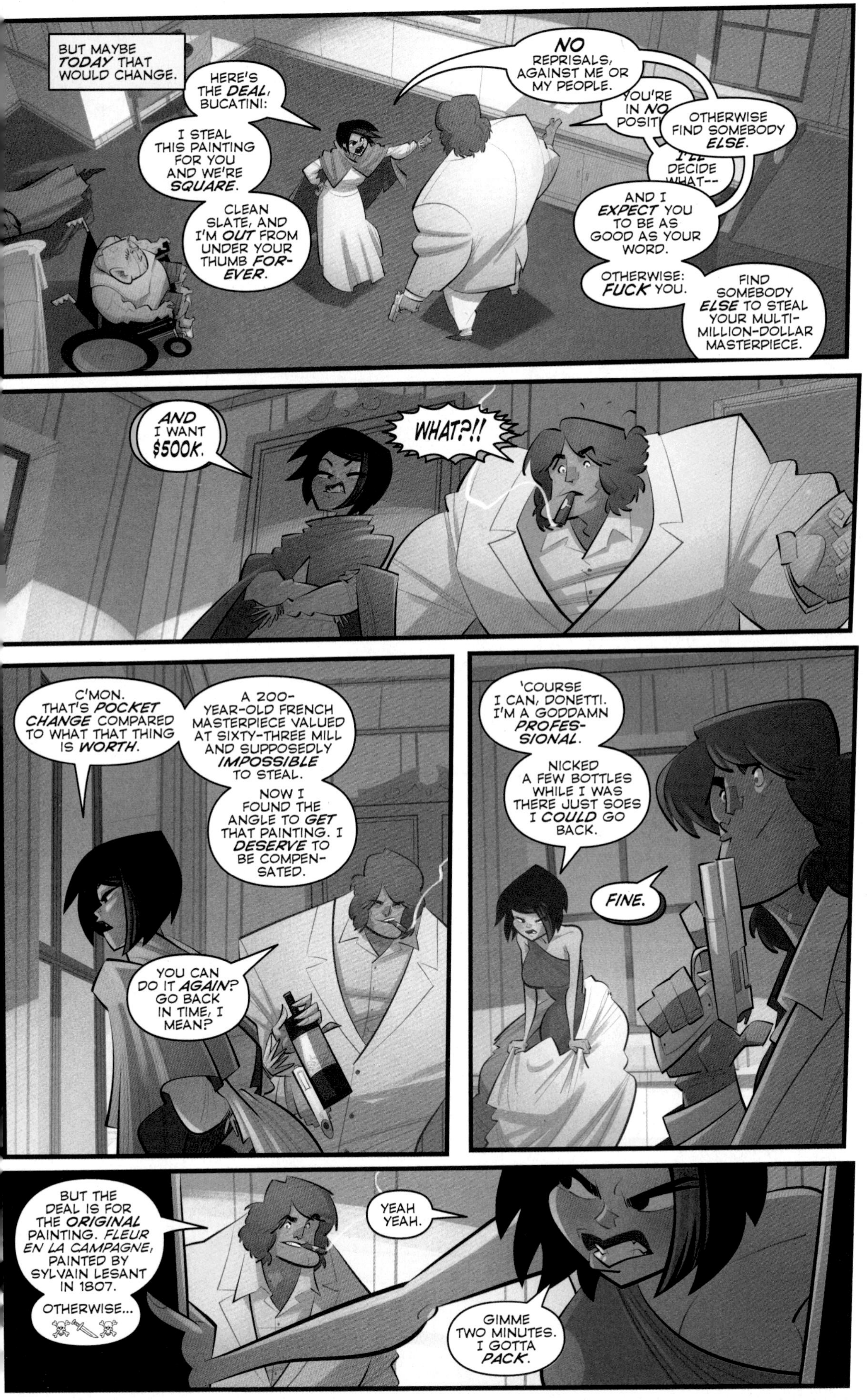
BUT MAYBE TODAY THAT WOULD CHANGE.
HERE'S THE DEAL, BUCATINI:
I STEAL THIS PAINTING FOR YOU AND WE'RE SQUARE.
CLEAN SLATE, AND I'M OUT FROM UNDER YOUR THUMB FOR-EVER.
NO REPRISALS, AGAINST ME OR MY PEOPLE.
YOU'RE IN NO POSIT
OTHERWISE FIND SOMEBODY ELSE.
I'LL DECIDE WHAT--
AND I EXPECT YOU TO BE AS GOOD AS YOUR WORD.
OTHERWISE: FUCK YOU.
FIND SOMEBODY ELSE TO STEAL YOUR MULTI-MILLION-DOLLAR MASTERPIECE.
AND I WANT $500K.
WHAT?!!
C'MON. THAT'S POCKET CHANGE COMPARED TO WHAT THAT THING IS WORTH.
A 200-YEAR-OLD FRENCH MASTERPIECE VALUED AT SIXTY-THREE MILL AND SUPPOSEDLY IMPOSSIBLE TO STEAL.
NOW I FOUND THE ANGLE TO GET THAT PAINTING. I DESERVE TO BE COMPEN-SATED.
YOU CAN DO IT AGAIN? GO BACK IN TIME, I MEAN?
'COURSE I CAN, DONETTI. I'M A GODDAMN PROFES-SIONAL.
NICKED A FEW BOTTLES WHILE I WAS THERE JUST SOES I COULD GO BACK.
FINE.
BUT THE DEAL IS FOR THE ORIGINAL PAINTING. FLEUR EN LA CAMPAGNE, PAINTED BY SYLVAIN LESANT IN 1807.
OTHERWISE...
YEAH YEAH.
GIMME TWO MINUTES. I GOTTA PACK.

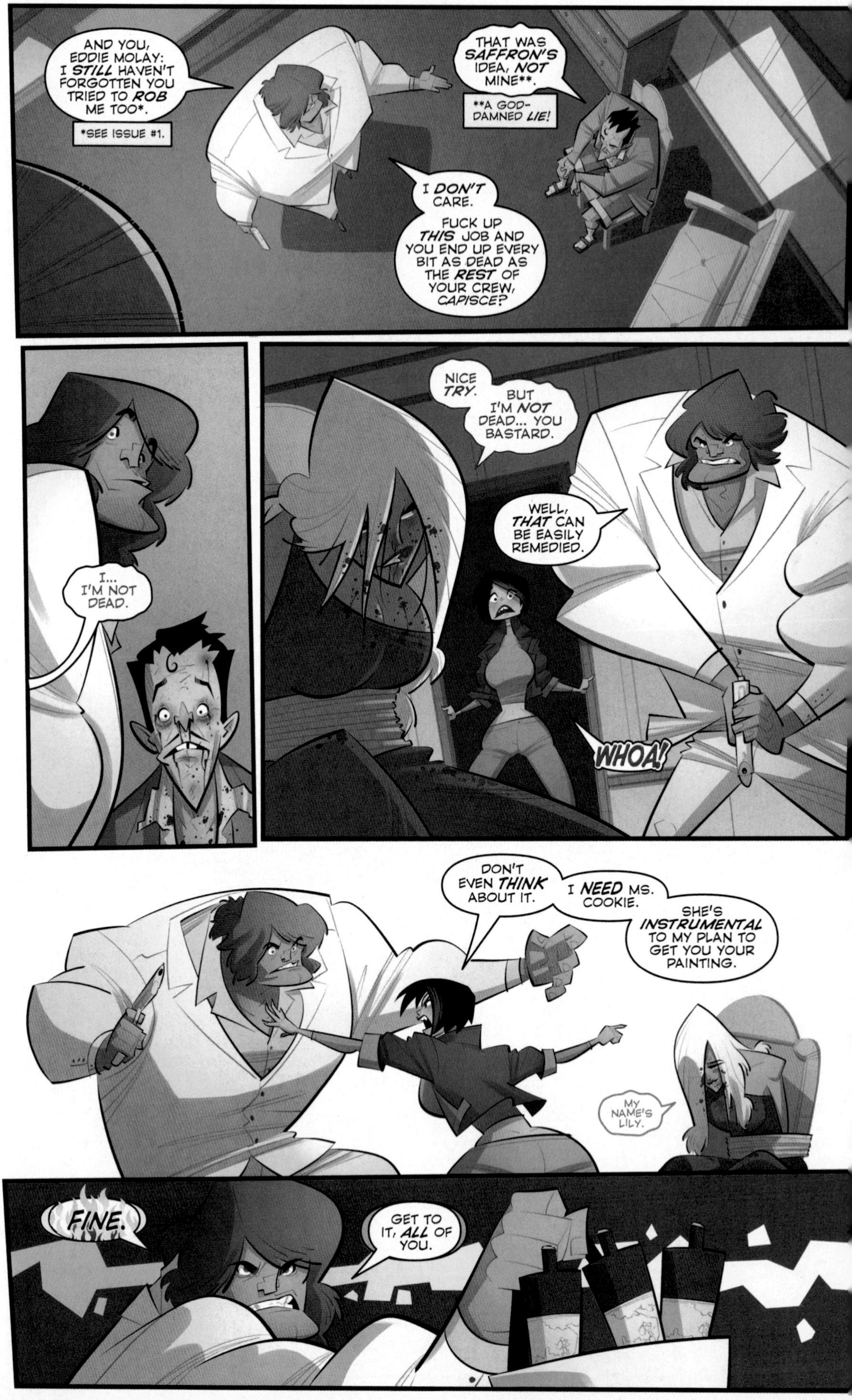

AND YOU, EDDIE MOLAY: I STILL HAVEN'T FORGOTTEN YOU TRIED TO ROB ME TOO*.
*SEE ISSUE #1.
THAT WAS SAFFRON'S IDEA, NOT MINE**.
**A GOD-DAMNED LIE!
I DON'T CARE.
FUCK UP THIS JOB AND YOU END UP EVERY BIT AS DEAD AS THE REST OF YOUR CREW, CAPISCE?
I... I'M NOT DEAD.
NICE TRY.
BUT I'M NOT DEAD... YOU BASTARD.
WELL, THAT CAN BE EASILY REMEDIED.
WHOA!
DON'T EVEN THINK ABOUT IT.
I NEED MS. COOKIE.
SHE'S INSTRUMENTAL TO MY PLAN TO GET YOU YOUR PAINTING.
MY NAME'S LILY.
FINE.
GET TO IT, ALL OF YOU.

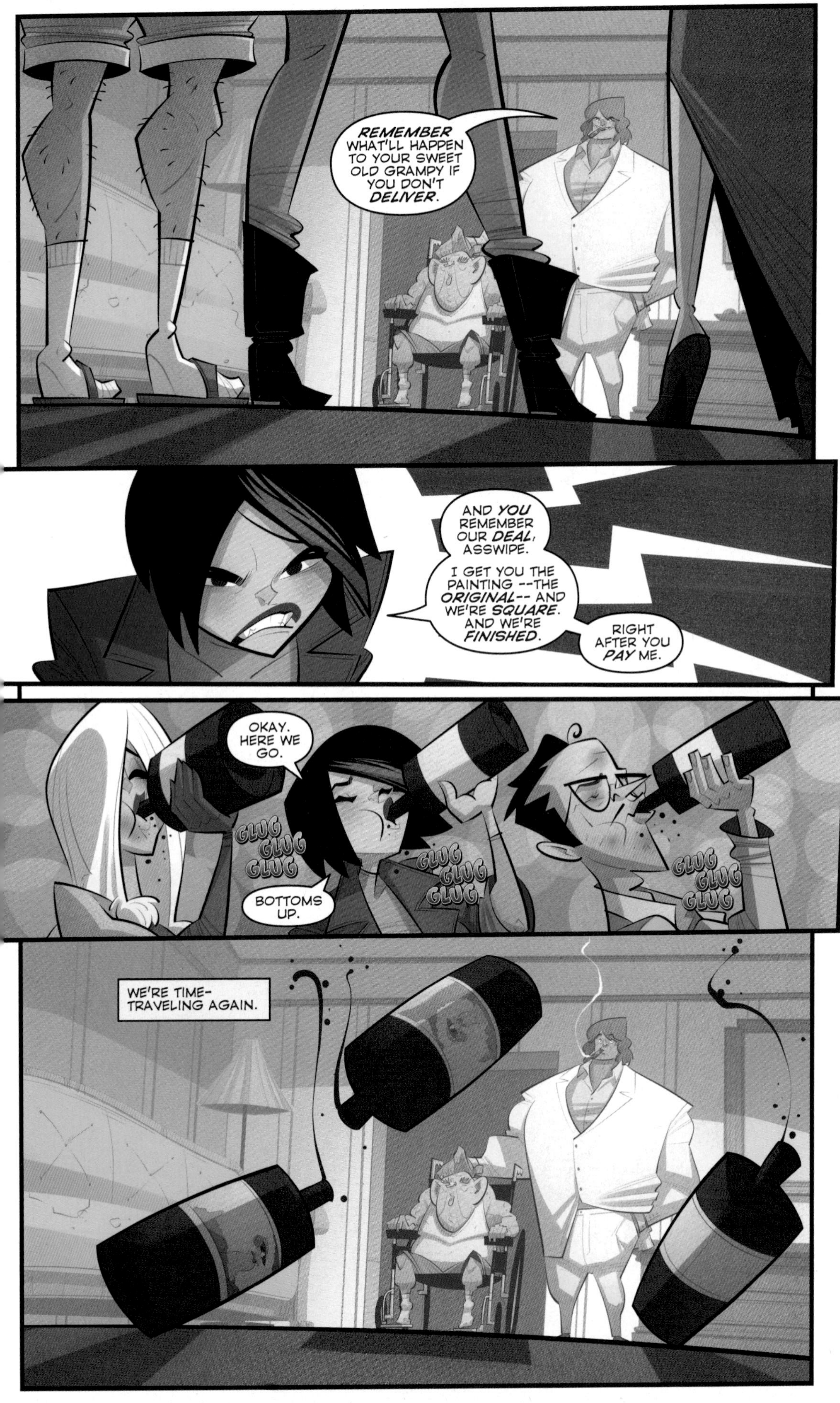
REMEMBER WHAT'LL HAPPEN TO YOUR SWEET OLD GRAMPY IF YOU DON'T DELIVER.
AND YOU REMEMBER OUR DEAL, ASSWIPE.
I GET YOU THE PAINTING --THE ORIGINAL-- AND WE'RE SQUARE. AND WE'RE FINISHED.
RIGHT AFTER YOU PAY ME.
OKAY. HERE WE GO.
GLUG GLUG GLUG
BOTTOMS UP.
GLUG GLUG GLUG
GLUG GLUG GLUG
WE'RE TIME-TRAVELING AGAIN.

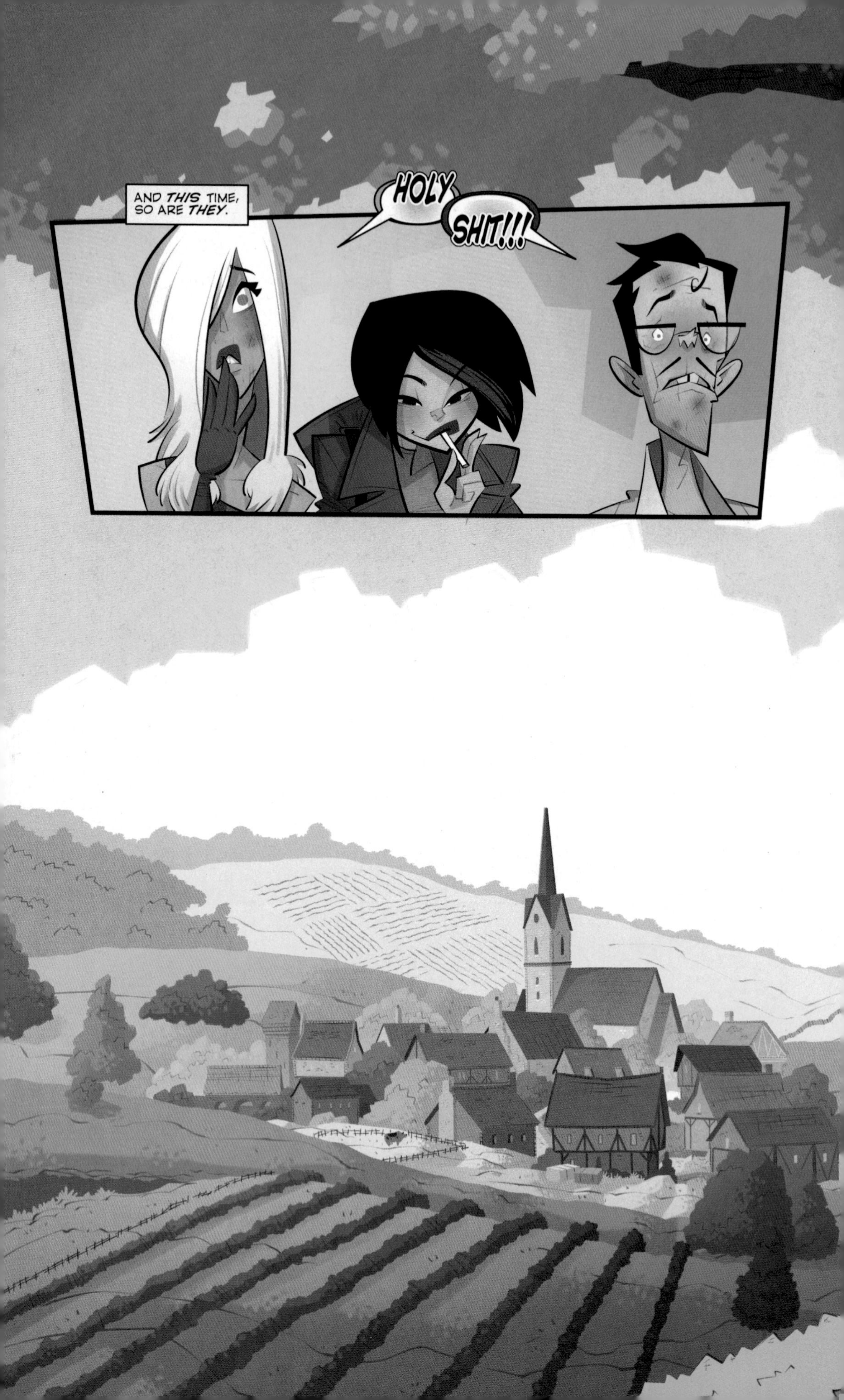
AND THIS TIME, SO ARE THEY.
HOLY
SHIT!!!

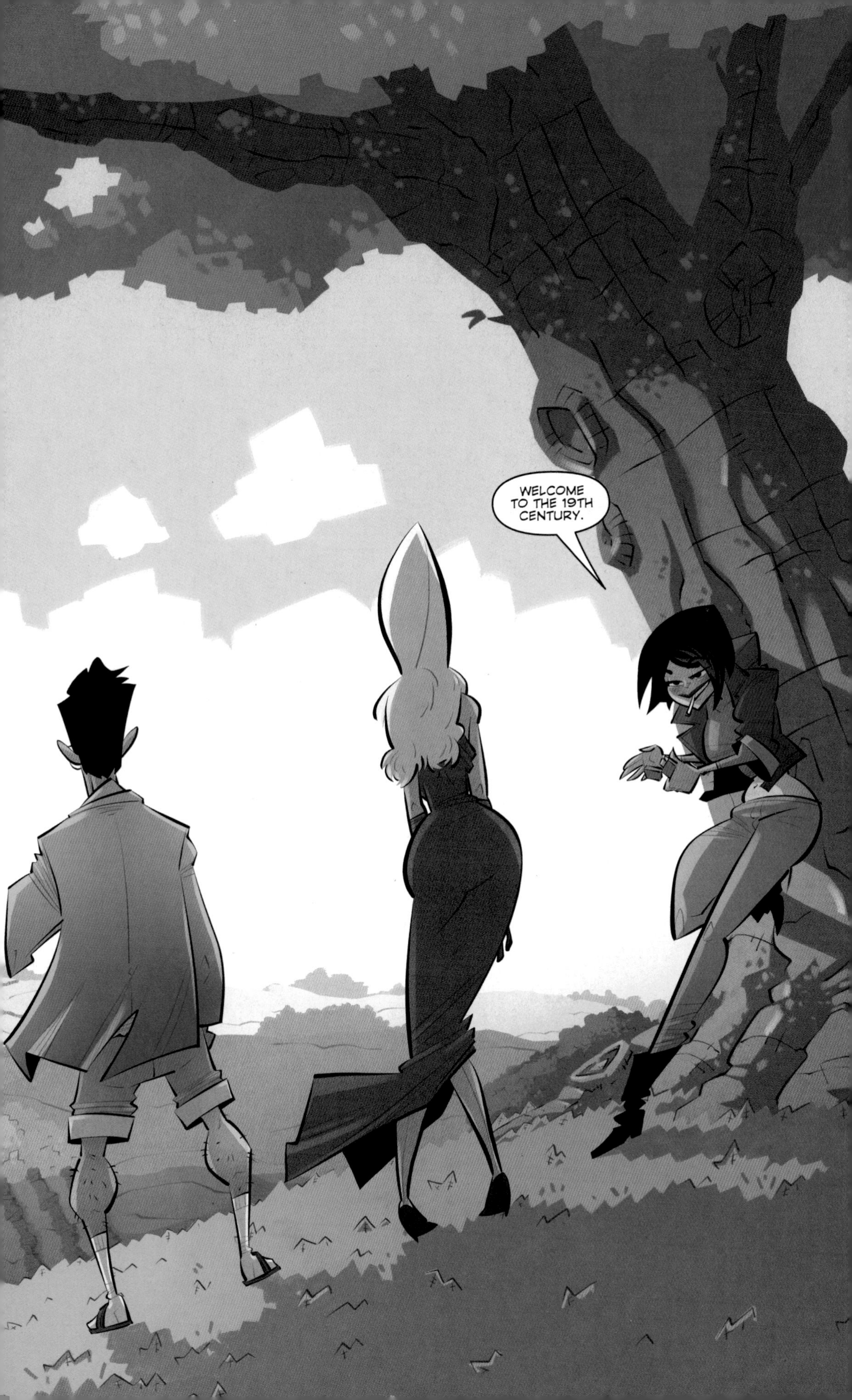
WELCOME TO THE 19TH CENTURY.

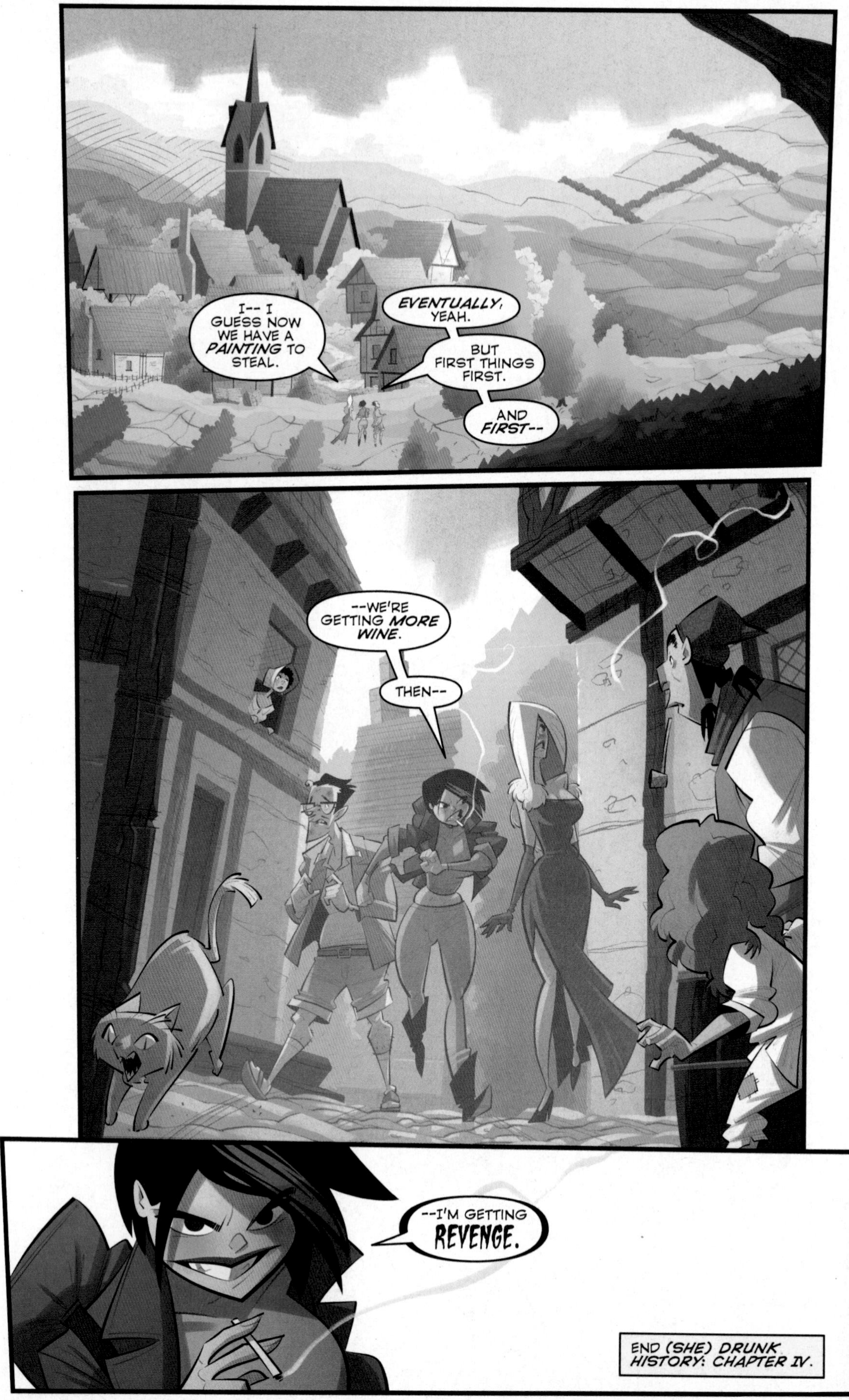
I-- I GUESS NOW WE HAVE A *PAINTING* TO STEAL.
EVENTUALLY, YEAH.
BUT FIRST THINGS FIRST.
AND *FIRST*--
--WE'RE GETTING *MORE WINE*.
THEN--
--I'M GETTING **REVENGE.**
END (SHE) *DRUNK HISTORY*: *CHAPTER IV*.

Chapter 5

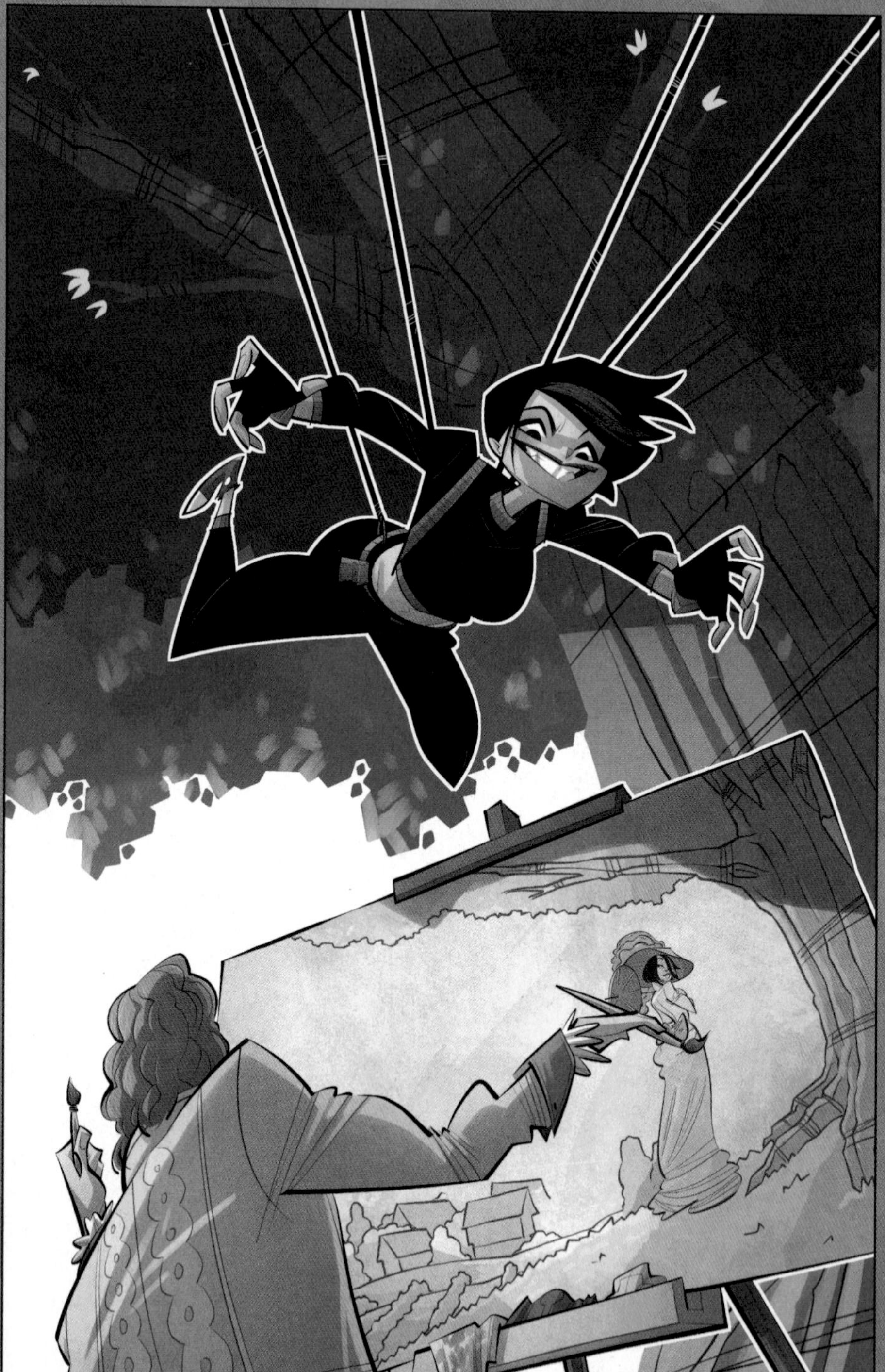

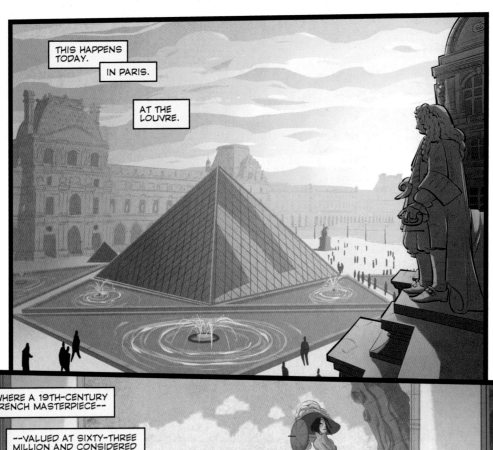

THIS HAPPENS TODAY.

IN PARIS.

AT THE LOUVRE.

WHERE A 19TH-CENTURY FRENCH MASTERPIECE--

--VALUED AT SIXTY-THREE MILLION AND CONSIDERED *IMPOSSIBLE* TO STEAL--

--SIMPLY *DISAPPEARED*.

:POOF:

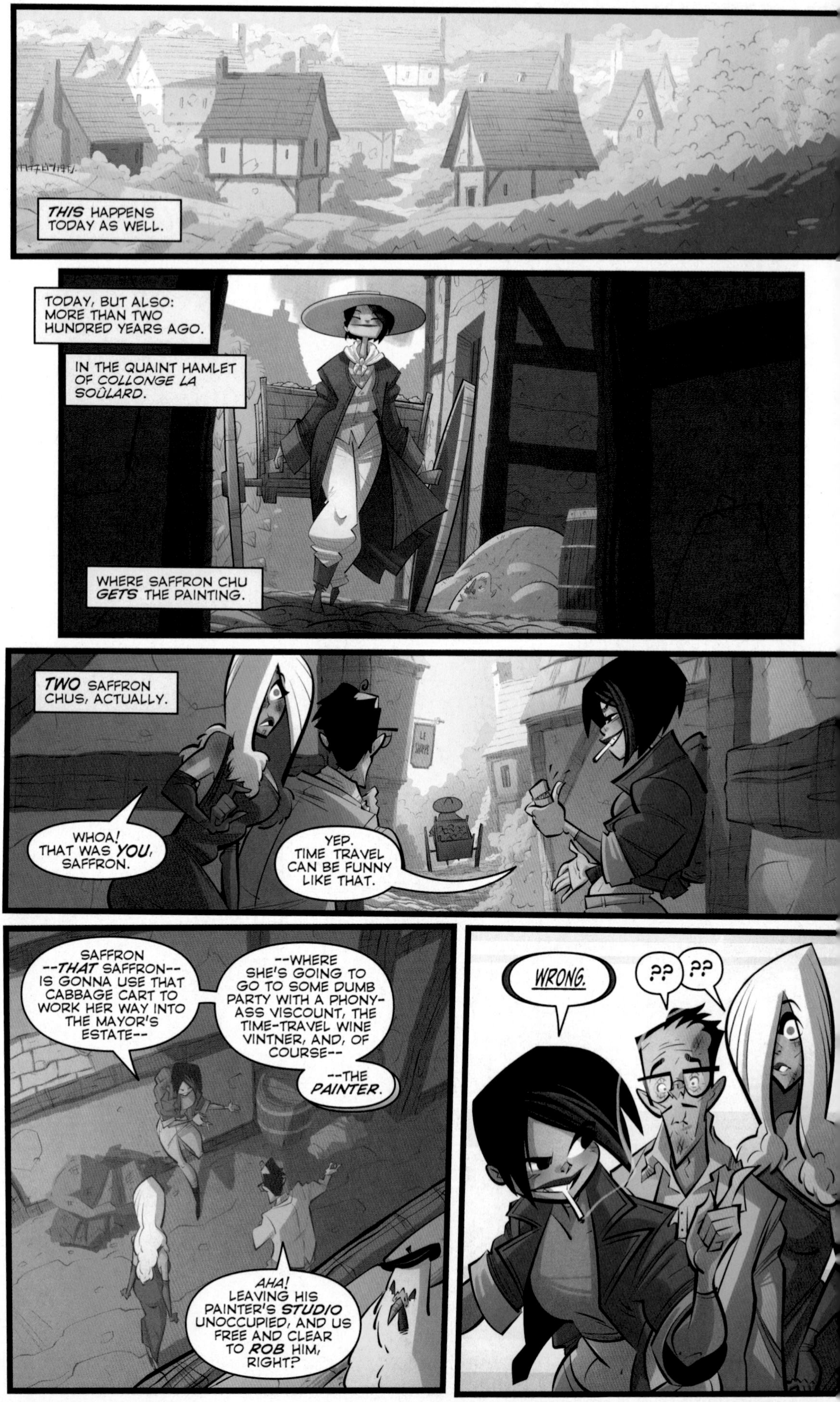
THIS HAPPENS TODAY AS WELL.
TODAY, BUT ALSO: MORE THAN TWO HUNDRED YEARS AGO.
IN THE QUAINT HAMLET OF COLLONGE LA SOÛLARD.
WHERE SAFFRON CHU GETS THE PAINTING.
TWO SAFFRON CHUS, ACTUALLY.
WHOA! THAT WAS YOU, SAFFRON.
YEP. TIME TRAVEL CAN BE FUNNY LIKE THAT.
SAFFRON --THAT SAFFRON-- IS GONNA USE THAT CABBAGE CART TO WORK HER WAY INTO THE MAYOR'S ESTATE--
--WHERE SHE'S GOING TO GO TO SOME DUMB PARTY WITH A PHONY-ASS VISCOUNT, THE TIME-TRAVEL WINE VINTNER, AND, OF COURSE--
--THE PAINTER.
AHA! LEAVING HIS PAINTER'S STUDIO UNOCCUPIED, AND US FREE AND CLEAR TO ROB HIM, RIGHT?
WRONG.
??
??

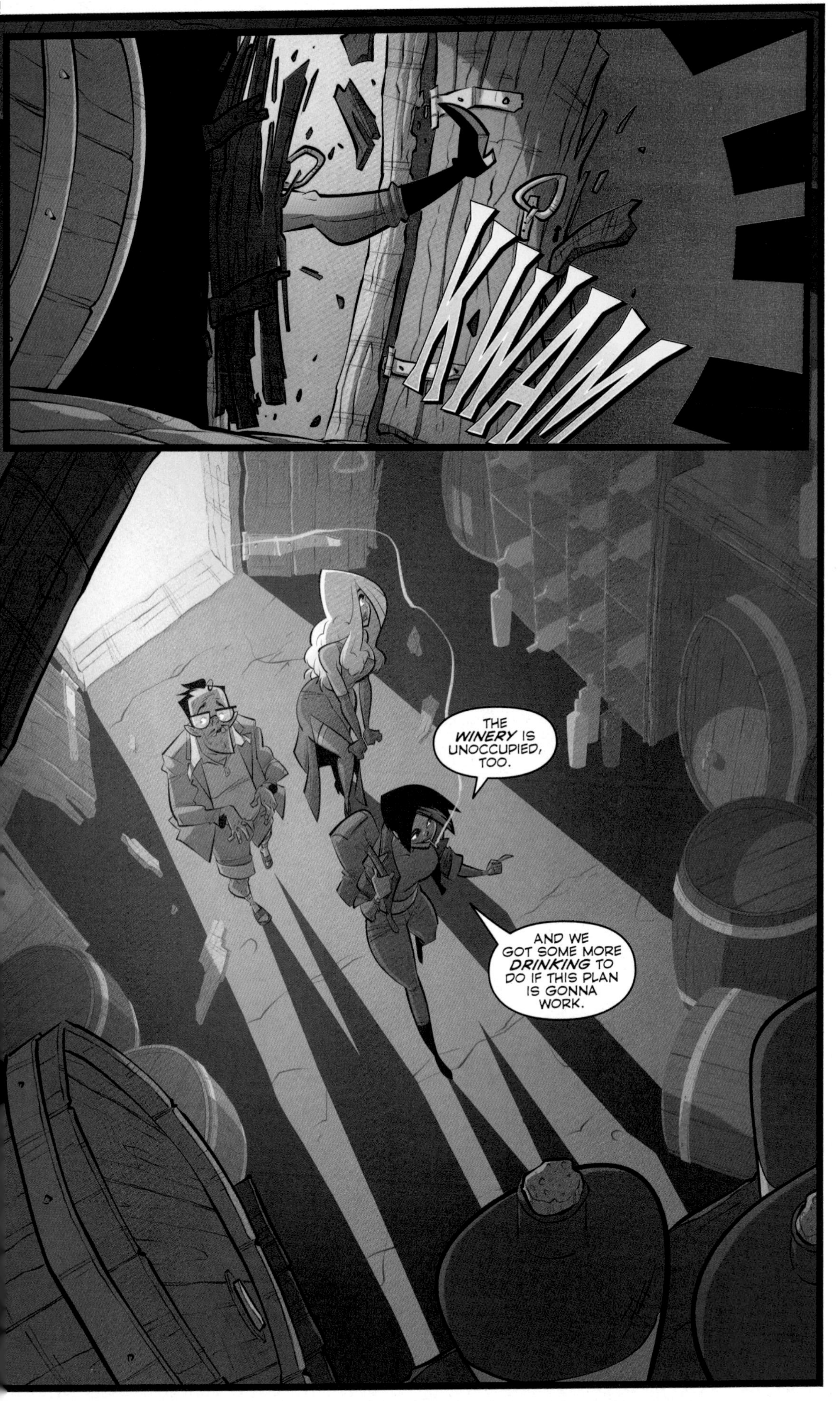
KWAM
THE *WINERY* IS UNOCCUPIED, TOO.
AND WE GOT SOME MORE *DRINKING* TO DO IF THIS PLAN IS GONNA WORK.

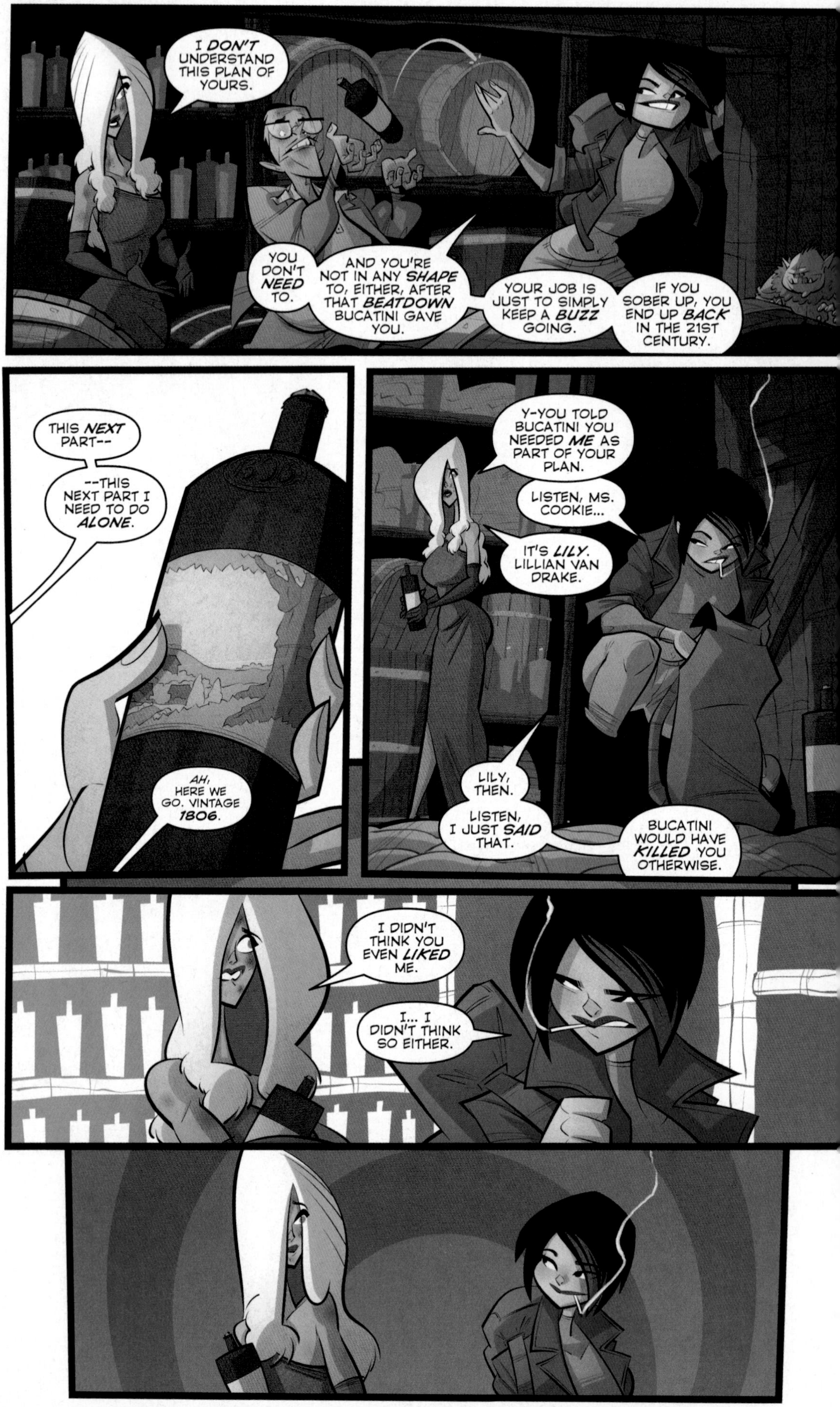
I DON'T UNDERSTAND THIS PLAN OF YOURS.
YOU DON'T NEED TO.
AND YOU'RE NOT IN ANY SHAPE TO, EITHER, AFTER THAT BEATDOWN BUCATINI GAVE YOU.
YOUR JOB IS JUST TO SIMPLY KEEP A BUZZ GOING.
IF YOU SOBER UP, YOU END UP BACK IN THE 21ST CENTURY.
THIS NEXT PART--
--THIS NEXT PART I NEED TO DO ALONE.
AH, HERE WE GO. VINTAGE 1806.
Y-YOU TOLD BUCATINI YOU NEEDED ME AS PART OF YOUR PLAN.
LISTEN, MS. COOKIE...
IT'S LILY. LILLIAN VAN DRAKE.
LILY, THEN.
LISTEN, I JUST SAID THAT.
BUCATINI WOULD HAVE KILLED YOU OTHERWISE.
I DIDN'T THINK YOU EVEN LIKED ME.
I... I DIDN'T THINK SO EITHER.

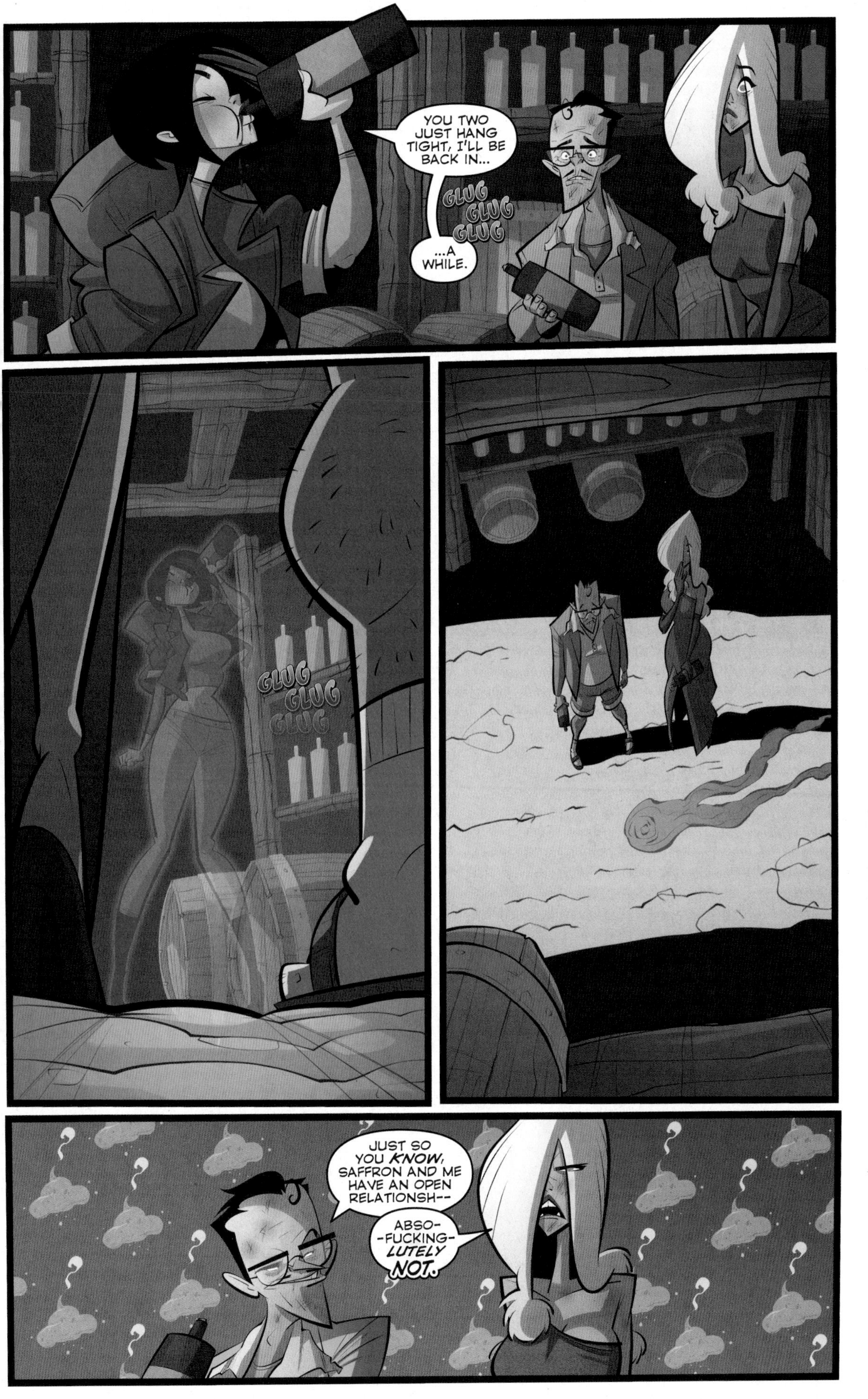
YOU TWO JUST HANG TIGHT, I'LL BE BACK IN...
GLUG GLUG GLUG
...A WHILE.
GLUG GLUG GLUG
JUST SO YOU *KNOW*, SAFFRON AND ME HAVE AN OPEN RELATIONSH--
ABSO- -FUCKING- ***LUTELY NOT.***

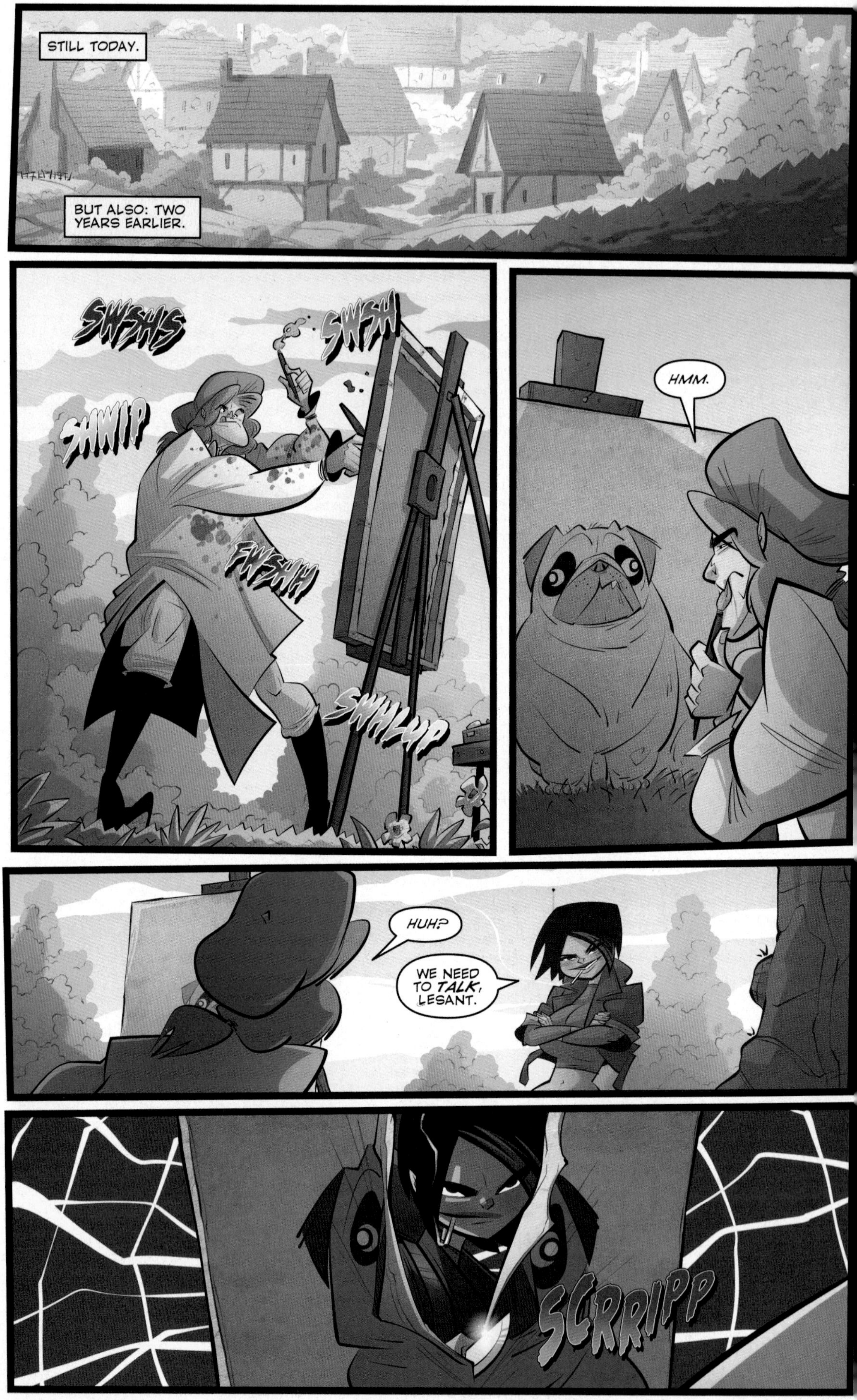
STILL TODAY.
BUT ALSO: TWO YEARS EARLIER.
SWSHS
SWSH
SHWIP
FWSHH
SWHLUP
HMM.
HUH?
WE NEED TO *TALK*, LESANT.
SCRRIPP

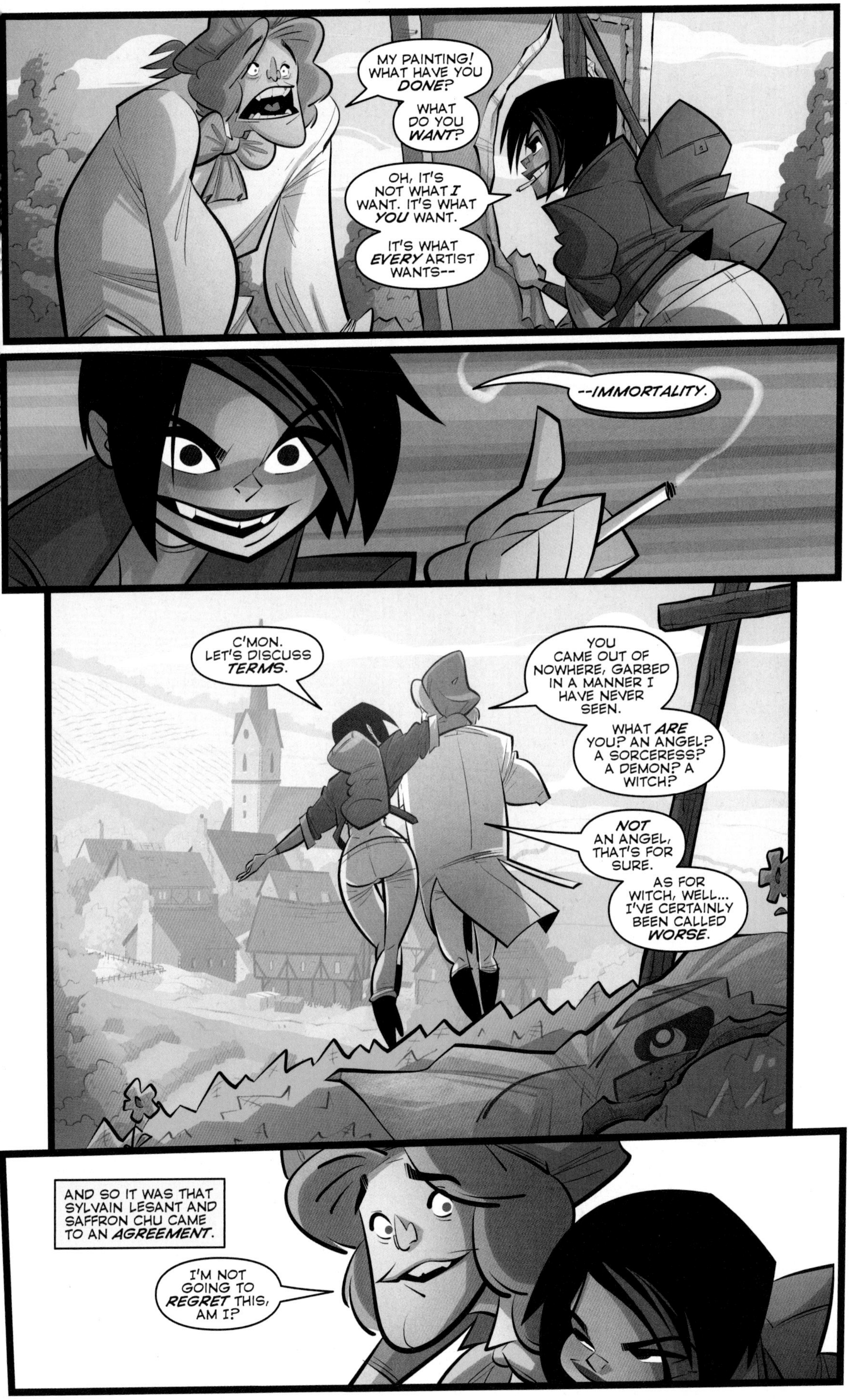
MY PAINTING! WHAT HAVE YOU DONE?
WHAT DO YOU WANT?
OH, IT'S NOT WHAT I WANT. IT'S WHAT YOU WANT.
IT'S WHAT EVERY ARTIST WANTS--
--IMMORTALITY.
C'MON. LET'S DISCUSS TERMS.
YOU CAME OUT OF NOWHERE, GARBED IN A MANNER I HAVE NEVER SEEN.
WHAT ARE YOU? AN ANGEL? A SORCERESS? A DEMON? A WITCH?
NOT AN ANGEL, THAT'S FOR SURE.
AS FOR WITCH, WELL... I'VE CERTAINLY BEEN CALLED WORSE.
AND SO IT WAS THAT SYLVAIN LESANT AND SAFFRON CHU CAME TO AN AGREEMENT.
I'M NOT GOING TO REGRET THIS, AM I?

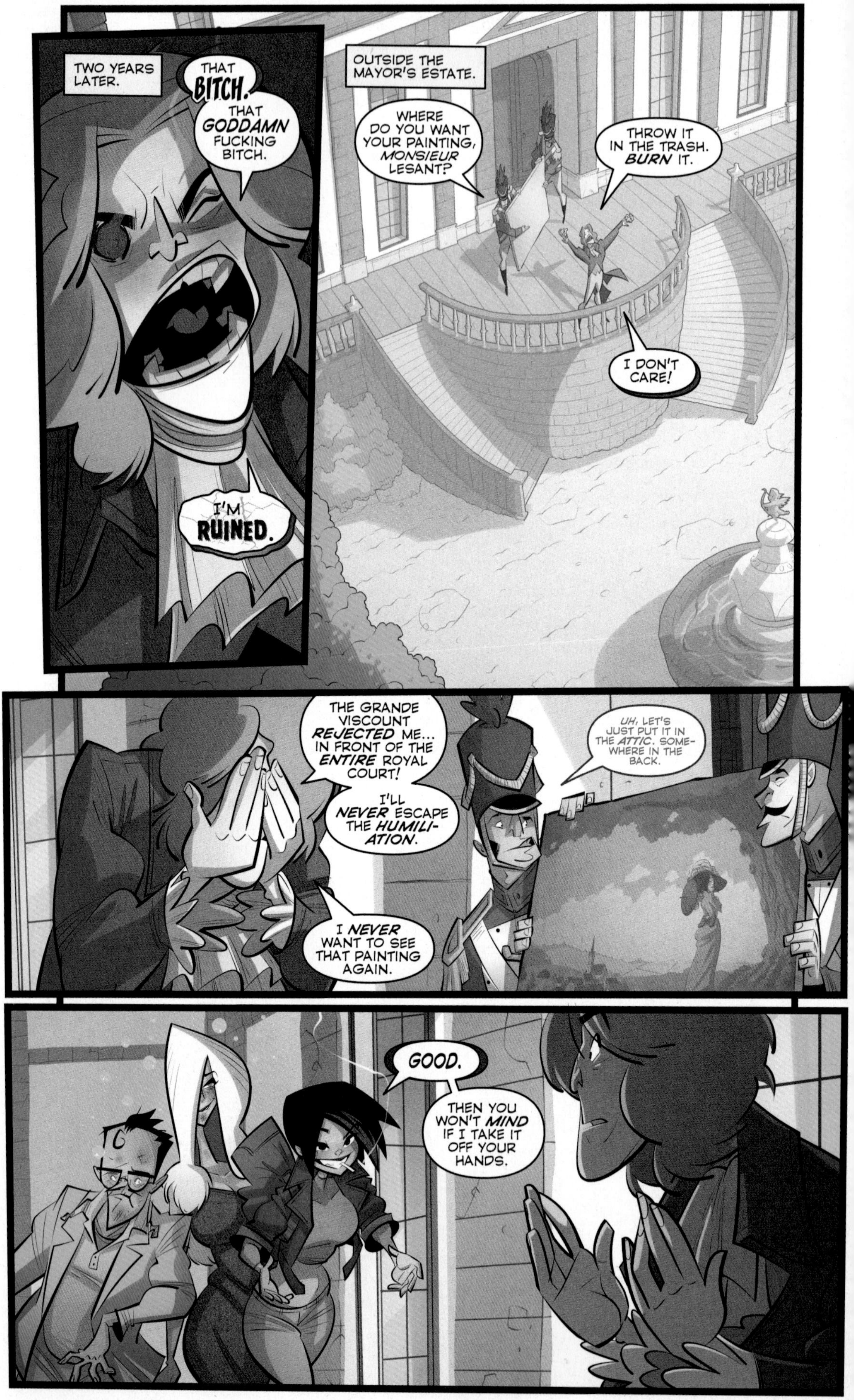
TWO YEARS LATER.
THAT BITCH.
THAT GODDAMN FUCKING BITCH.
I'M RUINED.
OUTSIDE THE MAYOR'S ESTATE.
WHERE DO YOU WANT YOUR PAINTING, MONSIEUR LESANT?
THROW IT IN THE TRASH. BURN IT.
I DON'T CARE!
THE GRANDE VISCOUNT REJECTED ME... IN FRONT OF THE ENTIRE ROYAL COURT!
I'LL NEVER ESCAPE THE HUMILI-ATION.
I NEVER WANT TO SEE THAT PAINTING AGAIN.
UH, LET'S JUST PUT IT IN THE ATTIC. SOME-WHERE IN THE BACK.
GOOD.
THEN YOU WON'T MIND IF I TAKE IT OFF YOUR HANDS.

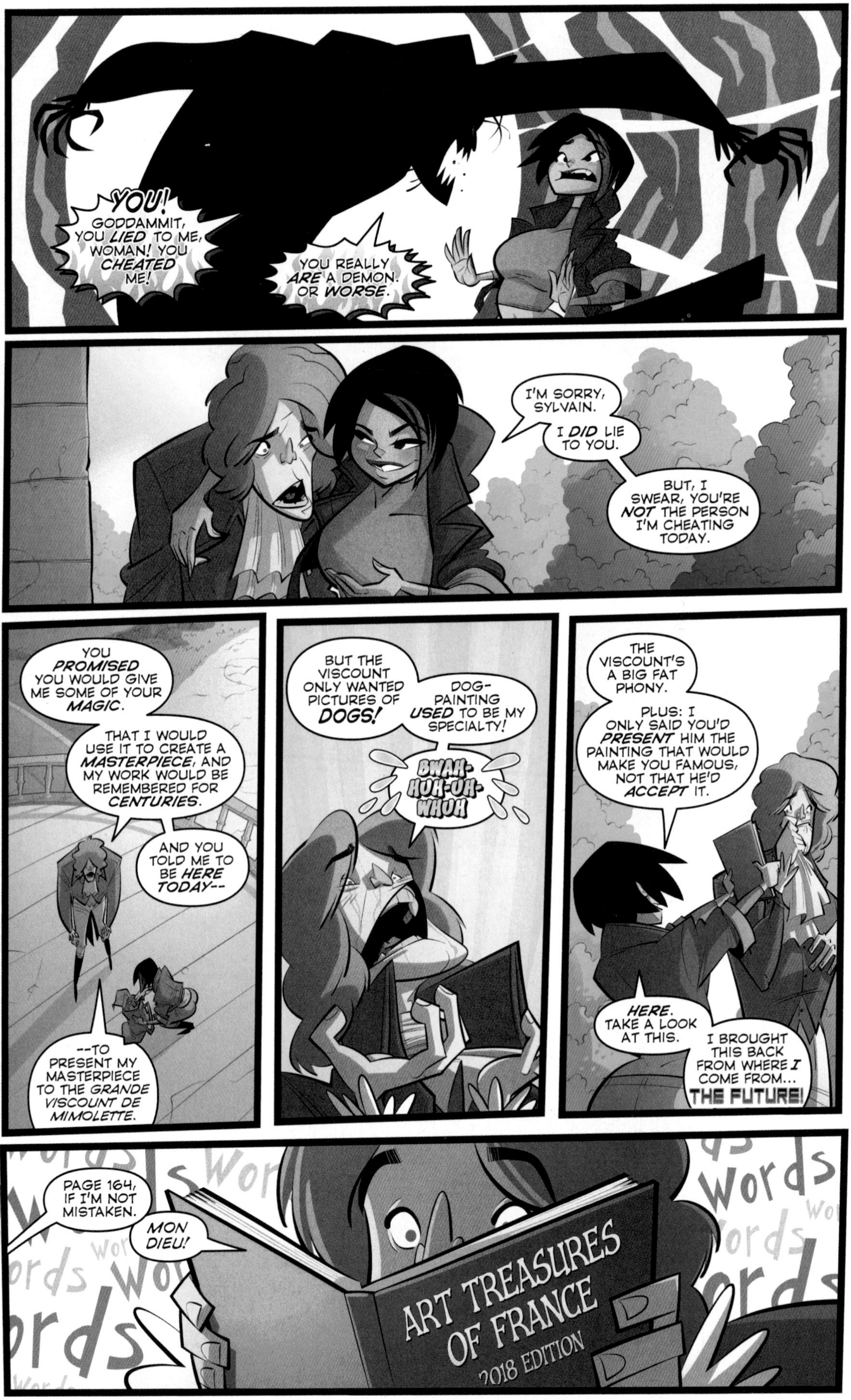

YOU! GODDAMMIT, YOU LIED TO ME, WOMAN! YOU CHEATED ME!
YOU REALLY ARE A DEMON. OR WORSE.
I'M SORRY, SYLVAIN.
I DID LIE TO YOU.
BUT, I SWEAR, YOU'RE NOT THE PERSON I'M CHEATING TODAY.
YOU PROMISED YOU WOULD GIVE ME SOME OF YOUR MAGIC.
THAT I WOULD USE IT TO CREATE A MASTERPIECE, AND MY WORK WOULD BE REMEMBERED FOR CENTURIES.
AND YOU TOLD ME TO BE HERE TODAY--
--TO PRESENT MY MASTERPIECE TO THE GRANDE VISCOUNT DE MIMOLETTE.
BUT THE VISCOUNT ONLY WANTED PICTURES OF DOGS!
DOG-PAINTING USED TO BE MY SPECIALTY!
BWAH-HUH-UH-WHUH
THE VISCOUNT'S A BIG FAT PHONY.
PLUS: I ONLY SAID YOU'D PRESENT HIM THE PAINTING THAT WOULD MAKE YOU FAMOUS, NOT THAT HE'D ACCEPT IT.
HERE. TAKE A LOOK AT THIS.
I BROUGHT THIS BACK FROM WHERE I COME FROM... THE FUTURE!
PAGE 164, IF I'M NOT MISTAKEN.
MON DIEU!
ART TREASURES OF FRANCE
2018 EDITION

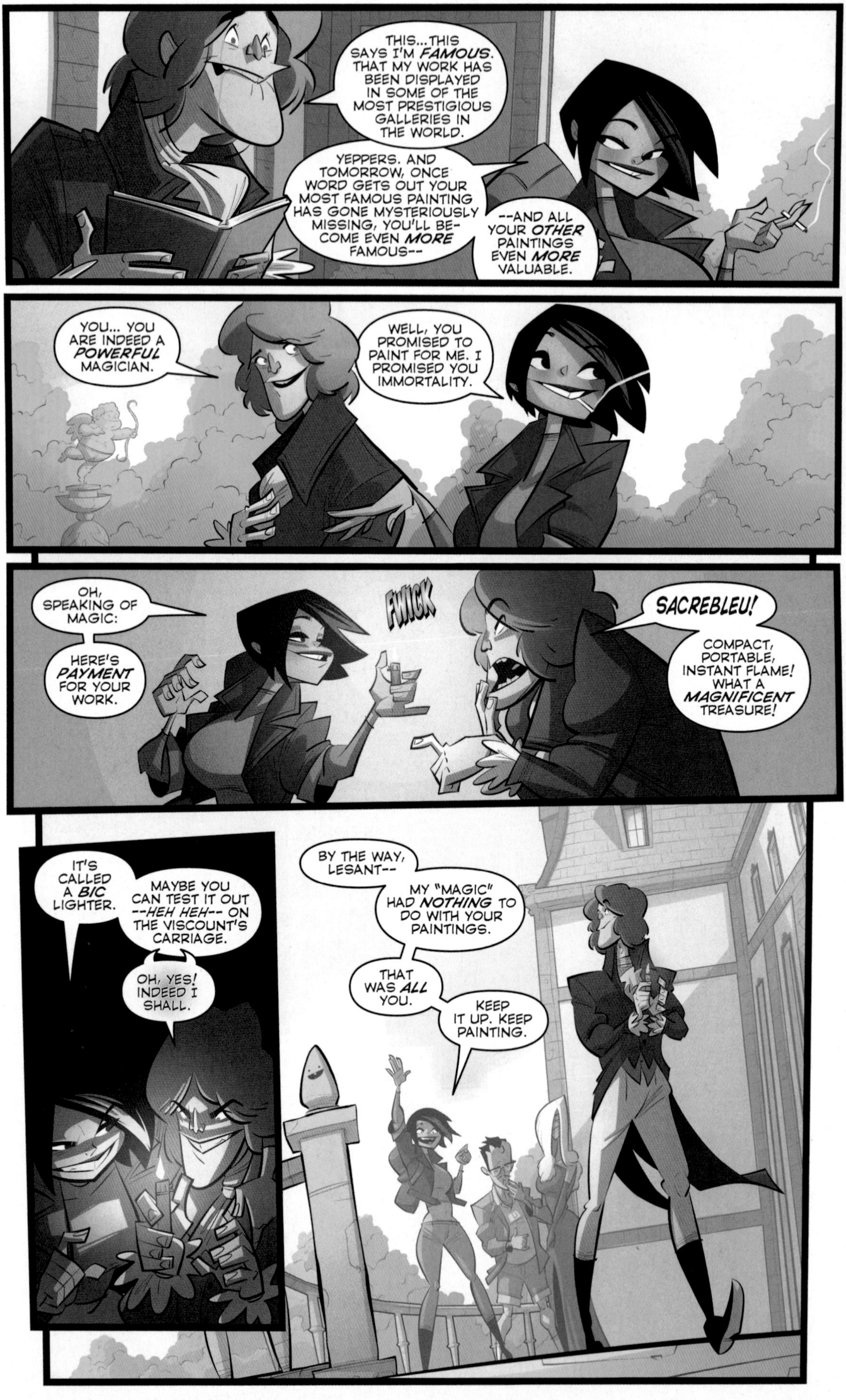
THIS...THIS SAYS I'M FAMOUS. THAT MY WORK HAS BEEN DISPLAYED IN SOME OF THE MOST PRESTIGIOUS GALLERIES IN THE WORLD.
YEPPERS. AND TOMORROW, ONCE WORD GETS OUT YOUR MOST FAMOUS PAINTING HAS GONE MYSTERIOUSLY MISSING, YOU'LL BE-COME EVEN MORE FAMOUS--
--AND ALL YOUR OTHER PAINTINGS EVEN MORE VALUABLE.
YOU... YOU ARE INDEED A POWERFUL MAGICIAN.
WELL, YOU PROMISED TO PAINT FOR ME. I PROMISED YOU IMMORTALITY.
OH, SPEAKING OF MAGIC:
HERE'S PAYMENT FOR YOUR WORK.
FWICK
SACREBLEU!
COMPACT, PORTABLE, INSTANT FLAME! WHAT A MAGNIFICENT TREASURE!
IT'S CALLED A BIC LIGHTER.
MAYBE YOU CAN TEST IT OUT --HEH HEH-- ON THE VISCOUNT'S CARRIAGE.
OH, YES! INDEED I SHALL.
BY THE WAY, LESANT--
MY "MAGIC" HAD NOTHING TO DO WITH YOUR PAINTINGS.
THAT WAS ALL YOU.
KEEP IT UP. KEEP PAINTING.

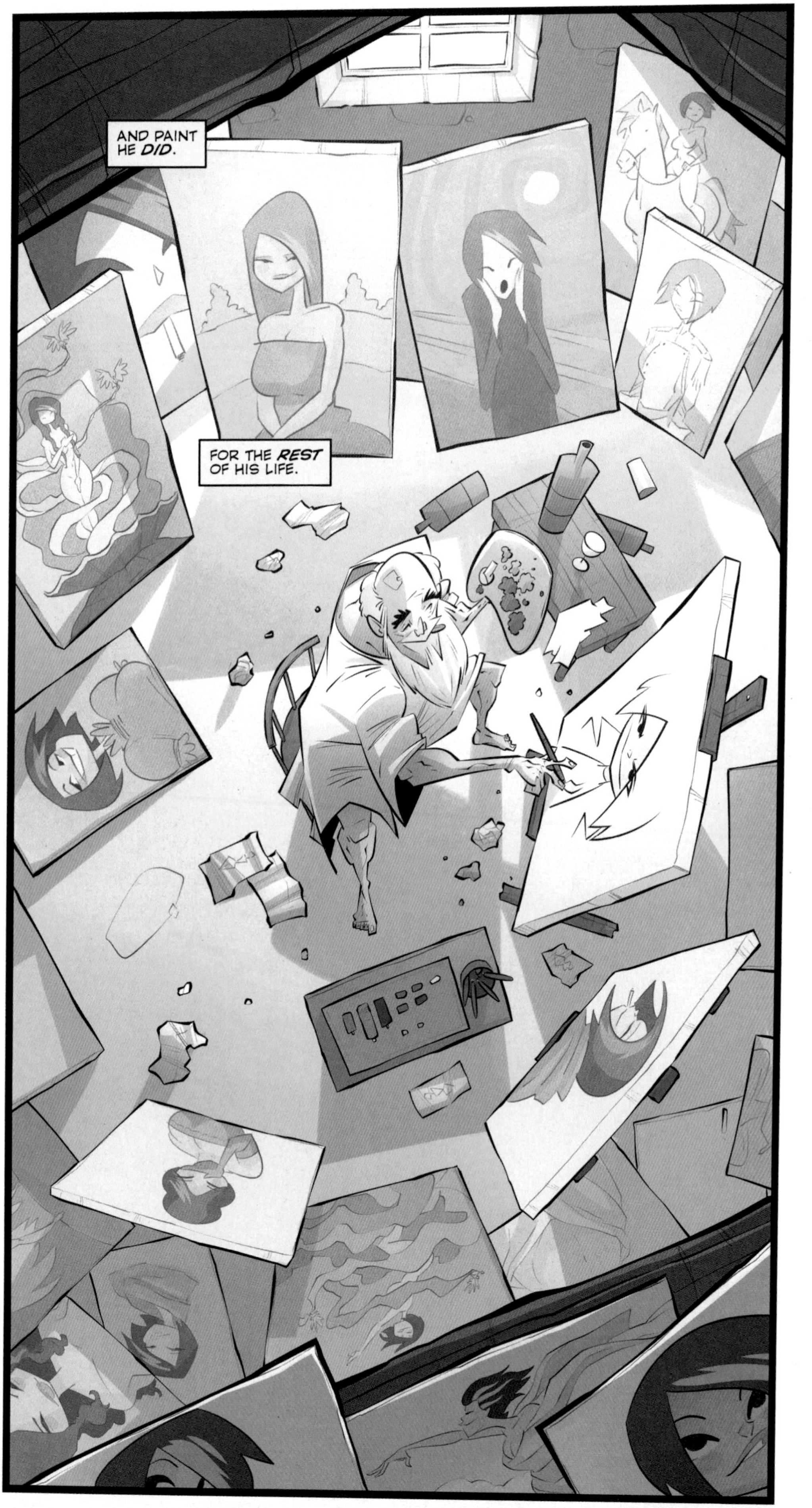
AND PAINT HE *DID*.
FOR THE *REST* OF HIS LIFE.

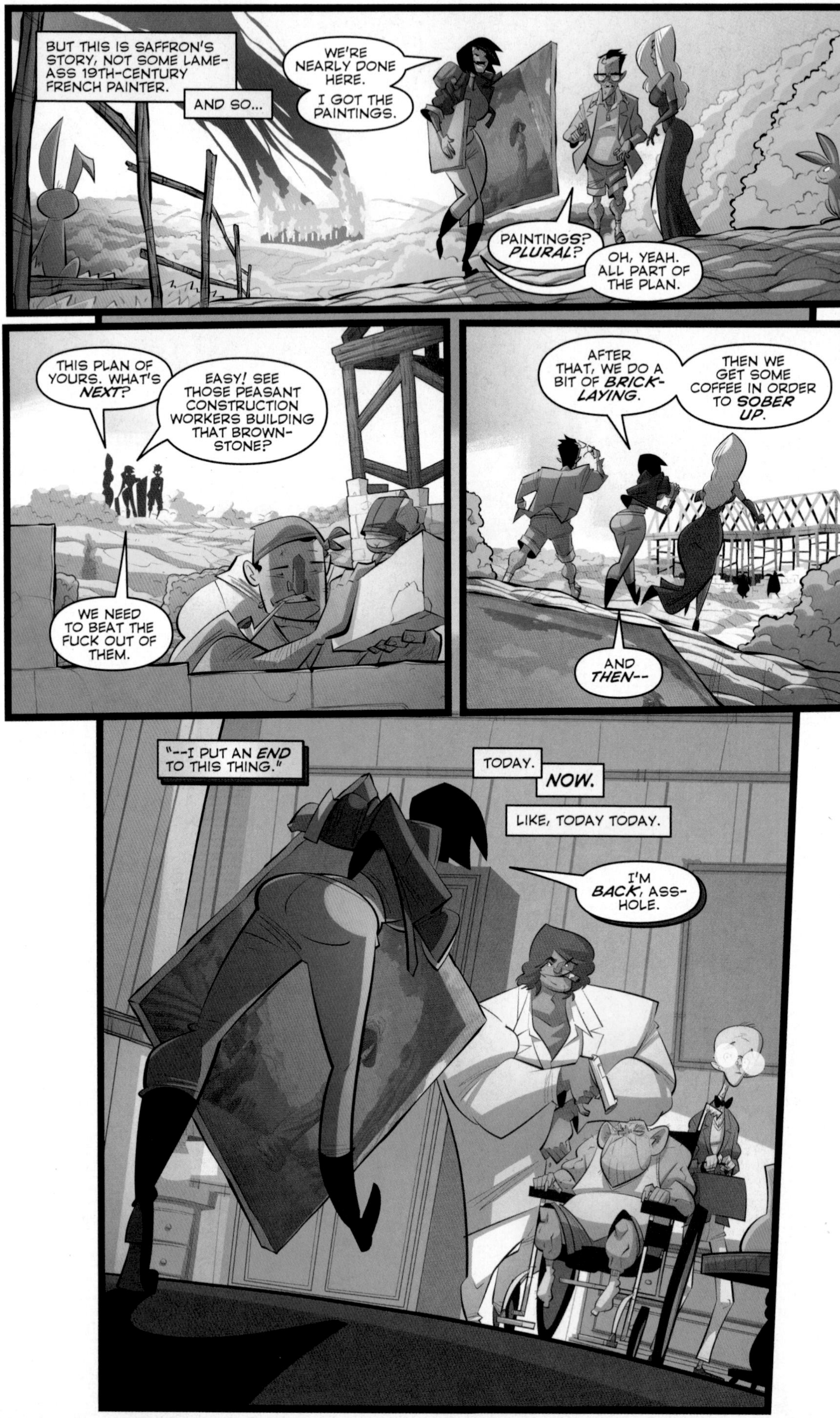
BUT THIS IS SAFFRON'S STORY, NOT SOME LAME-ASS 19TH-CENTURY FRENCH PAINTER.
AND SO...
WE'RE NEARLY DONE HERE.
I GOT THE PAINTINGS.
PAINTINGS? PLURAL?
OH, YEAH. ALL PART OF THE PLAN.
THIS PLAN OF YOURS. WHAT'S NEXT?
EASY! SEE THOSE PEASANT CONSTRUCTION WORKERS BUILDING THAT BROWN-STONE?
WE NEED TO BEAT THE FUCK OUT OF THEM.
AFTER THAT, WE DO A BIT OF BRICK-LAYING.
THEN WE GET SOME COFFEE IN ORDER TO SOBER UP.
AND THEN--
"--I PUT AN END TO THIS THING."
TODAY.
NOW.
LIKE, TODAY TODAY.
I'M BACK, ASS-HOLE.

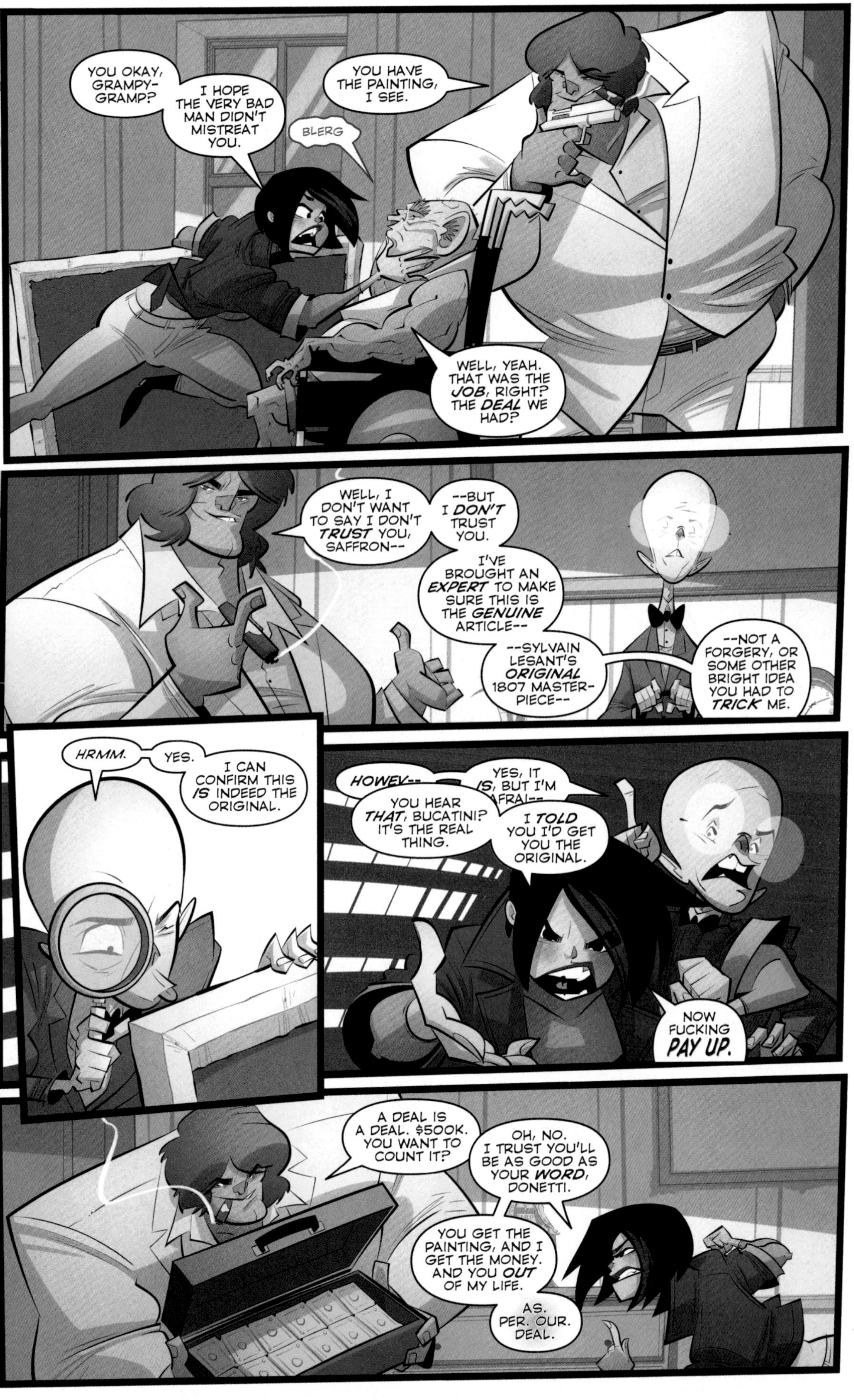
YOU OKAY, GRAMPY-GRAMP?
I HOPE THE VERY BAD MAN DIDN'T MISTREAT YOU.
BLERG
YOU HAVE THE PAINTING, I SEE.
WELL, YEAH. THAT WAS THE JOB, RIGHT? THE DEAL WE HAD?
WELL, I DON'T WANT TO SAY I DON'T TRUST YOU, SAFFRON--
--BUT I DON'T TRUST YOU.
I'VE BROUGHT AN EXPERT TO MAKE SURE THIS IS THE GENUINE ARTICLE--
--SYLVAIN LESANT'S ORIGINAL 1807 MASTER-PIECE--
--NOT A FORGERY, OR SOME OTHER BRIGHT IDEA YOU HAD TO TRICK ME.
HRMM.
YES.
I CAN CONFIRM THIS IS INDEED THE ORIGINAL.
HOWEV--
YES, IT IS, BUT I'M AFRAI--
YOU HEAR THAT, BUCATINI? IT'S THE REAL THING.
I TOLD YOU I'D GET YOU THE ORIGINAL.
NOW FUCKING PAY UP.
A DEAL IS A DEAL. $500K. YOU WANT TO COUNT IT?
OH, NO. I TRUST YOU'LL BE AS GOOD AS YOUR WORD, DONETTI.
YOU GET THE PAINTING, AND I GET THE MONEY. AND YOU OUT OF MY LIFE.
AS. PER. OUR. DEAL.

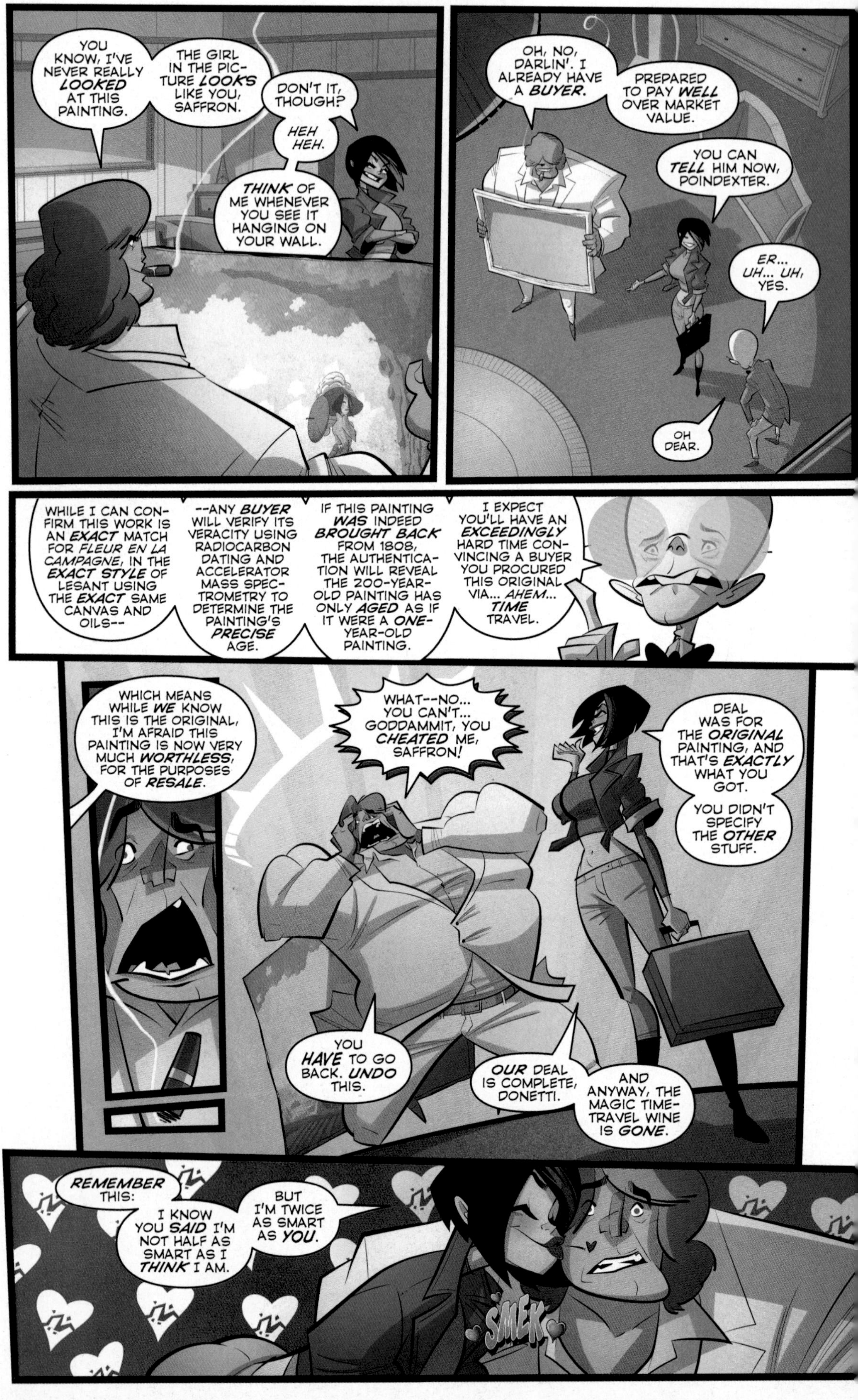
YOU KNOW, I'VE NEVER REALLY LOOKED AT THIS PAINTING.
THE GIRL IN THE PICTURE LOOKS LIKE YOU, SAFFRON.
DON'T IT, THOUGH?
HEH HEH.
THINK OF ME WHENEVER YOU SEE IT HANGING ON YOUR WALL.
OH, NO, DARLIN'. I ALREADY HAVE A BUYER.
PREPARED TO PAY WELL OVER MARKET VALUE.
YOU CAN TELL HIM NOW, POINDEXTER.
ER... UH... UH, YES.
OH DEAR.
WHILE I CAN CONFIRM THIS WORK IS AN EXACT MATCH FOR FLEUR EN LA CAMPAGNE, IN THE EXACT STYLE OF LESANT USING THE EXACT SAME CANVAS AND OILS--
--ANY BUYER WILL VERIFY ITS VERACITY USING RADIOCARBON DATING AND ACCELERATOR MASS SPECTROMETRY TO DETERMINE THE PAINTING'S PRECISE AGE.
IF THIS PAINTING WAS INDEED BROUGHT BACK FROM 1808, THE AUTHENTICATION WILL REVEAL THE 200-YEAR-OLD PAINTING HAS ONLY AGED AS IF IT WERE A ONE-YEAR-OLD PAINTING.
I EXPECT YOU'LL HAVE AN EXCEEDINGLY HARD TIME CONVINCING A BUYER YOU PROCURED THIS ORIGINAL VIA... AHEM... TIME TRAVEL.
WHICH MEANS WHILE WE KNOW THIS IS THE ORIGINAL, I'M AFRAID THIS PAINTING IS NOW VERY MUCH WORTHLESS, FOR THE PURPOSES OF RESALE.
WHAT--NO... YOU CAN'T... GODDAMMIT, YOU CHEATED ME, SAFFRON!
DEAL WAS FOR THE ORIGINAL PAINTING, AND THAT'S EXACTLY WHAT YOU GOT.
YOU DIDN'T SPECIFY THE OTHER STUFF.
YOU HAVE TO GO BACK. UNDO THIS.
OUR DEAL IS COMPLETE, DONETTI.
AND ANYWAY, THE MAGIC TIME-TRAVEL WINE IS GONE.
REMEMBER THIS:
I KNOW YOU SAID I'M NOT HALF AS SMART AS I THINK I AM.
BUT I'M TWICE AS SMART AS YOU.
SMEK

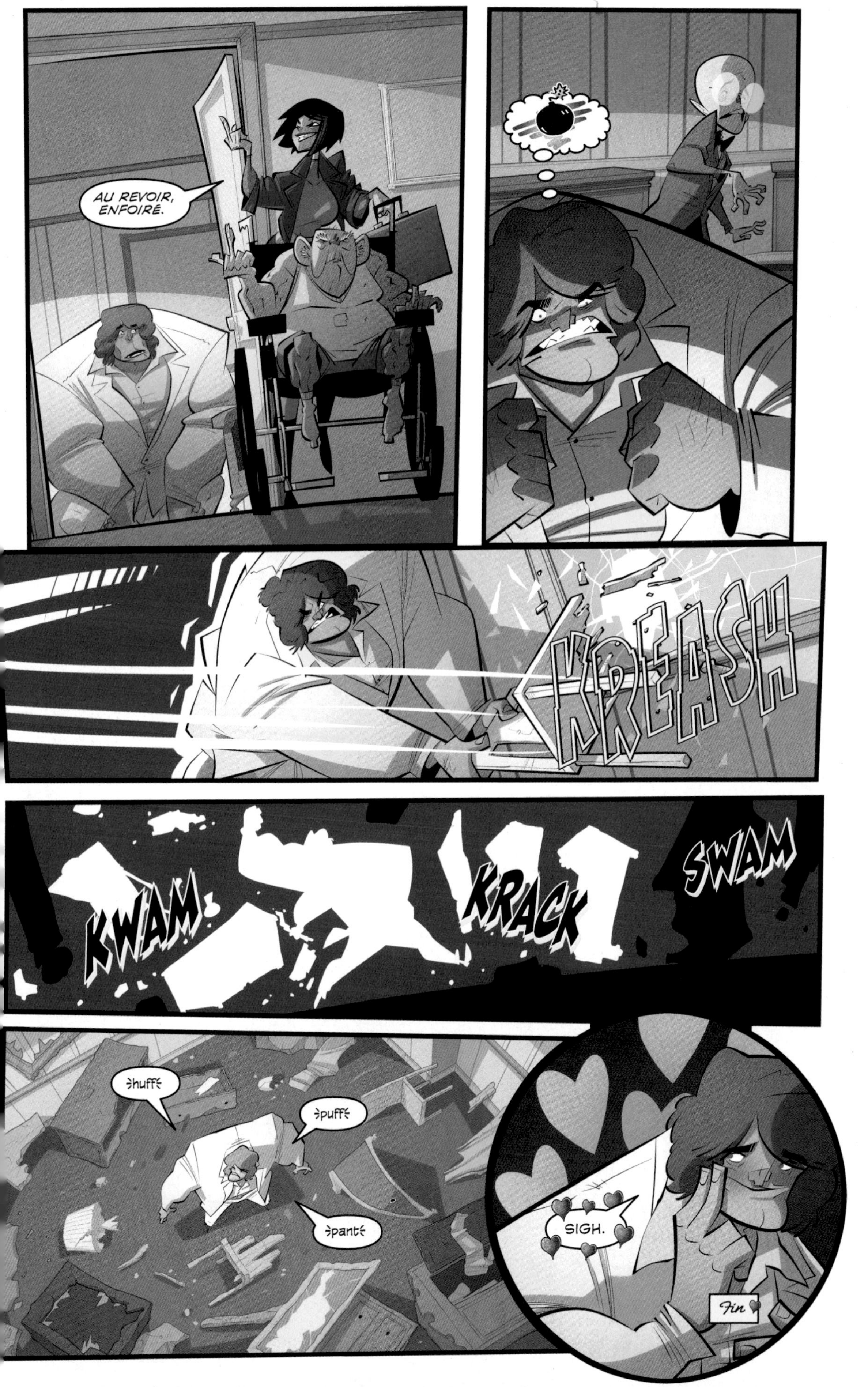
AU REVOIR, ENFOIRÉ.
KREASH
KWAM
KRACK
SWAM
huff
puff
pant
SIGH.
Fin

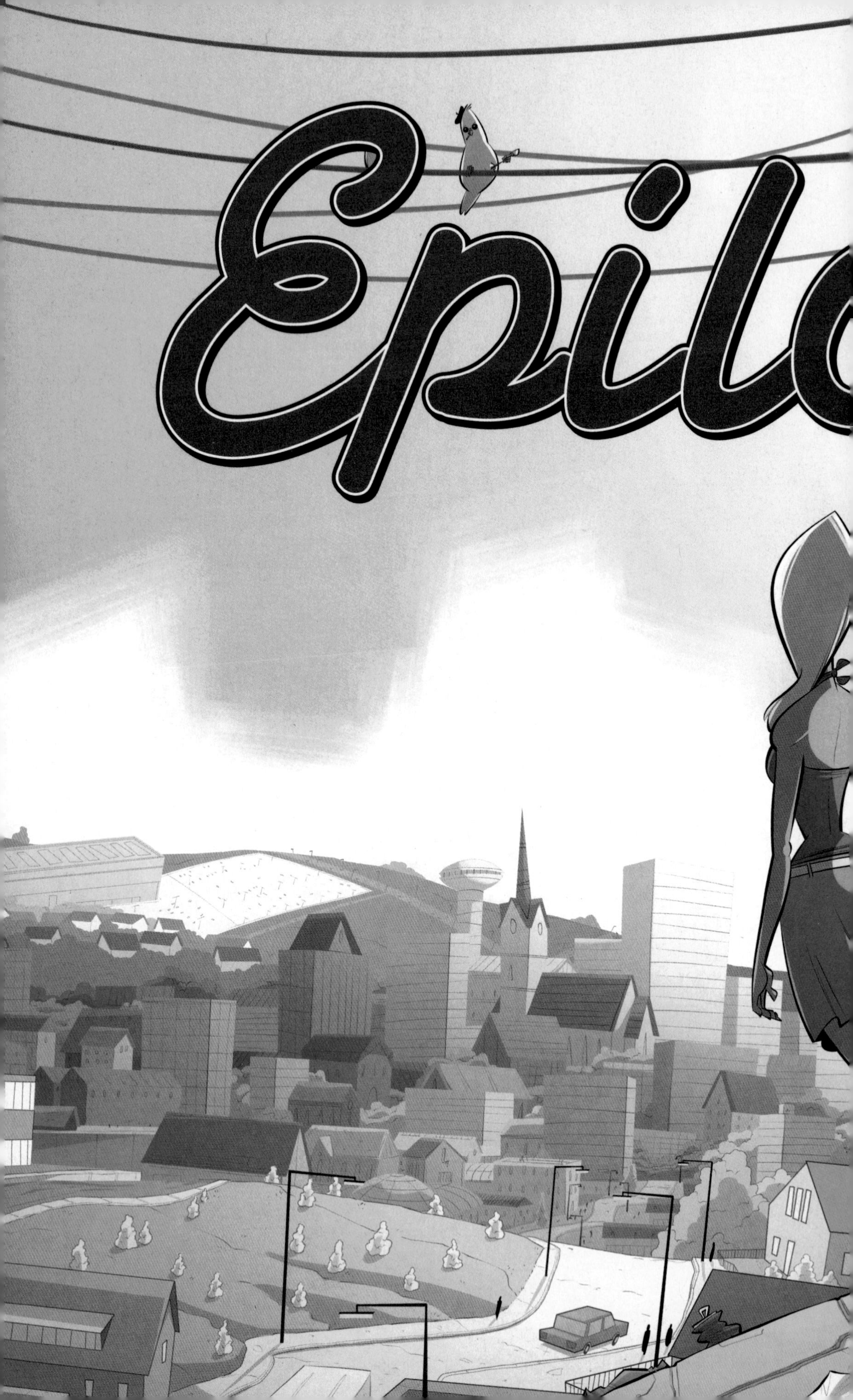
Epilo

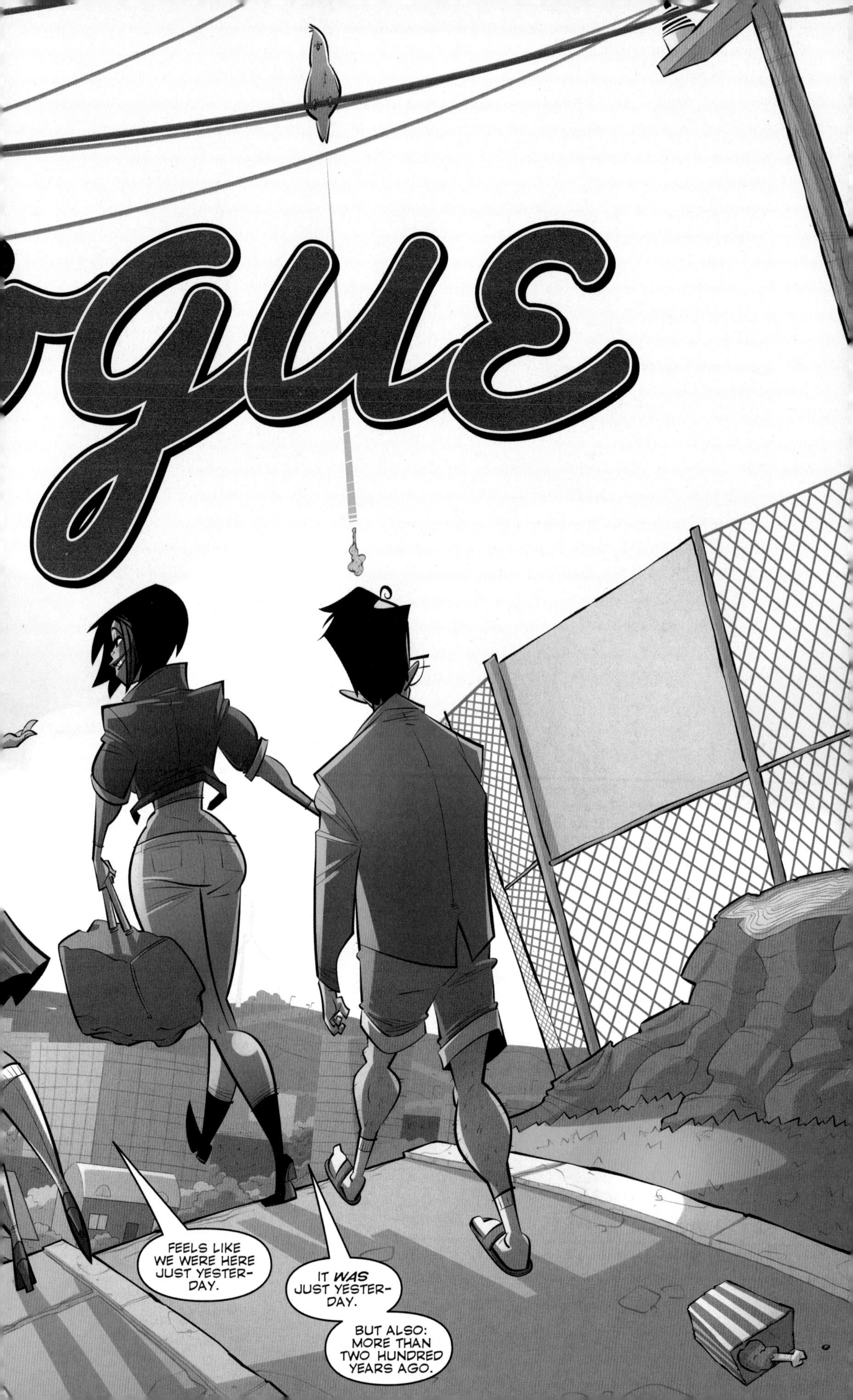

GUE
FEELS LIKE WE WERE HERE JUST YESTER-DAY.
IT *WAS* JUST YESTER-DAY.
BUT ALSO: MORE THAN TWO HUNDRED YEARS AGO.

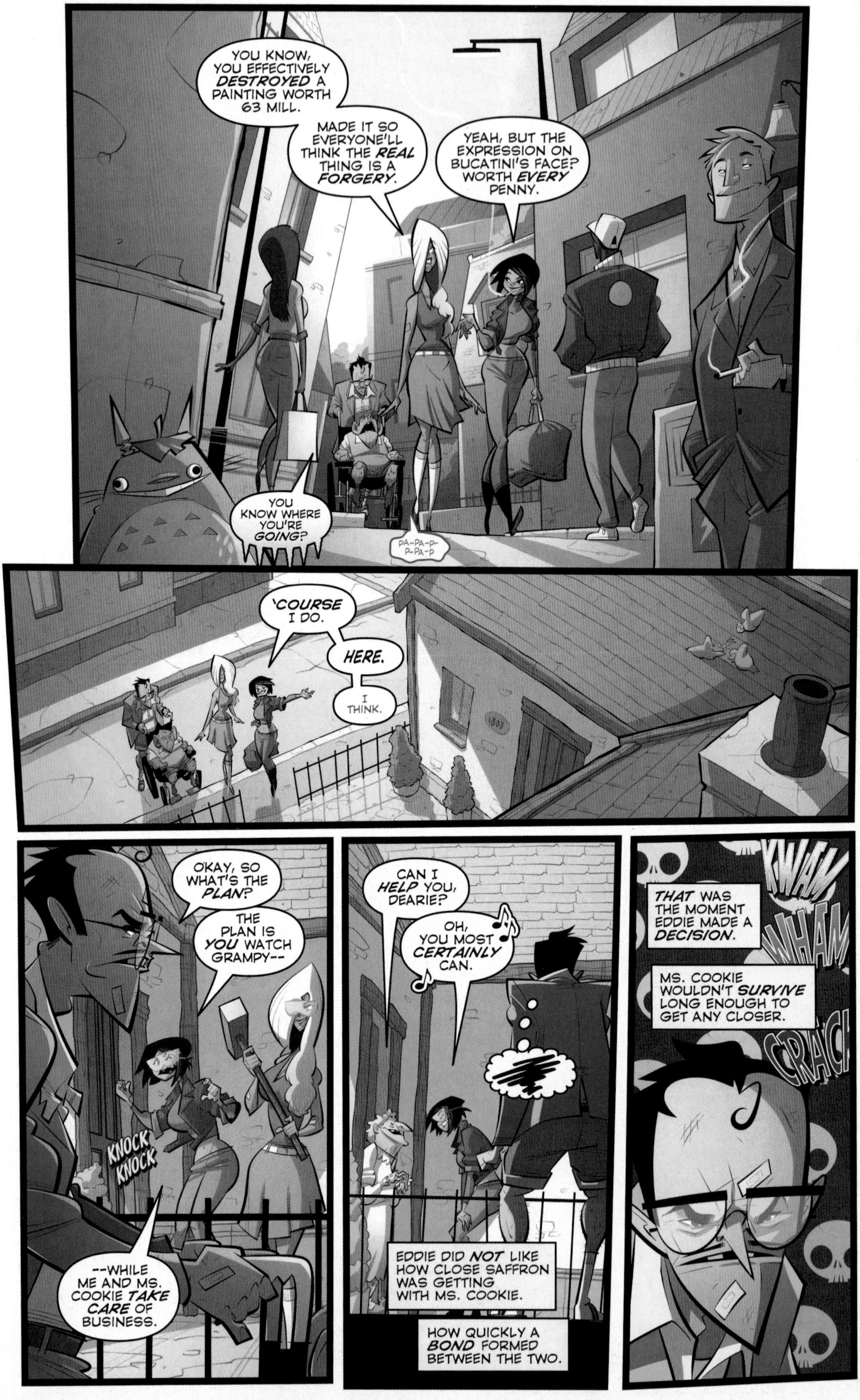

YOU KNOW, YOU EFFECTIVELY DESTROYED A PAINTING WORTH 63 MILL.
MADE IT SO EVERYONE'LL THINK THE REAL THING IS A FORGERY.
YEAH, BUT THE EXPRESSION ON BUCATINI'S FACE? WORTH EVERY PENNY.
YOU KNOW WHERE YOU'RE GOING?
PA-PA-P-P-PA-P
'COURSE I DO.
HERE.
I THINK.
OKAY, SO WHAT'S THE PLAN?
THE PLAN IS YOU WATCH GRAMPY--
KNOCK KNOCK
--WHILE ME AND MS. COOKIE TAKE CARE OF BUSINESS.
CAN I HELP YOU, DEARIE?
OH, YOU MOST CERTAINLY CAN.
EDDIE DID NOT LIKE HOW CLOSE SAFFRON WAS GETTING WITH MS. COOKIE.
HOW QUICKLY A BOND FORMED BETWEEN THE TWO.
KWAM
WHAM
CRACK
THAT WAS THE MOMENT EDDIE MADE A DECISION.
MS. COOKIE WOULDN'T SURVIVE LONG ENOUGH TO GET ANY CLOSER.

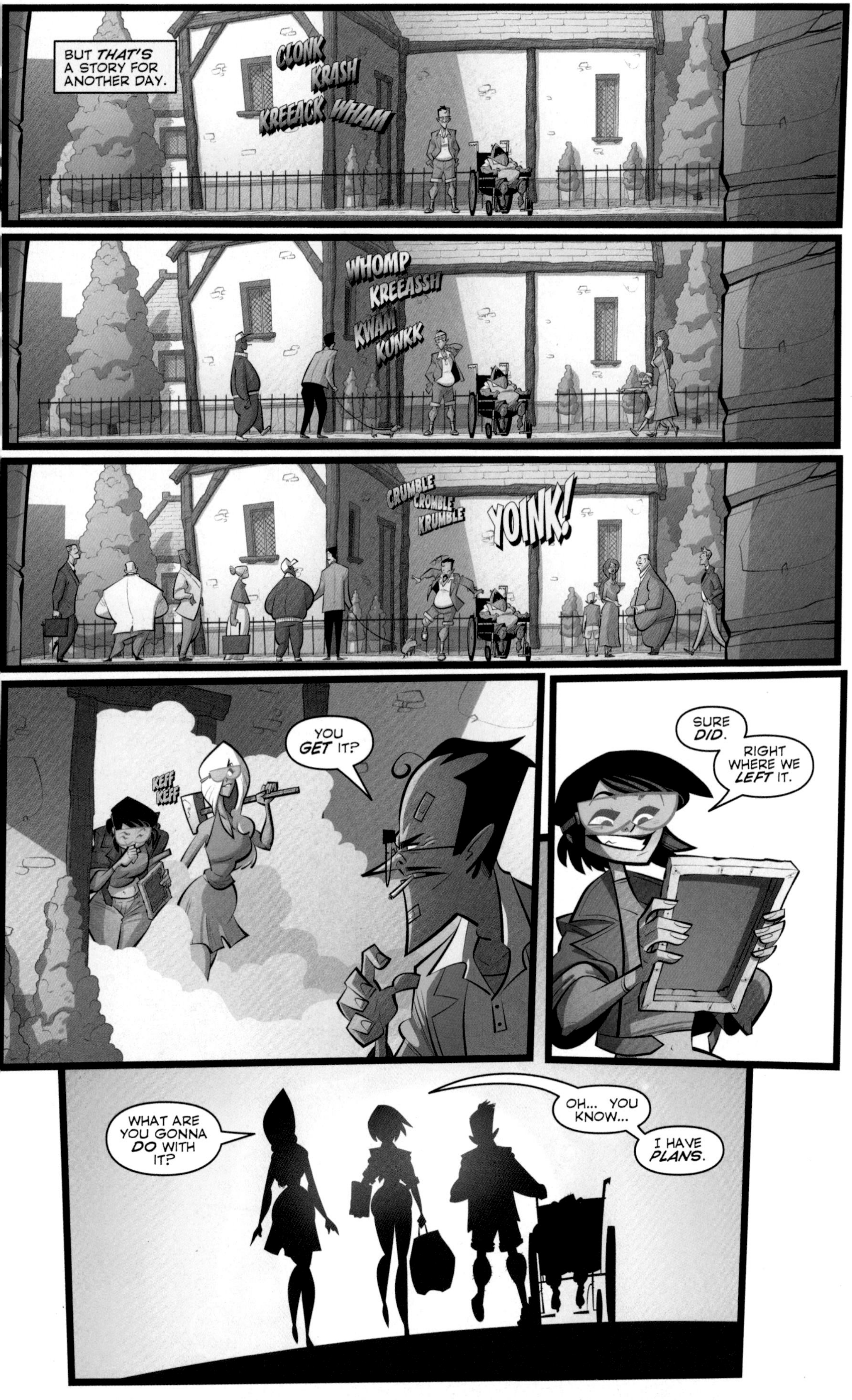
BUT *THAT'S* A STORY FOR ANOTHER DAY.
CLONK
KRASH
KREEACK
WHAM
WHOMP
KREEASSH
KWAM
KUNKK
CRUMBLE
CROMBLE
KRUMBLE
YOINK!
KEFF KEFF
YOU *GET* IT?
SURE *DID*.
RIGHT WHERE WE *LEFT* IT.
WHAT ARE YOU GONNA *DO* WITH IT?
OH... YOU KNOW...
I HAVE *PLANS*.

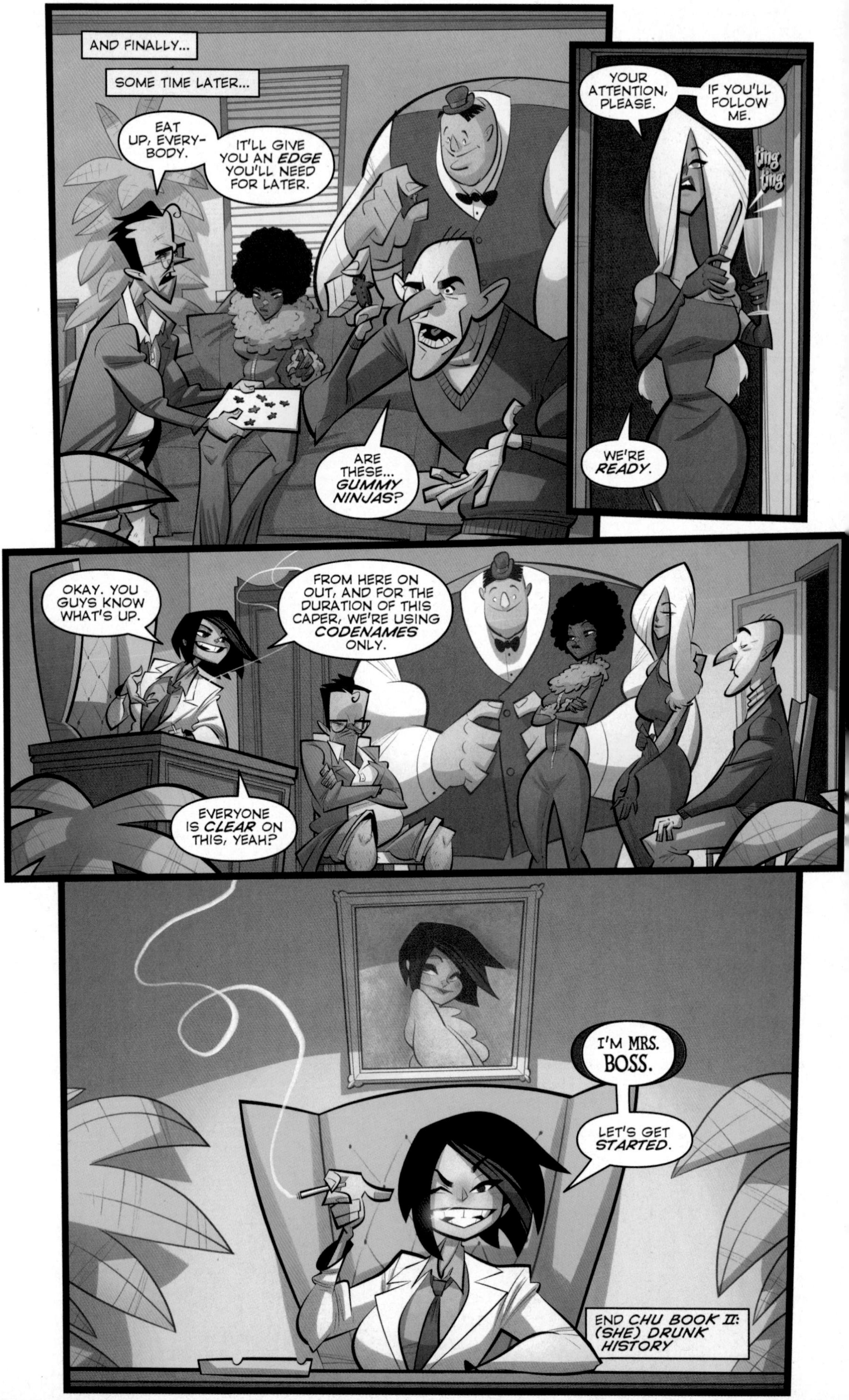
AND FINALLY...
SOME TIME LATER...
EAT UP, EVERY-BODY.
IT'LL GIVE YOU AN EDGE YOU'LL NEED FOR LATER.
ARE THESE... GUMMY NINJAS?
YOUR ATTENTION, PLEASE.
IF YOU'LL FOLLOW ME.
ting ting
WE'RE READY.
OKAY. YOU GUYS KNOW WHAT'S UP.
FROM HERE ON OUT, AND FOR THE DURATION OF THIS CAPER, WE'RE USING CODENAMES ONLY.
EVERYONE IS CLEAR ON THIS, YEAH?
I'M MRS. BOSS.
LET'S GET STARTED.
END CHU BOOK II: (SHE) DRUNK HISTORY

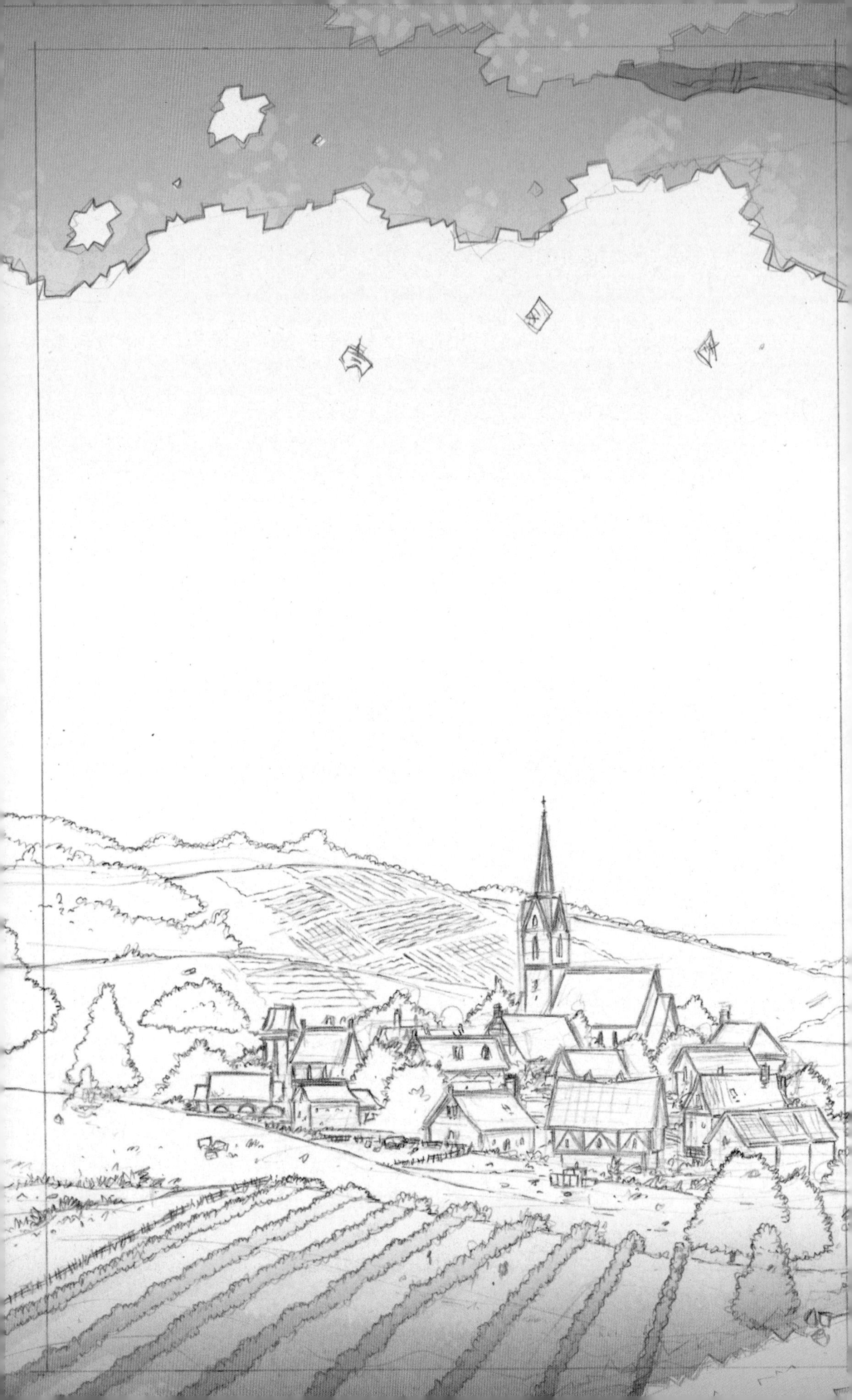

Extras

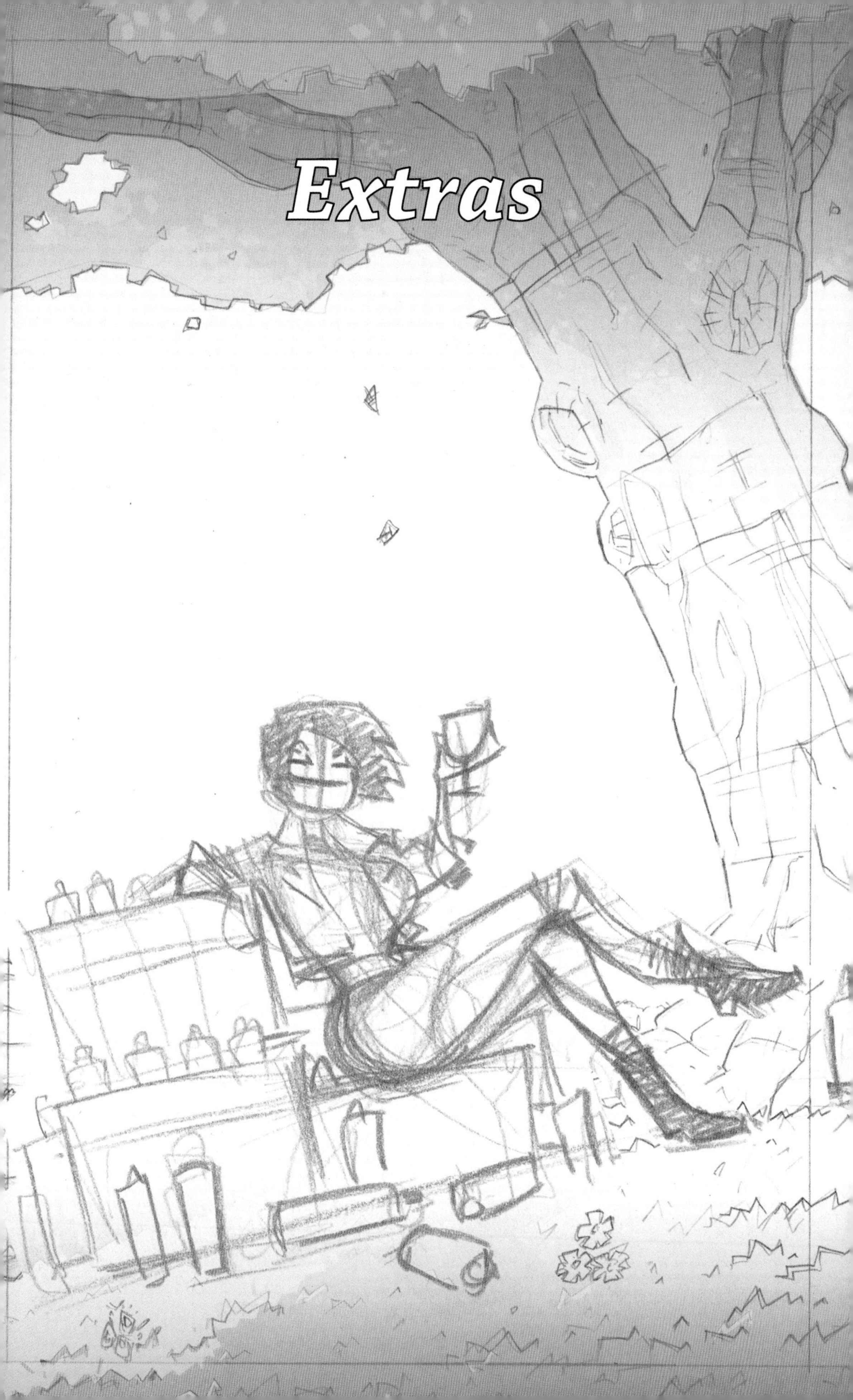

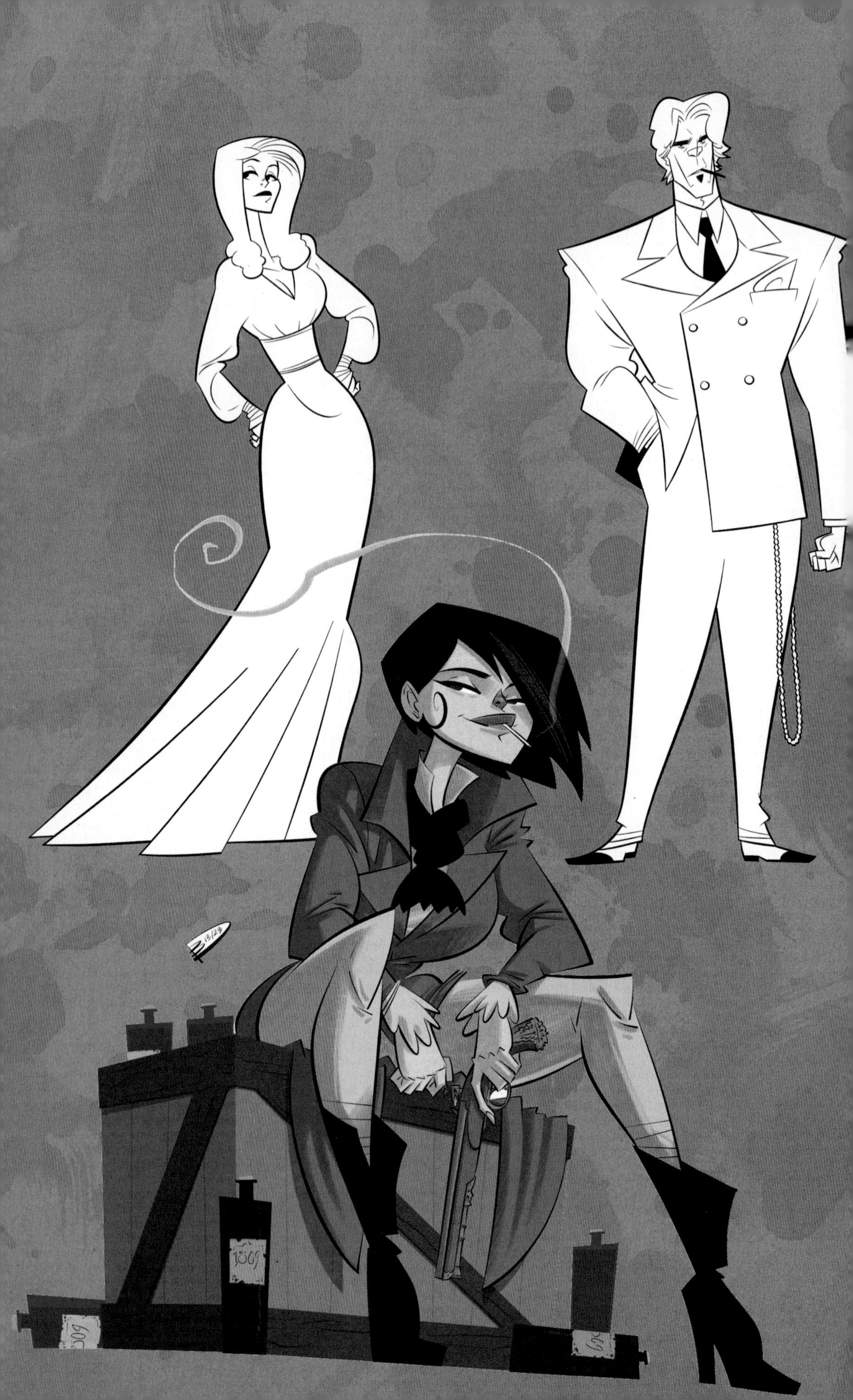

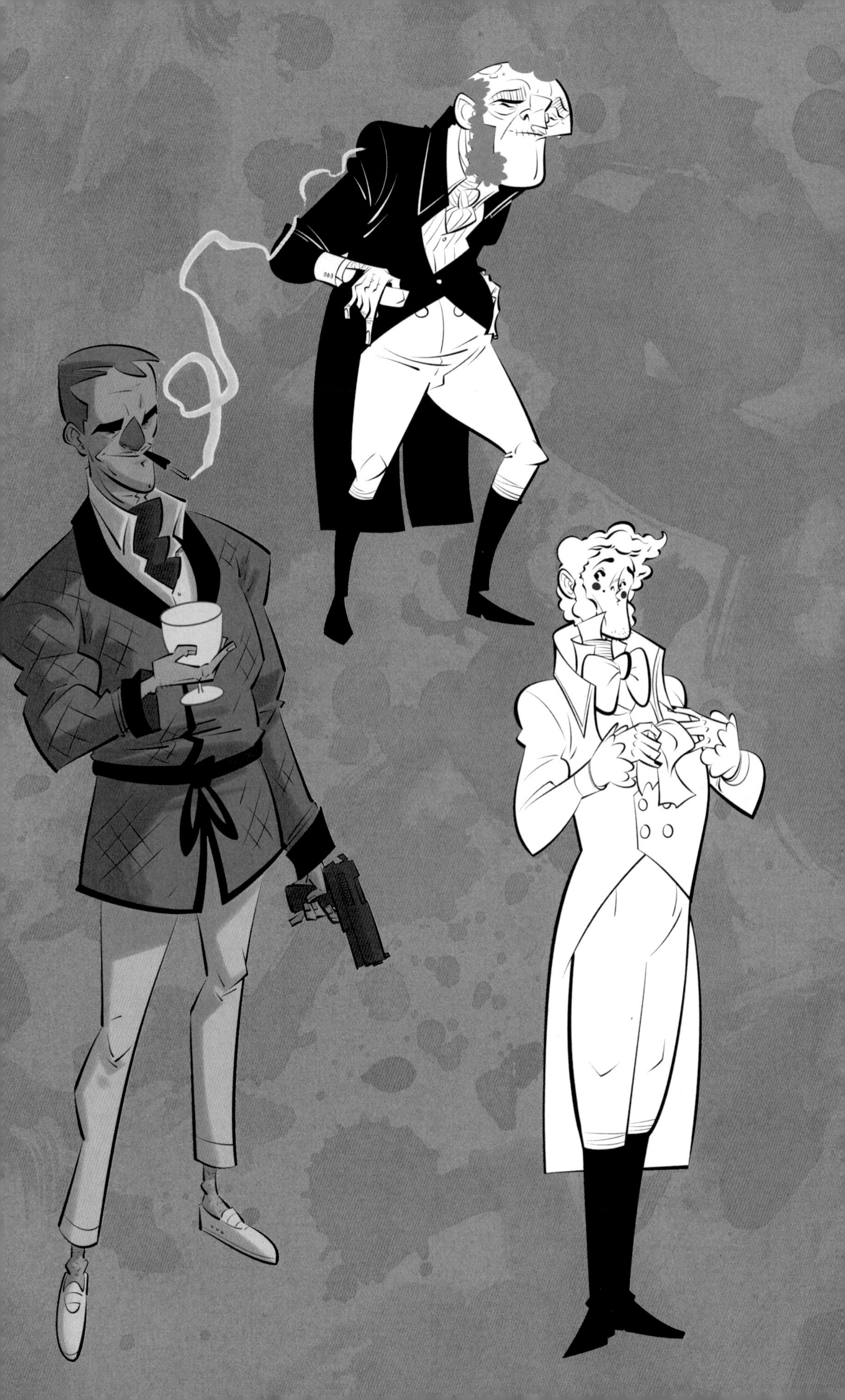

CHU

(She) Drunk History #2
(of 5)

AKA CHU #7

By John Layman
For Dan Boultwood

PAGE ONE
PANELS 1, 2 and 4 are widescreen and equal-sized. Your call what you want to do with Panel 3, Dan.

PAGE ONE
We're on a city street corner in afternoon Paris, a very *French* street filled with French pedestrians going on their way, and a small car or scooters or bikes whizzing by on road. Prominently featured is Eddie Molay and wheelchair-bound Grampa Ong. As captions suggest, Eddie is standing behind Ong, standing close into the street, giving the insensible old man a dirty look.

I don't know how well you know France, Dan. Let me know if you need reference, though I image you can use Google as well as I can.

Eddie is wearing Airpod type headphones, through we don't need to see it.

CAPTION: NOTHING WOULD MAKE EDDIE MOLAY HAPPIER THAN TO <u>PUSH</u> OLD ONG CHU INTO THE ONCOMING TRAFFIC.

ONG (WOOZY):   T-TA-T-TA-T-T

CAPTION: EDDIE <u>HATED</u> GRAMPA ONG.

PANEL TWO

Similarly composed panel. Eddie and Ong continue to stand in the sidewalk as people, not moving as people and vehicles pass by.

CAPTION: HATED DRAGGING HIM AROUND EVERYWHERE.

CAPTION: HATED <u>SMELLING</u> HIM AND CLEANING UP AFTER HIM.

ONG (WOOZY):   V-VA-V-V

CAPTION: THE OLD MAN HAD BEEN JABBERING NONSTOP EVER SINCE THEY GOT TO PARIS, <u>NEVER</u> MAKING <u>ANY</u> SENSE.

PANEL THREE

Either another similarly composed panel, or maybe vary the shot and have Eddie looking down in simmering revulsion toward Grampa, like he is actual contemplating murder.

CAPTION: PLUS, SOMETIMES EDDIE GOT IN A <u>MOOD</u> AND SIMPLY <u>WANTED</u> TO <u>KILL</u> SOMETHING.

ONG (WOOZY):   T-TA-T-TA-T-T

PANEL FOUR

Similarly composed panel to Panels 1 and 2, as Eddie suddenly shoves Grandpa Ong's wheelchair into the street (it will cause a fender-bender, but leave the old man ultimately unscathed. Which is to say: we are faking out the reader here into thinking Eddie might be murdering old Grampa, when in fact he is running a scam, which the elderly con man is complicit in.)

Grampa Ong has a wide-eye look of surprise on his face, mostly to enhance the comic effect, but also this is the first time we see any actual signs of life from Grampa (story note: Grampa is going to "wake up" more and more over the series as a return to criminal life rejuvenates him. Like our hint in the last arc, this is another sign ol' Gramps ain't as catatonic as he may often appear.)

CAPTION: SO WHEN THE VOICE IN HIS HEAD TOLD HIM TO "<u>GO</u>"--

CAPTION: --HE WAS MORE THAN HAPPY TO GIVE THE OLD FUCKER A

SOUND FX (overlapping with caption):   SHOVE!

EDDIE: WITH PLEASURE.

GRAMPA: !!   ***

PAGE TWO

Two big panels, top and bottom, with two smallish panels in the middle of the page.

PANEL ONE

Big panel, half the page or more. Jump cut to Saffron on the rooftop of a French building (something not TOO tall, 3 or 4 stories. Not, like, a skyscraper.) She's dressed for burglary, all in black, with a black knit cap, the purple streak of her hair is peaking from. She's got some rope slung around her shoulder and a grabbling hook crossbow in hand. She's wearing airpods too, which she is speaking (to Eddie) from, maybe touching her earpiece to drive home the point she's giving the order.

SAFFRON: GO.

FLOATING ELECTRONIC: With pleasure.

PANEL TWO

Smallish on Saffron, cocking her head and listening, hearing some welcome sounds of a traffic accident from the nearby city street below. Sounds like maybe an old man just got pushed into traffic!

SOUND FX (overlapping):   HONK HONK HOONK KREEASH

PANEL THREE

Smallish on Saffron, maybe closing one eye while taking aim and letting loose with her grappling hook gun. (Hook attached to rope, which she can use in next panel to run from building to building.)

SOUND FX: TONK

PANEL FOUR

Big, widescreen panel, Saffron having run a rope from one building rooftop to another via grabbling hook and is stealthily and skillfully tight-rope walking/running across from one Parisian rooftop to another.
--SILENT PANEL

                    ***

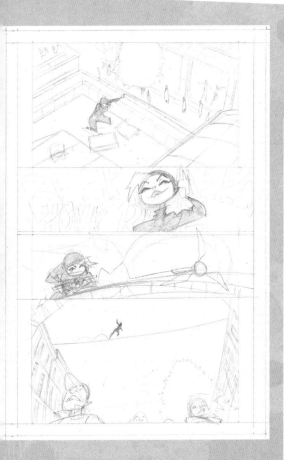

PAGE THREE

<u>PANEL ONE</u>
Cut down to the street, Eddie helping Ong Chu up. Overturned wheelchair in the street nearby. There is a car nearby that rear-ended another car, and its engine is smoking. Probably from slamming on his brakes to stop from running down Ong Chu. Pedestrians stopping and looking on. If there is room, people from the upper story office building looking down at the street below.

EDDIE.   YOU OKAY, OLD FELLA?

EDDIE (SEPARATE FROM PREVIOUS): THAT WAS A NASTY--

EDDIE (VERY SMALL):   --AND <u>COMPLETELY</u> ACCIDENTAL--

EDDIE.   --SPILL YOU JUST TOOK.

<u>PANEL TWO</u>
On Saffron, sneakily climbing into an office window while people who work in the office are looking out a *different* window, distracted by what's going on in the street below.

SMALL, FLOATING: DON'T WORRY, FOLKS.

SMALL, FLOATING: *NE SOIS PAS ALARME.*

SMALL, FLOATING: I THINK HE'S OKAY!

<u>PANEL THREE</u>
Back on Eddie, setting old Ong back into his now uprighted wheelchair. French people still looking on. Eddie wears a sly look, know he just pulled of *his* part of this mini caper.

EDDIE: LET'S GET YOU BACK IN THAT CHAIR, MISTER.

EDDIE: YOU <u>REALLY</u> NEED TO BE MORE <u>CAREFUL</u>, ELDERLY TOTAL STRANGER.

ONG (woozy):   v-Va-v-v

<u>PANEL FOUR</u>
Back to the office, Saffron behind a desk, stealthily rifling through a drawer and maybe pulling out a file while everybody else is gawking out the window.
--SILENT PANEL

<u>PANEL FIVE</u>
Small panel, Eddie with his back to us, pushing Grampa down the street. Mission accomplished.

EDDIE: <music note>

ONG (small, woozy):   t-t-ta-t   ***

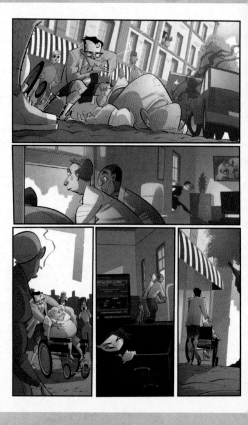

PAGE FOUR

PANEL ONE
Biggest panel of the page. Saffron is outside leaning against a wall on some nearby city street just a bit later, smoking and looking satisfied, looking through the file she just nicked, as Eddie and Grampa approach in the background. Saffron has taken off the knit hat so she no longer looks like a cat burglar. She just looks... French.
--SILENT PANEL.

PANEL TWO
Eddie (pushing Gramps,) approaches Saffron, who holds up a file with a look of cocky satisfaction.

EDDIE: YOU GET IT, SAFFRON?

SAFFRON: *OUI, MONSIEUR!*

SAFFRON: SECURITY SPECIFICS. GUEST LIST. SCHEDULE. FULL INVENTORY OF THE WINES BEING AUCTIONED, ALONG WITH PRICES THEY'RE EXPECTED TO FETCH.

SAFFRON: EVEN THE CATERER'S MENU.

PANEL THREE
Just on Eddie, looking perturbed.

EDDIE: GO BACK TO THE WINES, SAFFRON.

EDDIE: YOUR MAN PALMOIL SAID THE WINE BOTTLES HE WANTED TO STEAL COULD BE WORTH TENS OF MILLIONS.

EDDIE: BUT ALL OUR INFORMATION SAYS THESE BOTTLES ARE WORTH TENS OF THOUSANDS, TOPS.

PANEL FOUR
Saffron is on one side of the panel, looking through the file, as in the background Eddie is putting a ratty blanket over Gramp Ong's legs (we'll see why, next page,) but Grampa is looking over at Saffron, once again looking (mildly) alert, like Saffron just said something that got his attention.

SAFFRON: YEAH, I DON'T UNDERSTAND EITHER. FILE SAYS THE SAME THING.

SAFFRON: *CABERNET CAMEROIS.* BOTTLED 1808 IN COLLONGE LA SOÜLARD.

SAFFRON: VINTED AT *CHATEAU DEVERAUX,* BY GASPARD DEVERAUX, NOTED *VINETEMPORUS.*

SAFFRON (SMALL): WHATEVER THAT IS.

GRAMPA: !!

PANEL FIVE
Small, closer on Saffron, looking at the papers in the open file with a look of furrowed brow concentration, trying to figure out what she missed.

SAFFRON: THERE'S AN ANGLE HERE.

SAFFRON: I JUST HAVE TO FIND IT.
                 ***

PAGE FIVE

PANEL ONE

Angle favoring Grampa, who has a ratty blanket on his lap and a ratty hat on the ground with a few coins in it, and a sign begging for money. Basically, Eddie is presenting Grampa as a homeless street beggar and they are leaving him to panhandle while they run their caper. Eddie is looking at Grampa disdainfully, as Grampa looks over to Saffron and continues to make noise, a little more urgently that previously.

The assumption here is he's leaving him out alone in the cold to fend for himself, but Grampa, as we'll see, actually has something to say of importance.

SIGN (crudely handwritten with dollars signs around) :

Le homeless et malodorant.
Necesité beacoup moolah. Merci.

LE HOMELESS ET MALODORANT.
NECESITÉ BEACOUP MOOLAH. MERCI.

EDDIE: AH, SHUT YOUR GODDAMN YAP, YOU OLD BUZZARD.

EDDIE: WE'RE ONLY LEAVING YOU OUT HERE FOR A FEW HOURS.

EDDIE: MAYBE TRY AN' BUM A FEW BUCKS. BE USEFUL FOR ONCE.

GRAMPS (larger):   t-T-ta-t-t

PANEL TWO

Saffron kneels so she is eye level with her Grandfather and looks sympathetically looks at him. She is inexplicably fond for the old man.

SAFFRON: I'M SORRY, GRAMPY.

SAFFRON: BUT WE CAN'T EXACTLY HAVE YOU AT THE SAFE HOUSE DURING THE MEET, CAN WE?

SAFFRON: I'LL COME GET YOU AS SOON AS THE JOB IS DONE, I PROMISE.

GRAMPS (woozy):   V-v-vi

PANEL THREE

Small panel. Pan in, with Saffron start to lean in to better hear what Grampa is saying.

SAFFRON: WHAT'S THAT, GRAMPY?

GRAMPS (SMALL, WOOZY):   V-V-*VINETEMPORUS.*

PANEL FOUR

Small panel. Even closer. Close-up as Grampa cups a hand and whispers to Saffron, who has leaned close to see what he says. Make it an homage to the CHEW #40 cover. That is, compose panel similarly: https://images.app.goo.gl/5QqxAWn8EjJ86LocA

GRAMPS (super small, woozy):   whisper whisper

PANEL FIVE

Now pull back, to see Saffron is wide-eyed with stunned surprise at what she heard (and the audience did not.) Eddie calls to her, but it does not matter if he is on panel or not. (We'll find out what Grampa Ong said at the end of the issue.)

SAFFRON: Holy shit.

EDDIE (biggish):   Saffron!

PANEL SIX

Eddie impatiently taps his watch. Can't afford to be late for tonight's robbery!

EDDIE: WE GOTTA GO

EDDIE: THIS IS MY FIRST TIME RUNNING A CAPER AS A BOSS.

EDDIE: AND WE NEED EVERYTHING TONIGHT TO GO PERFECTLY.

CAPTION: SPOILER: EVERYTHING TONIGHT WOULD NOT GO PERFECTLY.

          ***

Hungry for more? Help yourself to--

--THE CHEW BACKLIST

TWELVE SOFTCOVER TPBS!!

**VOL 1.
TASTER'S
CHOICE**

**VOL 2.
INTERNATIONAL
FLAVOR**

**VOL 3.
JUST
DESSERTS**

**VOL 4.,
FLAMBÉ**

**VOL 5.
MAJOR LEAGUE
CHEW**

**VOL 6.
SPACE CAKES**

**VOL 7.
BAD APPLES**

**VOL 8.
FAMILY
RECIPIES**

**VOL 9.
CHICKEN TENDERS**

**VOL 10.
BLOOD
PUDDIN'**

**VOL 11.
THE LAST
SUPPERS**

**VOL 12.
SOUR
GRAPES**

SIX HARDCOVER "OMNIVORE EDITIONS"!!!

VOL 1.

VOL 2.

VOL 3.

Don't forget Saffron's first adventure!

VOL 4.

VOL 5.

VOL 6.

**VOL 1.
THE FIRST
COURSE**

JOHN LAYMAN

Born during _____ , John _____ Layman left
<small><historical event></small> <small><flower></small>

his native land of _____ and moved at the tender age of
<small><country></small>

____ to _____ to pursue a career as a _____
<small><number></small> <small><city></small> <small><occupation></small>

before discovering a profound _____ for comics. A
<small><emotion></small>

_____ writer, he has worked on a multitude of comic
<small><adjective></small>

properties over the years, including _____ and
<small>< superhero></small>

_____, though his dream is to write
<small><cannibal FDA agent></small>

_____. In his spare time Layman enjoys
<small><pop culture character></small>

_____, _____, _____, and
<small><hobby></small> <small><hobby></small> <small><type of bloodsport></small>

_____ with _____.
<small><obscene gerund></small> <small><noun (plural)></small>

DAN BOULTWOOD

Born some time ago, Dan Boultwood draws things. Some of it's even been quite good. Has anybody got any gin?